Governance
in the
21st Century

OECD

ORGANISATION FOR ECONOMIC CO-OPERATION AND DEVELOPMENT

ORGANISATION FOR ECONOMIC CO-OPERATION AND DEVELOPMENT

Pursuant to Article I of the Convention signed in Paris on 14th December 1960, and which came into force on 30th September 1961, the Organisation for Economic Co-operation and Development (OECD) shall promote policies designed:

- to achieve the highest sustainable economic growth and employment and a rising standard of living in Member countries, while maintaining financial stability, and thus to contribute to the development of the world economy;
- to contribute to sound economic expansion in Member as well as non-member countries in the process of economic development; and
- to contribute to the expansion of world trade on a multilateral, non-discriminatory basis in accordance with international obligations.

The original Member countries of the OECD are Austria, Belgium, Canada, Denmark, France, Germany, Greece, Iceland, Ireland, Italy, Luxembourg, the Netherlands, Norway, Portugal, Spain, Sweden, Switzerland, Turkey, the United Kingdom and the United States. The following countries became Members subsequently through accession at the dates indicated hereafter: Japan (28th April 1964), Finland (28th January 1969), Australia (7th June 1971), New Zealand (29th May 1973), Mexico (18th May 1994), the Czech Republic (21st December 1995), Hungary (7th May 1996), Poland (22nd November 1996), Korea (12th December 1996) and the Slovak Republic (14th December 2000). The Commission of the European Communities takes part in the work of the OECD (Article 13 of the OECD Convention).

Publié en français sous le titre :
LA GOUVERNANCE AU XXIe SIÈCLE

Foreword

In the run-up to the preparations for EXPO 2000 – the World Exposition in Hanover, Germany – the OECD Forum for the Future organised a series of four conferences to take place beforehand around the theme of "People, Nature and Technology: Sustainable Societies in the 21st Century". The series considered four key areas of human activity: technology, economy, society and government. The conferences explored possible evolutions of key variables and analysed different development paths in order to expose some of the main policy implications and options. Each conference provided analysis of underlying trends and policy directions. However, the overall aim of the series was to build a comprehensive foundation for assessing the critical choices likely to face citizens and decision makers in the next century.

The entire series benefited from special sponsorship by EXPO 2000 and four German banks – Bankgesellschaft Berlin, DG BANK Deutsche Genossenschafts-bank AG, NORD/LB Norddeutsche Landesbank, and Westdeutsche Landesbank Girozentrale (WestLB). Additional financial support was provided by numerous Asian, European and North American partners of the OECD Forum for the Future.

This book deals with the fourth and final conference in the series, hosted by the NORD/LB Norddeutsche Landesbank in Hanover, Germany on 25-26 March 2000. The theme was "21st Century Governance: Power in the Global Knowledge Economy and Society".

Three main messages emerged from the discussions and analyses that are summarised in the pages that follow. First, old forms of governance in both the public and private sectors are becoming increasingly ineffective. Second, the new forms of governance that are likely to be needed over the next few decades will involve a much broader range of active players. Third, and perhaps most importantly, two of the primary attributes of today's governance systems – the usually fixed and permanent allocations of power that are engraved in the structures and constitutions of many organisations; and, the tendency to vest initiative exclusively in the hands of those in senior positions in the hierarchy – look set to undergo fundamental changes.

Harbingers of changes in the first attribute can be found in highly supple organisations, both public and private, that are capable of regularly redistributing responsibility according to the nature of the task rather than on the basis of a rigid authority structure. That spontaneous determination of the most appropriate level for wielding power and taking responsibility goes hand in hand with the weakening of the second attribute of most prevailing governance systems, a decline in hierarchical or top-down methods for determining goals and means.

Gradually, at the leading edge of many economies and societies – particularly in areas where the production of intangibles and personal customisation are becoming dominant – initiative is shifting to the people who have detailed knowledge of what is desired and what is possible. Traditional leaders in either the workplace or the public sphere can no longer specify in advance exact outcomes or methods. Instead, in the context of shared missions and common rules, the objectives and techniques are being left to the unforeseeable innovations and creativity of the individuals and groups that have a deeper understanding of the specific needs and resources.

Organisational and creative liberty, however, has very exacting preconditions. In the future, more diffused approaches to governance in all parts of society will only work if there are frameworks in place that assure very high levels of transparency, accountability and integrity. At the same time, for public authorities and society more broadly, the ability to put new forms of governance into the service of realising people's collective good will depend on a common commitment to democratic values, human rights and equality of opportunity. Even with these frameworks and values in place, the emergence of new forms of governance will still depend fundamentally on the capacity of individuals and groups to participate actively in making and implementing decisions.

Meeting these challenges of individual and group capabilities will, at least from the perspective of government policy, probably entail a two-pronged thrust. One is to implement policies that foster, in ways laid out by the previous books in this series, technological, economic and social dynamism. The second approach, discussed in this volume, concerns policies that target improvements in three areas: the full range of learning infrastructures, the frameworks that are crucial for establishing confidence, and the standards (mission/values) that provide the common basis within which a society functions. By improving the capacity to make and implement decisions throughout society, these policies are likely to provide one of the main stepping stones to the realisation of people's individual and collective aspirations in the 21st century.

This publication brings together the papers presented at the meeting as well as an introductory contribution prepared by the Secretariat. The book is published on the responsibility of the Secretary-General of the OECD.

Table of Contents

Chapter 1

Governance in the 21st Century:
Power in the Global Knowledge Economy and Society

by
Wolfgang Michalski, Riel Miller and Barrie Stevens
OECD Secretariat, Advisory Unit to the Secretary-General

Gradually throughout human history, the power to steer society has diffused away from the chieftain or king towards a broader base of elected representatives, managers, bureaucrats and interest group leaders. Movement along this long-run trend has been far from linear or painless, and no one decision-making model has prevailed. Over time, however, economic growth has combined with changing values and institutions to reshape the nature, scope and means of exercising authority throughout society – in government, firms, associations and families.

Recently, there has also been a growing recognition that the ability or power of collective institutions to chart a particular course depends to an increasing degree on the active involvement of the governed. Looking to the future, there are signs that the governed of yesterday could become the governors of tomorrow. This does not mean that every citizen or worker would become a politician or manager. Instead, tomorrow's dynamic societies, less governable by the old methods of command and obedience, may set and achieve both individual and broad social goals by enhancing decision-making capacities generally.

Such a change would mean a radical break with past as well as with most prevailing governance models. Traditionally, decisions have been made and implemented using centralised, top-down and predetermined structures operating in rigidly defined fields of action – whether in a family, a firm or a nation. Despite today's general tendency to assign formal power to citizens and shareholders, in practice the choice of goals and of the means for reaching them remain largely delegated, centralised and hierarchical. As will become clear over the following pages, it is plausible and even desirable to consider the longer-term prospects for a major transition in the institutions, rules and culture that shape practical governance in all parts of society.

7

Prospects for such large-scale transformation of the ways in which freedom and responsibility are distributed will depend on a broad, interlocking set of changes in underlying technological, economic and social conditions. The characteristics, plausibility, desirability and policy requirements for these changes were explored in the previous books in this series. All three also envisioned a future that breaks with the patterns and methods of yesterday and today.

21st Century Technologies: Promises and Perils of a Dynamic Future established a strong case for the view that tomorrow's technological advances could have as wide-ranging an impact as past inventions such as printing, the steam engine and electricity.

The Future of the Global Economy: Towards a Long-Boom? underscored the possibility of a sustained period of above-average rates of growth and wealth creation due to the exceptional confluence of three sets of powerful changes – the shift to a knowledge economy, much deeper global integration, and a transformation in humanity's relationship to the environment.

The Creative Society of the 21st Century concluded that trends towards much greater social diversity, both within and between countries, may be sustained well into the future.

The prospect of discontinuity across so many dimensions is not unprecedented. There have been similar periods in human history, such as the transition from agricultural to industrial society. However, what distinguishes these shifts from previous ones is that they will largely depend on the emergence of a mutually reinforcing relationship between, on the one hand, a significant diffusion throughout society of governance capacities and, on the other, higher degrees of technological, economic and social dynamism. These two sets of developments could give rise to a powerful virtuous circle.

At the root of this symbiosis is the expectation that desirable changes will be both a consequence and a cause of the diffusion of power and responsibility. Consequence, because unlocking the positive potential of tomorrow's technological breakthroughs, deeper economic interdependence and greater social diversity seems unlikely to occur without a much broader dispersion of initiative and accountability. Cause, because the technological, economic and social changes that seem best suited to fulfilling society's aspirations also seem likely to provide many of the tools and experiences needed to enhance governance capacities and thereby make the reallocation of power more practical.

The nature of the possible changes in governance, the forces that might drive such changes, and the policies likely to facilitate movements in a positive rather than negative direction are the topics of this book. This introductory chapter offers an overview of each, in summary form.

Long-run governance trends: The end of authority?

Looking at governance as the general exercise of authority, it seems that over the long run there has been a clear reduction in the absolute or unconstrained power of those in positions of power. This has been a marked trend both at the macro-political level, where the state attempts to effect society-wide governance, and at the micro level, where firms and families have experienced important changes in the exercise of authority.

At the macro level, determination of the objectives, laws and methods meant to direct the collective future of society has, in most parts of the world, moved away from absolutism, authoritarianism and even the autarkic conception of the modern nation state. The decay of traditional notions of sovereign authority has now reached the point where in many circumstances universal principles, such as those of human rights and environmental sustainability, are becoming both more legitimate and more effective than rules imposed by appealing to national prerogatives. Similarly, the trend at the micro level of firms and families has been away from the unconstrained authority of the owner and father over employees and family members.

In broad strokes, four sets of historical developments have influenced these profound shifts in authority relationships. First is the direct impact of struggles to introduce greater democracy and competitive markets. The second set concerns the ways in which changes in economic productivity and material wealth alter both the aims and methods of governance – in the household, enterprise or government. A closely related third category of forces involves the rules and belief systems that serve as the implicit and/or explicit guides to decision making and implementation in all parts of a society. And the fourth category of general factors that alter governance systems relates to innovations and/or transformations in institutional design, organisational structure and administrative operation.

Looking to recent history, the 20th century has seen significant movement in all four of these overarching categories.

First of all, democratic approaches to collective governance have either directly overthrown absolutist and authoritarian regimes, or through superior economic and social performance have convinced by example. Power has also been pried away from vested interests by the advance of competitive approaches to wealth creation. Open trade and competitive markets, when serious efforts are made to combat the tendency towards the accumulation of monopoly power, have been very subversive with regard to existing authority structures. Combined, democracy and competition have had a further corrosive impact on the character of governance

9

systems by significantly increasing economic, social, and cultural interdependence. Here it is the micro-level interactions of firms and individuals that have operationalised and consolidated the links opened up by trade agreements, low-cost transportation, migration and new means of communication. Far-flung commerce, social mobility and global television – not to mention the swelling role of the internet – have been breaking down barriers and revealing powerful common interests that often pay little attention to the rules and prohibitions of conventional authorities.

Secondly, spectacular economic growth has allowed major segments of humanity to shift their focus from the minimum requirements for survival in terms of food, clothing and shelter to the pursuit of goals that take physical subsistence for granted. Along with major increases in wealth, the previous century also witnessed significant increases in the average lifespan, historically unprecedented levels of society-wide investment in education, and rates of productivity growth that provided sufficient resources to fund sizeable public sector infrastructure and administration without seriously undermining other areas of capital accumulation. Looking first at the OECD countries, there is good evidence that the average person has gradually become more concerned with quality of life issues, ranging from work satisfaction and educational opportunities to home internet access and environmental conditions. Other parts of the world have not been as successful in leaving behind the preoccupation with basic subsistence. Nevertheless, the demonstration effect of improvements in living conditions in OECD countries has been very influential.

At the beginning of the 21st century it seems fair to observe that almost all countries and regions are striving to emulate the conditions for prosperity – including the aims and methods of governance – that are largely taken for granted in most OECD countries. Such convergence is perhaps best symbolised by the adoption, starting in the middle of the 20th century, of the Universal Declaration of Human Rights. This event can be seen as a landmark on a long voyage, still far from complete, towards the universal and full implementation of governance practices that both limit the arbitrary exercise of power and, in a variety of ways, render decision making throughout society open to questioning. Overall, individual and social aspirations – key drivers of the governance agenda – changed markedly during the 20th century, and not only for people and institutions in the wealthier parts of the world. Globally, there has been a steady if uneven transition away from passive acceptance of divine rights to active pursuit of human rights, and away from unquestioning obedience of patriarchal authority to a more egalitarian recognition of individual liberty. Such shifts in values have played an important role in altering the ends and means of governance.

Thirdly, over the course of the 20th century, similarly influential changes have occurred in the structure and organisational functioning of households, businesses and the public sector. For example, in many countries women entered the labour force, generating important changes in how household production was organised. Managerial paradigms in many enterprises were overthrown, initially by impressive efforts to perfect Taylorism and then, towards the end of the century, to find new, less hierarchical approaches that better fit the production of intangibles. Government too has seen, at least in OECD countries, the generalisation throughout much of the century of advanced administrative models as well as continuous efforts at reform – including the most recent initiatives to "reinvent" government. All told, the changes in the techniques used to manage daily activities, from household chores to welfare payments, have also contributed to the transformation of governance in the 20th century. Although the application of these organisational changes has hardly been uniform, here again demonstration effects or the diffusion of techniques through organisational learning have played an important role.

Finally, in discussing the general, long-run forces influencing governance, it is important to note that all of these trends have also been transforming decision making at an international level. The scope and methods for exercising power in three types of transborder institution have gone through significant changes during the 20th century. The first set covers organisations where national governments meet to work together, like the United Nations, the OECD or the WTO. The second group involves private sector corporations that function and make choices that go beyond the confines of national boundaries. And the third category encompasses global-level civil society institutions such as the International Confederation of Free Trade Unions (ICFTU), Greenpeace, and – of more recent vintage – the Internet Corporation for Assigned Names and Numbers (ICANN). All three of these different types of extranational, governmental and non-governmental institutions have evolved along with the 20th century's upsurge in economic growth, more democratic values and innovative management techniques. Although once again the stories are not linear or uniform, there can be little doubt that most international institutions have made impressive advances in both the range and quality of decision making.

Taken as a whole, the findings in this book and the conference discussions support the view that passivity, either enforced by powerful authorities or chosen by engrained habit, is in long-run decline. This does not mean that it is impossible to imagine events that could lead to a situation where a few hierarchically organised powers make and implement the decisions that actually shape future society-wide outcomes. Still, there appears to be a consensus that the long-run trend is towards a broader, much less hierarchical distribution of the capacity for effective action. Changes in this general direction are seen as having a good chance of prevailing in the longer term as long as there is a continued extension and deepening of democracy, fully competitive open markets, and the rule of law.

If this trend continues, then many parts of the world can be expected to experience, albeit from very different starting points, fairly radical breaks with the institutions and behavioural patterns which underpin the governance traditions that currently dominate most aspects of daily life. Whether in the family, firm or public sphere, the legitimacy, reach and exercise of authority seem unlikely to stay the same. Of course there have been and continue to be strong counter-tendencies that attempt to conserve time-honoured power relations. At the macro level, for instance, there are still many who believe that the nation state has the right to conduct its internal affairs without any regard for universal or global considerations. At the micro level, there is a backlash familiar from around the world of those hoping to defend male privileges, deny children's rights, or retain the Taylorist division of conception and execution typical of the industrial era enterprise management.

Such counter-tendencies gain support from at least two types of major conflict. The first and most obvious is that both those who lose and those who gain from change have difficulty – particularly in a period of significant economic and social transition – working out the nature and mechanisms of compensation. As a result, those who lose from change usually make every effort to preserve the governance and authority structures of the past, while those who gain consider that the institutions and compensation arrangements of the past should no longer apply. Secondly, transition periods often give rise to deep-seated differences in the perception of risk or, more prosaically, the extent of people's feelings of insecurity. Typically, those who are not actively creating the new rules and power structures tend to perceive major changes as driven by the uncontrollable workings of exogenous and dangerous forces. In public and private spheres fear becomes a major obstacle to change and to the emergence of the genuinely innovative forms of governance that are appropriate to new circumstances.

Indeed, the outset of the 21st century looks to be fraught with many of these transition-induced conflicts and fears. Confidence is ebbing in the established forms of governance that are unable to claim either the effectiveness or the legitimacy required to advance society towards its goals. At first glance, it looks like the inadequacies of existing forms of governance will just compound the already major challenges likely to be posed by the technological, economic and social changes that might occur over the coming decades. Indeed, this risk does seem significant and the potential for damage serious. One path that could possibly avoid this danger, as this conference series has revealed, would involve the introduction of policies that encourage the virtuous circle between improvements in governance capacity and positive technological, economic and social change.

21st century technological, economic and social dynamism: Prospects for governance

Technological, economic and social forces seem poised to thrust both greater freedom and greater responsibility on people's shoulders. Two main reasons are advanced for expecting a diffusion of decision-making prerogatives and duties. First, if realised, tomorrow's technological, economic and social dynamism will probably share the dual characteristic of enhancing the scope of feasible action and breaking down many of yesterday's constraining institutions and rules. Second, taking full advantage of future innovative tools, new ways of organising economic activity, and highly heterogeneous social orders is likely to call for a redistribution of power within and across governments, companies, communities and families. This diffusion of decision-making responsibilities is likely to be both a cause and a consequence of more dynamic, productive and sustainable societies in the future. Indeed, as already mentioned, there is potentially a virtuous relationship between changes in governance and greater dynamism – one that finds sustenance in the capacity to be creative.

The brief analysis, over the following pages, of the prospect that such changes will occur in the early decades of the 21st century can be divided according to the three principal topics for analysis covered so far in this conference series: technological possibilities, the advance of the global knowledge economy, and the movement towards more complex and diverse social orders.

Technological dynamism

As underscored by the first volume in this series, *21st Century Technologies: Promises and Perils of a Dynamic Future*, people have always depended on knowledge, and the technologies in which it is so often embedded, for survival. Furthermore, humanity has stood on the threshold of pervasive technological change before. Indeed, it does not seem likely that the impact of future technologies can surpass that of previous breakthroughs like writing, printing, or antibiotics. Still, there is no reason to belittle the technological developments that appear feasible within the next decades. On both scientific and societal grounds, the changes made possible by future innovations in info- and bio-tech, at a minimum, look to be on par with prior technological breakthroughs that have diffused throughout all areas of human activity, such as the wheel and electricity.

Certainly the technologies now at research stages have the potential not only to replace or improve on existing products and processes, but also, crucially, to give rise to a wide range of unanticipated uses, skills and desires. Equally important, there are four main areas in which the new wave of technological transformation will probably both depend on and facilitate improvements in decision-making capacity.

First, tomorrow's technologies are likely to contribute to a broader process of enhanced transparency and easier acquisition of information. Advances in information technology will allow for vastly better filtering, anticipation and interaction, using a variety of techniques including so-called intelligent agents, global databases and entirely speech-/video-based interfaces. The introduction of these more efficient tools

13

for managing information has the potential to generate entirely new options for decision makers as well as improving the processes for making such choices.

A second field where technological changes are likely both to require and to help cultivate improved governance capacities involves further intensification of technology's integration into daily life. There are three aspects to this trend. One is the extent to which daily life depends on more numerous and complex layers of tools and techniques. On this score developments could diverge, as people in poorer parts of the world shift out of a relatively direct relationship to the land while in richer regions people seek to eliminate intervening layers of technology that they perceive as reducing quality of life. The second dimension of technological intensity, which has been on an upward trend for a long time, has to do with the accumulated or embedded knowledge contained in tools, techniques and products. Here the pace of scientific advance and technical innovation promises a phase of almost exponential growth. The third dimension is the personal one, again likely to be marked by a strong upward trend as technology continues to become more individualised as well as more integrated into people's bodies and psyches.

A third terrain where realisation of long-run technological possibilities may jointly depend on and encourage the evolution of governance capacity has to do with solving specific problems, such as malaria, tuberculosis, species extinction and excessive production of CO^2. Most experts are fairly certain that with the appropriate incentives for undertaking research, development and deployment, there is a good chance that technologies now on the horizon could end up making major contributions to either overcoming or seriously mitigating these problems. What is less clear is how to introduce the incentives to generate and diffuse these technologies. In the past, decisions concerning areas where markets could not be expected to respond fully fell almost exclusively to governments. In the future, a broader approach that spreads the incentives throughout society may be more effective in harnessing all the available knowledge on the demand and supply sides. However, such a path is only feasible if those empowered to make and implement the decisions – ranging from individuals and local communities to corporate managers and international organisations – can develop governance capacities that are adequate for the task.

Lastly, a related fourth area where advances in technology and governance will probably be co-determining concerns culture, or the perceptions people have of their place and power in society. Not for the first time, science and its technological fruit seem poised to call into question some of humanity's basic cultural reference points – like the definitions of life, evolution, and our place in the universe. In the future, it seems probable that the introduction of fully functional nano technologies, artificial intelligence and genetic engineering will both depend on and provoke the insights that advance the social capacity to assess and make judgements on difficult ethical questions. In what almost looks like a fortuitous coincidence, the development and diffusion of future technologies could simultaneously impose and facilitate the acquisition by citizens, managers and public officials of the requisite capacities to judge and govern the ever more pervasive tools humanity invents. Only, if this co-evolution comes to pass it will be as an integral part of the transition to a global knowledge economy and society, where technology-enabled interdependencies combine with a significant diffusion of governance authority and responsibility.

Overall then, technological dynamism seems likely to provoke new forms of governance because it entails a fundamental shift in the capacity to make and implement the choices that shape future technological developments. Perhaps the most obvious example of this co-dependence is in the field of biotechnology. This is not because there is something unique about the ethical and technical dilemmas posed by genetic engineering, or because in the future there will suddenly be much less apathy than in the past. Previous technological advances, like those in nuclear science in the 20th century, also called into question the future of the species and elicited considerable political activism by concerned citizens. What makes developments in biotechnology different from breakthroughs in the past is that the vast range of radical applications made possible by genetic engineering are only likely to emerge in a context where many more people have and want the authority, knowledge and tools needed to take an active part in deciding how this technology develops and is used.

In other areas such as personal nutrition, health and the surrounding environment there are also clear signs that people want to gain greater direct and informed control. Similarly, when it comes to the threats posed to privacy and copyright by information technology, there is an evident co-dependency between advances in technology and governance capacities. This is why the challenge for policy makers in the longer term will be to foster the rules, institutions and behavioural patterns that take into account the mutual contingency between technological dynamism and governance – with the aim of sparking a virtuous circle between the two.

Economic dynamism

Over the coming decades, as emphasised in the second book in this series – *The Future of the Global Economy: Towards a Long-Boom?* – there is a chance that economic changes will bring a continuation of the long-run trend towards the extension and deepening of market relationships in a world where transaction costs of all kinds are falling. In this more competitive and highly interdependent context, the rules and behaviour that shape the making and implementation of decisions could also undergo major changes.

Like the waves of technological breakthroughs discussed above, this is not a new phenomenon. Market-driven economic transformation has been a potent force in the past, regularly outpacing the regulations and habits that entrench authority. Leading sectors and firms, managerial strata and techniques, dominant production

15

methods and skill patterns have all been shaken up on a regular basis. What may distinguish the coming period of economic dynamism from previous transitions is, in a manner similar to the preceding discussion of technology, the coincidence of future economic changes with new forms of distributed and flexible governance.

In particular, economic dynamism in the early part of the 21st century may propel two general trends with special implications for governance. The first relates to a shift in the predominant source of value-added in the economy as a whole, away from mass production for an impersonal market to a production process where the consumer plays a direct and personal role. The second general trend involves the long-run deepening of economic interdependence, only this time potentially under conditions of much greater transparency and on a global basis.

Turning to the first trend, what distinguishes the knowledge economy from preceding periods is the centrality of creativity (in the sense of personal expression, not unprecedented artistic uniqueness) as the source of value-added. An economy dominated by one-off personalised products and services will require new ways for both producers and consumers to add knowledge to the final output. This is in contrast to the passivity expected of most people when daily life is dominated by mass production and mass consumption. In the future, attaining the decentralisation of learning, initiative, innovation and design, necessitated by unique production and consumption, is likely both to demand and help enable a fairly radical reworking of the decision-making range and capacity of almost all members of society.

In turn, this leap in importance of initiative and interdependency is likely to demand a significant shift from values such as obedience, conformity and exclusivity – as sustained by various strains of state-centric nationalism, Taylorism, and paternalism – to more tolerant, self-directed and egalitarian perspectives. Indications that these decision-making values and methods are changing can be seen in the declining status and effectiveness of certain institutions, laws and ways of organising people. There is a chance that in most OECD countries the 21st century will witness the passing of 19th and 20th centuries' institutional and organisational innovations, such as the standardised employee-employer contract and production process that follow Taylorist principles, government bureaucracies for administrating centralised welfare state programmes, and nuclear families centred on one male income-earner. Although the exact contours of future values and institutions remain to be determined, there is a good chance that the distribution and exercise of authority will shift – partly through decentralisation towards individuals and smaller collectivities, and partly through the development of means for articulating truly planet-wide goals and tasks.

This latter issue is the second area of co-dependency between economic dynamism and governance. Technological advances that shrink distance and the interdependencies that arise from much wider and deeper global economic integration will tend to confront decision makers with new possibilities and responsibilities. Already there is a growing awareness on the part of governments, firms, associations and individuals that in the 21st century global power will no longer be the exclusive domain of imperial nations or the largest multinational corporations or the dominant religious orders. As a result, the requirements for sustaining the legitimacy – both for internal constituencies and for external "clients" – of decisions taken at the international level are changing.

Decision makers are being pushed to reconsider traditional aims and methods of governance. The people in positions of authority in many existing international organisations, be they ministers in national governments or directors of the board or activists that make up an NGO, are in the midst of redefining the power they wield. Not necessarily because a sovereign state lacks military capabilities or a board director the formal legal right to vote independently, but because the nature of global action is changing. These changes, like the emergence of new planetary issues and new constituencies that lie outside the mandates and/or competencies of existing international organisations, could be significant enough to call into question the ways in which authority is exercised at a global level.

Should these two general trends dominate future economic change, there is a chance that the hierarchical forms of governance that have predominated in many areas of human activity will be turned upside down. Typically, within the firm and in markets, authority has been organised according to the familiar pyramid structure – even if there has been intermittent shuffling of the pecking order. Firms in general have been subject to a steady strengthening of hierarchy as those in positions of authority usually followed a Taylorist logic that attempts to control every step of the production process. Markets that have in practice been relatively closed due to various "imperfections" or barriers (tariff, transport, information, scale) have also been characterised by the hierarchical structures associated with different degrees of oligopoly.

In the future, the generalisation of personalised creation and deeper interdependence could overthrow hierarchical forms of organisation, both within the firm and in the market-place, by transforming three relationships that have largely defined governance structures in the market economy.

First, the further deepening of interdependence is likely to be accomplished in part through major reductions in the cost of high-quality information (greater transparency). As a result, it may become possible to reduce significantly the cost advantages of co-ordinating production within the conventional firm. This could create a situation where dis-integration is feasible. In turn, this would allow relationships that were once subject to the authority of a rigid command structure to be openly negotiated (in the market-place or through new types of task-specific organisations with variable authority structures).

Making this leap will not be easy, partly because moving towards a dis-integration of the hierarchical division of labour within the enterprise will depend on fundamental change to a second basic relationship – the separation of conception and execution. Without going into full detail, this is a corollary of the shift to the personalisation of production and consumption. The implication is that future competitive success will demand products – tangible and intangible – that capture much more completely two knowledge sets, those of the supplier and of the consumer. Without the capacity to fully utilise the available knowledge, customisation and on-the-spot innovation become much more difficult.

However, fulfilling this imperative almost certainly calls into question the basic premise of Taylorism, which is to extract and codify *in advance* the exact attributes of both the production process and the final product. In the context of personalised output, control and responsibility shift, altering the basic power relations that have underpinned the organisation of much of economic life. Both the individual consumer and producer take on new roles that are close to the opposite of what prevailed in the world of mass production and mass consumption. Passivity is no longer the watchword.

Moving to this type of activist, personal economy will also entail changes to a third basic economic relationship – supply networks will need to take on much more reconfigurable and competitively open patterns. Parallel with the dis-integration of the firm and the advent of personalised production and consumption, a creative economy will depend on a vast and flexible network of supply-side responses. If market-places remain relatively closed off, dominated by oligopolistic hierarchies, then the incentives that would make spontaneous personalisation feasible are unlikely to emerge. Most firms will have little reason to relinquish control or break with traditional patterns of managerial authority when there are few competitors. Most consumers will not even bother to cultivate the creativity that personalisation requires if the chances of finding the spontaneous, once-off suppliers are low or the search too costly.

Major advances in institutional and behavioural frameworks will be necessary to usher in a world without bosses or monopolies, with seamless supply networks and creative personalisation as the source of most wealth creation. In such a world, where predetermined allocations of authority or initiative are significantly reduced, the challenge for policy makers will be to introduce sufficient levels of transparency, confidence and competition. Then people's experience of inventing rather than following, of being active rather than passive, can be expected to significantly enhance the desire and capacity to govern. Continuously gathering the knowledge that comes from wielding power and taking responsibility might be just the ingredients that fuel the virtuous circle between economic dynamism and new forms of governance.

Social dynamism

In coming years, as detailed in the third publication in this series, *The Creative Society of the 21st Century*, most people will probably experience significant changes in their sense of identity or in the identity expressed by many of the people directly around them. Around the globe, from a wide range of departure points, there are likely to be major alterations in two of the key determinants of self-identity: social status (income, age, profession, etc.) and authority structures (nation, family, religion, etc.). Such transformations in identity are, in turn, closely tied up with the ways in which people make and implement decisions. New identities, for instance ones that are less obedient, less passive and assume greater responsibility – or the opposite – have profound implications for governance.

Once again, this kind of social dynamism is not a new phenomenon. Changes in the nexus of status, authority and identity have been associated with some of the most painful and hopeful episodes of human history. However, this time around there is a chance that future social dynamism may be distinguished from such periods in the past by the extent to which the construction of identity will be left up to the individual. This would be a significant departure from earlier ways of forming identity that have leaned very heavily on a relatively limited number of overbearing and inflexible sources.

Four possible society-wide trends that look set to propel future social dynamism might also push this radical change in the methods used to build identity: growing demographic diversity, transitions in the dominant socio-economic systems, widespread institutional decline and renewal, and major strides in developing individual capacities. Each of these four trends has the potential to act as both a solvent on the old frameworks and a catalyst for new, potentially less hierarchical ways of forging socially functional identities.

First, the tendency towards greater demographic diversity reflects a variety of factors, from changing age structures to immigration. Not for the first time, both within and across different parts of the world, demographic shifts are breaking down old constituencies and opening up the possibility of creating new ones. What is perhaps unique this time is that the churning of demographic attributes is occurring in a world where there is less insistence or efficacy in the efforts of established authorities to impose identity on people. Should such openness prevail, there is probably a better chance that those who are willing and able to forge their identities outside the traditional hierarchies of social status and authority will succeed. This should serve as a springboard for further diversity and give pride of place to open, non-hierarchical forms of governance that can not only accommodate but encourage social differentiation.

Secondly, socio-economic transitions also tend to shake up existing hierarchies. For instance, the wrenching process of industrialisation that is bringing mass

19

production, mass consumption and mass government to many poorer parts of the world regularly runs roughshod over traditional hierarchies. The three other societal transitions already under way, from command planning to rule-based markets, from post-industrial to knowledge-intensive, and from global trade to global integration, are all equally callous when it comes to uprooting the formerly entrenched categories of social status and sources of authority. Overall, there are grounds for expecting that if democracy and the rules meant to ensure competitive conditions prevail, then the trend will be towards less authoritarian, less hierarchical outcomes. However, much will turn on what happens to the capacities of institutions and individuals.

Thirdly, on the institutional side there are signs of a possible trend break. For a long time diversity, originating in the scattered nature of human settlement and ingrained inequality of opportunity, has been subject to the homogenising influences of efforts to establish national monoculture, corporate conformity and uniform social services. The pursuit of these objectives will only diminish gradually as the 20th century preoccupation with socio-cultural uniformity gives way to a recognition and encouragement of individual uniqueness and heterogeneity.

The problem is that most of the old institutions are ill-suited for new forms of governance. A lack of legitimacy and effectiveness plagues many organisations attempting to adapt to emerging circumstances. For instance, national governments and international intergovernmental organisations are finding it difficult to gain credibility and achieve stated goals in the global arena. Similarly, enterprises and non-governmental organisations cannot garner the necessary legitimacy or power to fill global or local stages while lacking transparent democratic accountability. In effect, the pressures of technological, economic and social dynamism call into question the capacity of existing institutions without providing clear avenues for the emergence of new ones. Here the source of innovation is likely to be found in the next trend.

The fourth trend, that both propels social dynamism and plays a major role in changing the relationship between identity and authority, concerns improvements in the capacity of individuals to engage or participate in new ways of making and implementing decisions. Once again, this is a continuation of a long-run process that has provided a growing number of people with the capacity to resist and eventually to break free from arbitrarily imposed rules and patterns. Over time, greater knowledge has been wielded to gain independence, despite the regular and dire warnings of those who argue that grasping such freedom will bring insecurity and chaos.

For governance the prospect of such significant societal transformation brings both risks and opportunities. On the one hand, the coexistence of extreme variations in degrees of power and the capacity to wield it can considerably complicate certain decisions and at the same time threaten to provoke destructive social conflict. On the other hand, the diversification of the aims and methods of governance that emerge from a more heterogeneous society can help create a climate that is hospitable to difference and encourages the development of innovative choices. Overall, the movement towards greater social heterogeneity is likely to be, once again, both a cause and consequence of changes in the capacity of people to govern themselves and the society around them. Indeed, greater diversity in society and the diffusion of decision making probably go hand in hand – not in a linear fashion but in ways that correspond roughly with the type of societal transitions that are under way.

In this sense, each of the four trends that seem likely to propel social diversity over the next decades are also likely to pose different types of opportunities and risks for governance. For instance, in the case of the shift from a mass-based to knowledge-based economy and society there seem to be few precedents for such a broad diffusion of decision making. Efforts will be needed to guard against the centrifugal forces that threaten, as some commentators fear, a destructive fragmentation and dissolution of the social order. Policies will be needed to buttress not only access to the physical networks made up of fibre optic cable and computer software, but also the social networks that are based on mutual understanding. In these cutting-edge communities the magnitude of the challenge of ensuring the integrity, trustworthiness and interoperability of diverse networks will probably be compounded by a continued decoupling of the 19th and 20th centuries' fusion of nation, as an identity, and state, as an administrative unit.

For other countries and regions, only beginning to make the transition from a command or rural economy with usually isolationist, non-elected regimes to rule-based market democracies, the governance aims, if not the means, are more familiar. However, as the transition difficulties experienced by a broad range of countries demonstrate, the transformation of society-wide decision-making systems is easier said than done. Restoring and creating the required social capital means addressing the needs for new discourses, new assumptions and new networks for individuals, families, firms and governmental bodies. With such wide variation in the points of departure and the specific aspirations that guide choices, it seems unlikely that any one model will fit all the circumstances. Instead it is possible that the 21st century will leave behind the restrictive, homogenising tendencies of the "modern" nation state.

There is some hope that the imperatives of militarism and nationalism may be sufficiently attenuated to allow diversity to serve as a source for the experimentation and innovation upon which prosperity is likely to be built. However, given the scale and scope of the societal transitions likely to mark the outset of the 21st century, it is important not to neglect the heightened risks of conflict due to the possible polarisation that frequently accompanies the passing of old social orders and the emergence of new ones. Policy choices will be the determining factor in minimising this friction and encouraging the potential synergies. The challenge will

21

be to combine the flexibility that innovation and creativity demand with new ways of providing people with a sense of security. Here again, the co-dependency of knowledge and the power to use it as a decision maker could be the antidote to insecurity and one of the main sources for tomorrow's creativity.

From this perspective, appeals to the simplicity or efficiency of less complex and slower ways of living ignore the fact that today's multifaceted and fast-paced world is but the fruit of human desires pursued with the greater capacities offered by more knowledge and better tools. Indeed, it is at this level, where individuals make the countless decisions that reproduce daily life, that the innate human desire to gain control over events could combine with a steadily improving capacity to do so. New forms of governance, including the renewal of the rituals and institutions that foster a sense of security, could be the outcome. Overall then, the challenge for policy makers is to target initiatives likely to encourage the development of both individual capacities and the virtuous circle between new forms of governance and technological, economic and social change.

Learning how to govern and governing to enhance learning

Recently, considerable interest has been expressed in the topic of governance. Most often the focus is on the role and methods of governments. Understandably, parallels are drawn between the changes taking place in the private sector, such as the advent of e-business models facilitated by the internet, and what might be done to improve the delivery of government services – including electoral politics. "Reinventing government" or how to set up and realise the potential of e-government is certainly an important issue. However, this book addresses a broader question: how might societies in the future become more effective in arriving at desirable collective outcomes.

The answer, echoed in the results from the previous conferences in this series, is that creating a desirable future will depend on provoking a virtuous circle between new forms of governance and technological, economic and social dynamism. Historically, it would not be the first time changes in governance were intimately tied with fairly sweeping societal transformation. What does distinguish the current conjuncture is the nature of changes in governance that will be needed.

As the preceding analysis underscores, establishing the complementarity between future dynamism and new forms of governance entails two major, interdependent shifts in how decisions are made and implemented throughout society. The first, more macro-level dimension involves replacing predetermined and rigid organisational schema with much more spontaneous, fluid and task-based approaches. The second, more micro-level dimension concerns the need to overcome the hierarchical relationships, habits and traditions that have been so ingrained in how people behave and think.

Both of these changes will call for major advances in the practical skills and rules used in daily life by organisations and individuals, whether operating alone or in concert, locally or globally, in a government, workplace or household context. Thus, the common challenge for policy makers, in public and private sectors, is to ensure that people will have the capacity to exercise their liberty and to manage the constraints that come with the adoption of a common set of basic principles or values. Furthermore, policies will need to address the interdependency of the micro and macro dimensions of this challenge that arise, because the requisite skills and institutional frameworks are the outcome of efforts at both the collective and individual levels.

Despite the extremely wide disparities between different parts of the world, two basic and overlapping policy thrusts are likely to be crucial for improving governance capacities in the 21st century. The first approach is relatively indirect since it depends on encouraging technological, economic and social dynamism. The second, more direct approach involves efforts to upgrade the primary ingredients – the skills, infrastructure, frameworks, values and goals – that determine individual and institutional capacity to make and implement the decisions that govern the future.

The first set of policies has been laid out in some detail in the previous conferences in this series, including the different areas where policy continuity, major reforms and new directions need to be considered. Nowhere will new forms of governance evolve without the positive contributions made by new technologies, the greater specialisation and wealth arising from deeper and more extensive economic interdependency, and the creativity inspired by further social differentiation. This means that advances in governance will depend considerably on the success of policies meant to encourage the ongoing transitions that are leaving behind traditional agriculture and command planning for either mass-based or creative knowledge-driven societies. These changes are crucial sources of necessary tools and experiences.

Which still leaves a second set of policies to consider since the pursuit of technological, economic and social dynamism does run the risk of disintegrating into chaos and conflict if governance capacities are not also addressed directly. Allowing the improvements in learning, confidence and common mission that effective governance requires to simply be the unconscious by-products of societal transition is probably inadequate to the task. Three general areas can be identified where policy makers, for the purposes of this chapter primarily in government, could contribute directly to the evolution of governance capacities – and thereby also assist with increasing the rates of sustainable technological, economic and social dynamism.

Learning infrastructure

The first framework that plays a central role in creating and enhancing society-wide decision-making and implementation capacities involves the basic infrastructure that makes learning possible: universal access to initial education; adequate sanitation, health care and nutrition; mechanisms for insuring individuals against certain uncontrollable risks and the vagaries that can accompany ageing; and political stability. There is no underestimating the importance of these foundations. Without the underpinnings of literacy, physical health and a minimum sense of security, learning is seriously impeded. Without learning there can be little expectation of improvements in the quality of decision making at home, on the job or in the community at large.

Recognising the universal importance of this basic infrastructure does not mean uniform policy responses are in order. On the contrary, the vast differences in the starting points of nations and social groups when it comes to the quality and accessibility of this infrastructure demand highly differentiated approaches. For instance, in many parts of the world, as emphasised previously in this conference series, efforts to combat poverty need to be given the highest priority. In wealthier countries the stress needs to be on policies that, for example, transform education so it is no longer a process that schools young people to be obedient and responsive to given problems. Instead, it should develop the sense of autonomy and self-worth that underpins initiative and imagination.

Factory-era school systems, along with status-screening mechanisms like the high school diploma, are probably inimical to the development of the learning methods and incentives upon which a knowledge-intensive economy and society can thrive. Similarly, the various services that are essential for assuring good health and a sense of social security can be provided through a variety of mechanisms – including hybrid public-private systems. Encouraging sufficiently high levels of learning and security depends on finding the right balance between incentives and disincentives in the context of a particular society's unique culture, history and institutions.

Confidence

The second policy-relevant framework that supports and guides the governance capacities of a society has to do with the nexus of confidence, legitimacy and trust. Quality decision making and the learning that it requires are expensive and inefficient in a world fraught with distrust. If people cannot easily access and verify information, then learning is much more costly. If decisions are made behind closed doors it is difficult to establish accountability. Barriers to gathering quality information and determining accountability erode the incentives and disincentives that are involved in the maintenance of integrity and legitimacy.

The transparency, accountability, integrity and legitimacy of the institutions, rules, practices and values upon which a society functions are essential determinants of the quality of decision making. Of course all of these attributes are relative – there is no such thing as absolute transparency or accountability in social and economic affairs. But what is crucial from a policy point of view is to encourage the development of the tools, organisations and expectations that improve what might be called, in a general way, the degree of confidence people have in their society. Once again, the initiatives likely to succeed in strengthening this framework will differ significantly across and within countries.

Many places lack the rules and/or mechanisms for the sufficiently impartial enforcement needed to make contracts trustworthy, guarantees reliable, politicians or managers accountable and the institutional fabric of society legitimate. In such places, transactions – from market exchange to sharing knowledge – can be burdensome to the point of economic and social breakdown. Under these circumstances the policy agenda takes as its primary aim the restoration or establishment of confidence in the laws and institutions that structure daily life. For societies where rule of law and institutional legitimacy have reigned for considerable periods of time, the challenge is how to deepen or renew confidence *vis-à-vis* higher aspirations.

In this sense the scale of the hurdles, or people's perceptions of their difficulties, remains relative. There is still a long way to go, even in very confident societies, to achieve the degree of transparency and accountability necessary to effectively govern the challenges posed by technological change and the emergence of the global knowledge economy. For instance, as already noted in the discussion of technological dynamism, when it comes to genetically modified organisms or privacy and security on the internet, existing rules and institutions are not capable of creating sufficient transparency and accountability to inspire trust and legitimacy. Similar governance deficiencies plague businesses trying to inspire worker creativity and engage stakeholders ranging from local communities to ethical mutual funds.

Perhaps one of the highest-profile examples of where transparency, accountability and legitimacy are insufficient to create confidence is in the global arena. Experience shows that there is little reason to expect the top-down imposition of decision-making systems to be successful when it comes to global environmental co-operation, the introduction of a more information-rich and trustworthy financial architecture, or a multilateral treaty on foreign direct investment. Here there is a considerable gap between the failed efforts of old governance systems and the still-limited capacity of future decision-making networks.

Indeed, beyond a world structured by a hierarchy of authority and predetermined aims is a realm of considerable ambiguity, where the process can in many cases be the product. Judgement and creativity, facilitated by improvements in transparency and accountability, become cornerstones for generating social sustainability in circumstances where the precise means and ends emerge from the network. Policy, in this context, must also relinquish its hierarchical mantle to become the invention of goals, rules and procedures by all social actors that are willing both to abide by network standards and to subscribe to a common mission.

Mission

One final ingredient, without which a creative learning society would likely collapse, is the overarching and shared mission statement. Allegiance to a common code is the prerequisite not only for maintaining the standards upon which diversity thrives, but crucially for establishing the minimum set of shared values that would make improvements in governance capacity feasible. Basic parameters or values that could serve as standards within which human expression flourishes are slowly being put into place. Future implementation (not just recognition) of the already mentioned Universal Declaration of Human Rights of 1948, as well as other more recent initiatives like the Rio Declaration of 1992, will play an important part in setting the stringent limits within which spontaneity, fluidity and initiative can flourish.

Indeed, although it may appear paradoxical, it seems likely that as the world gets more complex, the most effective method for ensuring coherent and sustainable societies will be to pursue adherence to simple and universal rules – a solution that rests on the similarly paradoxical truth that freedom is based on accepting certain constraints. The need to reconcile these conflicting impulses highlights the danger that even if people have acquired the appropriate decision-making and implementation capacities, they will still need sufficient political will to reconcile some difficult trade-offs. For instance, abandoning industrialisation might save rural ways of living, but cuts off the possibility of introducing other desirable lifestyles. Similarly, stepping back from a more open and integrated planet might help to preserve tradition and autarky, but it would probably foreclose progress towards the greater tolerance, creativity and well-being that are likely to be the desirable outcomes of a more dynamic and tightly knit world.

Finally, it is important to acknowledge, by the same token, that success in introducing policies to encourage a virtuous circle between governance and technological, economic and social dynamism also means excluding other options – particularly preservation of the status quo. As a result, resistance can be expected from those who do not wish to subscribe to the necessary new frameworks or see the more hierarchical and fixed modes of governance come to an end. The message offered here is double-edged. On the one hand, there are strong analytical grounds for affirming the tremendous potential for positive change in the decades to come. On the other hand, actually realising such a trajectory will hinge on the success of exceptional efforts to introduce the appropriate policies. Complacency, rooted in the view that change is inevitable and that explicit collective choices – including those made by governments – are largely irrelevant, would almost certainly mean missing out on many of the highly promising possibilities of the 21st century.

Chapter 2

Wealth, Values, Institutions: Trends in Government and Governance

by
Daniel Tarschys
Stockholm University, Sweden

"The request which agriculture, manufacture and commerce present to governments, is as modest and reasonable as that which Diogenes made to Alexander: 'Stand out of my sunshine.' We have no need of favour – we require only a secure and open path."[*]

Some two centuries after Jeremy Bentham made this plea for minimal government, our appreciation of the linkages between politics and economics is much less straightforward. At a variety of levels – local, regional, national and supranational – political institutions play a crucial role in social and economic development, and the lessons drawn from the latter half of the past century have only enhanced our awareness of the complexity of their interaction. Consider the recent experience of governance in three parts of the world:

- In the industrialised countries, an unprecedented economic expansion has gone hand in hand with an equally unprecedented growth in the size of the public sector. While particular forms of government intervention, and the fiscal burden needed to sustain them, may well have reduced the growth rates of individual countries in certain periods, the main trend in the economies of the OECD area has been a mutually reinforcing expansion of both private and public activities.

- In the third world, meanwhile, much smaller public sectors have frequently been seen to be overstretched and thereby to impair the conditions for economic development. Reducing public commitments was long a standard ingredient in the structural adjustment programmes prescribed by international

---

[*] Jeremy Bentham, quoted in Alan Bullock & Maurice Shock, *The Liberal Tradition from Fox to Keynes* (1967), Oxford: Oxford University Press, p. 29.

financial institutions. Recently, a more favoured approach has been to give more emphasis to measures intended to bring about "good governance".

- As the Soviet bloc collapsed, one of the great surprises was the remarkable weakness of the government apparatus left behind. With its comprehensive and highly intrusive political machinery, the Soviet system had appeared to be the very epitome of "the strong state", but many of the foundations of this structure, not least the moral ones, turned out to be so fragile that the whole edifice rapidly crumbled. Rebuilding a stable institutional framework of governance is now widely recognised as one of the key preconditions for the successful transition of the former Soviet-type economies to market conditions.

What is thus clear from just a quick glance in three different directions is that governance has become a central component in any explanation of economic and social development. It is both cause and effect, covering both independent and dependent variables in the evolutionary process. It is also linked to several different sides or aspects of our common history: to the formation and propagation of *values*, to the creation and distribution of *wealth*, and to the emergence and consolidation of *institutions*.

Although "governance" is sometimes used in a wider sense to cover steering and control activities in different spheres of society – enterprises, voluntary organisations, etc. – it refers principally to the exercise of authority in government and the political arena. This chapter will focus on four lines in 20th century thought on the topic, relating to 1) the scope of governance, 2) the units and levels of governance, 3) the use and abuse of governance, and 4) the techniques of governance.

1. The scope of governance

At the beginning of the 20th century, governments of European states extracted and spent something between 5% and 10% of gross national product. A large part of this went to the upkeep of the military machinery, which was still the most important pillar of state power. At the close of the century, between one-third and one-half of the gross national product of industrialised countries – in some Scandinavian countries as much as six-tenths – passed through the public coffers. Education, health care, public transport and operation of the physical infrastructure had become major industries, predominantly funded through taxes, compulsory contributions, and public user charges. Giant sums were also channelled through various public or semi-public mechanisms for income maintenance, such as sickness and unemployment insurance and public pension schemes.

Like the Industrial Revolution of the 18th and 19th centuries, the "Public Revolution" of the 20th century has thoroughly transformed the economies of the advanced nations (a theme developed further in Tarschys, 1983). Other notions employed to capture this transition – "post-industrialism", "the service economy", "the tertiary society", "the knowledge economy", "the information technology revolution", etc. – highlight a variety of its technical characteristics, which have also affected the balance between the private and public spheres of these societies. Not only have public budgets swelled; there has also been a growth in intervention as expressed in the increasing scope of regulation. The number of statutes issued by parliaments and national governments has increased; the sub-vegetation of by-laws adopted by local and regional authorities has become more dense; and rules adopted through intergovernmental or supragovernmental co-operation have proliferated. At the close of the century, the *"acquis"* of the European Union is assessed to consist of some 80 000 pages of union legislation.

What might account for this growth in the scope of governance? Before the first theory of a positive correlation between the level of economic activity and the size of the public sector was launched by Adolph Wagner in 1883, most expectations went in the opposite direction. The faith in progress that emerged particularly with the Enlightenment was often combined with a conviction that the need for government action would gradually diminish through mankind's moral and economic advancement. Authority was required only in so far as people were unable to control themselves and manage their own affairs. As they matured, however, they would no longer need political guidance. The state that Hegel proclaimed to be the end of history was not an agency of economic intervention but rather a form of moral civilisation. To liberal economists and socialist utopians alike, state action held no promise of progress. As Adam Smith expressed it in The *Wealth of Nations*: "Though the profusion of government must, undoubtedly, have retarded the natural progress of England towards wealth and improvement, it has not been able to stop it" (quoted in Bullock and Shock, 1967, p. 26).

Against this predominant opinion, Wagner argued that an increase in public spending should be seen as a natural consequence of economic growth. Several processes accounted for this. First of all, the costs of defence would go up as all nations invested in more sophisticated weapons. Secondly, domestic protection would also become more expensive through industrialisation. The density of modern living would lead to more social frictions, and the complexity of an advanced economy would require new forms of public control. A third reason to increase public expenditure was the greater ability of government to meet certain income-elastic demands. Education and culture were fields where collective producers were by and large more efficient than private ones. The public sector would hence grow as basic needs were satisfied and patterns of consumption shifted in this direction. In some other areas such as rail transport, the capital required for investment would become so large that it could hardly be provided through private accumulation (Wagner, 1883).

Wagner's proposition inspired a wide range of hypotheses linking various technological and societal variables to growth in government activities. An Italian economist,

F.S. Nitti, was among the first to suggest that democratisation as such would inexorably boost public spending, through both increased demand for services and lower resistance to fiscal extraction. When the control of government rests with the people, he argued, they will no longer look upon taxation as a loss (Nitti, 1904). Arnold Brecht (1932) highlighted urbanisation as a prime force behind government expansion, linking population density to an increased demand for expenditures on housing, welfare, and security. G.S. Gupta (1969) has linked these perspectives together, tracing both the early expansion of the public sector and the later slowing-down of its growth rate to the cost-benefit analyses of the electorate. With a system of proportional taxation, the large majority will have an interest in the provision of more services as long as their benefits exceed their costs. Hence, the growth of the public sector is greatly stimulated by the extension of the franchise but then retarded when a point is reached where most citizens are affected by fairly severe taxation.

In the past century, the most abrupt impetus to government growth – as well as to government indebtedness – was undoubtedly provided by the two world wars. The downward adjustment of spending levels in the wake of the First World War, a major cause of the Depression, stimulated a study of macro-economic linkages that culminated in Keynes's *General Theory* (1936). Following the Second World War, the higher level of government activity was largely maintained, inspiring Alan T. Peacock and Jack Wiseman (1961) to their theory of the "displacement effect" or "ratchet effect" in public spending. Briefly stated, this hypothesis predicts that whereas public expenditure will be reasonably stable in normal times, it may be drastically boosted by wars and crises, and since its "stickiness" makes it easier to shift upwards than downwards, the higher levels are likely to remain. Over time, therefore, the curve of public expenditure as a ratio of the gross national product will resemble a staircase.

In the past half-century, the main force behind the expansion of public budgets has no doubt been the sustained growth of public service provision and income redistribution through the welfare state. Early steps were taken immediately after the war, but the most marked expansion followed rather in the latter part of *"les trente glorieuses"* with their unprecedented growth rates. Since the escalator effects built into the various transfer systems were strong enough to withstand the downward pressure ensuing from subsequent slower economic growth, public expenditure as a percentage of gross national product continued to rise in the following decades a well. As a result, many countries incurred exceptional budget deficits and policy makers were compelled to reconsider many components of the established welfare systems. The past two decades in particular have been a time of retrenchment and reorientation, with multiple efforts to "reinvent government" and introduce greater efficiency into programmes of redistribution and public services.

Even taking such efforts into account, one is struck by the resilience of "big government" in advanced industrial economies. There has been no lack of suggestions that growth rates would suffer irreparable damage if a particular level of government spending was surpassed. At the turn the century, French economist Leroy-Beaulieu calculated that the fiscal maximum a modern state could extract was 12-13% percent of gross national product. A few decades later, his Australian colleague Colin Clark set the fiscal ceiling of a thriving economy in the neighbourhood of 25% of its gross national product (Johansen, 1968-70). In recent decades, public choice economists in particular have sought to estimate the pernicious impact of tax wedges and "dead-weight loss" on the growth capacity of the economy.

Though it is more than likely that high levels and particular forms of taxation have indeed retarded the economic development of some countries, the experience of the 80s and 90s nevertheless clearly shows that market expansion and big government have by and large continued their peaceful if not symbiotic coexistence. The long list of ways in which public authorities, and the fiscal burden needed to sustain them, impede economic growth needs to be supplemented by a – probably not much shorter – list of ways in which the same agencies stimulate and facilitate private sector activities. The latter list would include not only basic services indispensable to enterprises (infrastructure, security, contract enforcement, risk control and management, etc.) but also human services necessary to sustain consumer demand, labour supply and social reproduction. There are reasons to doubt whether a high level of economic activity could be sustained without the ceaseless efforts of governments at various levels to organise collective demand and stimulate private demand through the transfer of purchasing power. Though we still have much to learn about the nature of the linkages between wealth generation and various forms of government institutions and activities, they are clearly more intricate and many-sided than was previously suspected.

2. The units and levels of governance

In December 1991, the heads of state and government of twelve independent nations met in Maastricht to form the European Union. Almost at the same time, at a meeting outside Minsk, another union was dissolved into twelve independent states. Other changes in the European state system in the early 90s were the emergence of five sovereign states on the territory of the former Yugoslavia and the peaceful dissolution of Czechoslovakia into two independent states. In other cases, requests for greater autonomy at sub-national levels of government were met with devolution of authority to regional institutions, as in Scotland, Wales and Northern Ireland. In Kosovo, similar claims were stubbornly rejected, eventually pushing the region into a vicious spiral of rebellion, repression and ethnic cleansing.

These recent examples illustrate the fluidity of the territorial organisation of governance. By the year 1500, there were around 1 500 sovereign political units in Europe. One and a half centuries later, at the conclusion of the Peace of Westphalia, there were some 300 independent territories, bishoprics and city-states in Germany alone. The empires which eventually swallowed many of these units, large and small, were highly heterogeneous not only in their ethnic composition but also in the degree to which political authority was exercised in different parts of the realm. Many versions of local immunity, liberty or autonomy survived in the imperial compounds. Yet there were also hegemonic and centralist tendencies that eventually endangered the survival of the vast empires, not least through the nationalist and separatist reactions they engendered.

The systems of governance that have been established in the modern world are inextricably linked to the different waves of nationalism that have swept through all continents in the last two centuries. The sequence of state-building and nation-building has differed in various countries; we have seen both "nations in quest of a state" and "states in quest of a nation". Yet the keenly felt need for a sense of social and cultural cohesion has underlain all efforts to consolidate legitimate political systems. What the anthropologist Benedict Anderson in a famous book-title has called "imagined communities" have played a large role strengthening the underpinnings of modern government.

A democracy cannot survive without a "demos". Unless the electorate is held together by a sense of *Schicksalsgemeinschaft*, or shared fate, a common legacy and a common destiny, the political authorities will encounter great difficulties in enforcing their decisions. While governments derive their legitimacy from multiple sources – such as the constitutional procedures by which they are elected or appointed, the quality of the services they deliver, and the respect they may command by demonstrating fairness and upholding the law – they cannot do without some measure of cultural allegiance of the citizens to the political community constituting the state.

Recalling Peacock and Wiseman's "ratchet effect", it seems reasonable to assume that the sense of national identity is heightened in wartime and that this enhanced community spirit can be carried over in some measure to the ensuing peacetime. In identifying the driving forces behind the welfare state that evolved in the latter half of the 20th century, one should pay attention not only to economic but also to institutional and ideological factors. Wealth was certainly crucial: this was the first society in history that could afford extensive education, health care, and income maintenance. Through the political and administrative machinery at hand, it could also organise these services. But values were also decisive. Apart from such undercurrents as an unrelenting faith in progress and a penchant for political technology and engineering, a key precondition for the welfare state – and not least the substantial fiscal levy required to erect and sustain it – was the sense of national cohesion and national solidarity that had taken root after many decades of state consolidation.

As systems of governance evolve and changes occur in the interplay between different levels of political authority, concerns have been raised about the effect these changes may have on citizens' sense of identity and loyalty. There is, however, no reason to believe that shifts in the citizens' support for and identification with the different units must occur within a zero-sum framework. The gradual emergence of a common European identity, closely monitored in periodic opinion studies, does not seem to have lessened the sense of allegiance with the nation state, nor is there necessarily any significant rivalry between local, regional and national identities. It is true that the tactics of some movements for regional autonomy have included vocal challenges to central institutions, but their long-term strategies normally aim at some form of accommodation with the national government. Identities and allegiances to territories of different size can very well be cumulative.

As to resources at the disposal of various levels of government, there is alas more justification for the suspicion that they are finite and must be shared in some orderly fashion. Advanced industrial states channel a considerable part of available public resources to the local level either through transfers of government revenue or through concessions of fiscal authority. Yet this does not prevent them from maintaining a relatively firm grip on many local activities through regulatory mechanisms, including inspection and monitoring procedures. The distribution of public spending between different levels of government does not adequately reflect the distribution of influence and authority. Nor can we rely on the familiar distinctions between unitary and federal constitutions or "Jacobin" vs. decentralist state traditions to reveal the real extent of local and regional autonomy. Despite the lack of accurate measures, there is a great deal of evidence to suggest that sub-national levels of government tend to gain ground in the long run, particularly in countries where the national government once exercised hands-on control of the minute details of providing public services.

Is this supposed loss of influence downwards matched by a similar deprivation of authority upwards? Some analysts portray the modern state as being squeezed between two competing forces: a more assertive local and regional level of government on the one hand and the dynamics of international and supra-national regulation on the other. In a variant of this hypothesis, the state is depicted as being pressured between various forms of market forces: from within by a restored individualism that proposes to re-privatise a variety of collective policy instruments, and from without by the inexorable thrust of economic globalisation that increasingly ties the hands of national policy makers.

Many facets of recent technological development seem to support these hypotheses. As mobility increases, and access to information expands explosively, and consumer demand for goods and services becomes ever more diversified as it climbs Maslow's famous staircase, one might well imagine that uniformity and homogenisation, which used to be standard products of governance in many different areas, are likely to meet with growing resistance. If people are less prepared to accept being "bossed around", there might be a weakening of traditional civic loyalty and submissiveness. At the same time, however, new technologies and growing economic interdependence also generate growing fears about potential abuses, concerns that quickly translate into requests for enhanced government control and supervision. Thus, we can note how a mounting aversion to being governed goes hand in hand with an increase in security concerns that stimulate the demand for more governance as a means of controlling other people.

3. The use and abuse of governance

This ambiguity with regard to governance is hardly a new phenomenon. Given the costs of compliance and the fiscal burden that government imposes on its subjects, it seems understandable that secular authority has often been accepted more as a necessary evil than as something desirable in itself. As entrepreneurs in protection, the rulers were endured because the alternative was far less palatable – either anarchy or another entrepreneur feared to be more ruthless and oppressive. Throughout the history of government we have also seen many regimes constituted through strategic social alliances, as when rulers combine with some economic stratum to support their resistance to the claims of other strata.

The grudging acceptance of governance as an insurance against less desirable forms of domination goes a long way to explaining the continual preoccupation with control mechanisms in political theory. Ever since Aristotle observed a regular pattern of regime degeneration, suggestions for methods and mechanisms to contravene such inherent tendencies in political systems have constantly been put forward. Early modern constitutionalism borrowed from physics the idea of checks and balances, from biology the concept of an organic division of functions in the body politic, and from jurisprudence the notion of contractual obligations in the public sphere. All of these metaphors provided inspiration for the invention of institutions and procedures aimed at constraining the exercise of political power, not least in the form of mechanisms for judiciary review of administrative decisions and representative bodies constituted through periodic elections.

With the relentless growth of state power in the 20th century, the twin doctrines of rule of law and pluralist democracy have become indispensable tools to circumscribe tendencies towards excessive zeal in governance. The idea of the rule of law (or *Rechtsstaat*, or *état du droit*) as developed in 19th century jurisprudence contains a set of requisites applicable to any civilised legal system, such as objectivity, predictability, a level playing field for different actors, and respect for the normative hierarchy which puts constitutional rules above ordinary legislation and requires political actors at all levels to abide by established rules of procedure (Forsthoff, 1968; Troper, 1993; Petersson, 1996). These basic premises have come to influence not only national legislation and jurisprudence but also international law, with the European Court of Human Rights as one of their foremost guardians.

In examining the impact of democratisation on 20th century governance, there are several dialectical processes to consider. In one perspective it is clear that the consolidation of parliamentary institutions has introduced constraints on the governments' freedom of action. But the extension of suffrage and the evolution of legislatures into more efficient and powerful representative bodies have also added legitimacy to the political systems and thus facilitated the unprecedented expansion of the public sector and the scope of governance. Parliamentary control has turned out to be a double-edged sword, cutting both against capricious governance and against resistance to extended political authority.

The proliferation of democratic institutions has been one of the most remarkable features of the history of the 20th century. When James Bryce undertook his (1921) study of modern democracies after the First World War, he found only six countries in the world matching his requirements. As late as the 1980s, a considerable part of the world was governed by one-party regimes claiming to have overcome the atavistic ideas of democratic pluralism. Today, only a handful of states still cling to this doctrine, even though one of them is the largest country in the world. Though this almost universal conversion to democratic ideals has not yet been accompanied by the consolidation of democratic institutions, procedures, habits and reflexes in all of the countries that have made the transition, an impressive start has nevertheless been made, and the foundations are being laid for new modes of interaction between electorates, legislatures and executive authorities.

In what way does this development affect the quality of governance? Democracies are certainly not immune to the abuse of authority, the exploitation of public means for private benefits, myopia in policy making, excessive state intrusiveness into the lives of the citizens, or other recognised forms of misgovernment. Political scandals in democratic states are standard ingredients in the news. While such reports may certainly impair the public confidence in politicians and political institutions, they nevertheless reflect the capacity of democratic systems for troubleshooting and self-correction.

Several features conspire to produce this effect. One is the important role played in democratic politics by a legitimate and protected opposition, which through its critical scrutiny instils a measure of healthy prudence in the performance of the government. Another key prerequisite for maintaining reasonable standards in governance is the freedom of the media, which of course can only be effective if the economic preconditions for making use of it are also fulfilled. A third component consists of particular institutions and procedures for control, such as constitutionally based auditing practices, ombudsmen, parliamentary inquiries and reporting requirements. None of these elements carries the same weight in authoritarian societies, where control mechanisms mainly serve the purpose of reinforcing the dominant position of the established leadership.

Through its capacity for self-correction, the democratic system of governance is far better equipped than other forms of government to absorb new information and adjust to changing circumstances. In his research on food supply in poor countries, Amartya Sen, the 1998 Nobel laureate in economics, found that famines were less a matter of natural disasters than of calamities occurring in non-democratic societies as a consequence of repressive policies or a skewed distribution of political resources. When harvests failed in democracies, the victims could not be as easily neglected and measures were therefore taken to provide emergency assistance (Sen, 1995).

While mechanisms of democratic control have proved to be indispensable tools for constraining excessive or misguided governance, increased exposure to competition has worked in the same direction. Though many government activities are still undertaken in a shielded, monopolistic environment, an increasing share of the public sector has become subject to different kinds of market pressure. As an employer, the government cannot neglect the conditions offered in the private labour market, and as a service provider it must also keep an eye on its competitors. With increasing physical mobility and with privatisation gaining momentum – particularly in recent decades – this type of constraint on government activities has grown in importance. To use Hirschmann's famous typology (1970), the "exit option" has come to exercise a stronger pressure on governance in many areas while the "voice option" retains its central role in all domains where public authorities still maintain a virtual monopoly.

4. The techniques of governance

Technologies of governance evolve in conjunction with other technologies. Five examples may illustrate this point:

- Innovations in arms production and military strategy have at several stages promoted the amalgamation of political units or creation of alliances by giving bigger countries or pacts an edge over smaller ones.

- The "numerical revolution" – the evolution of counting, accounting, registration, statistics and other quantitative techniques – provided governments with much better diagnostic information about their own societies as well as new methods of exercising control over subordinates, enterprises and subjects.

- New techniques for the quick duplication of documents (stencils, photocopies, etc.) have introduced an entirely new mode of deliberation into decision-making bodies by making huge amounts of information available to participants before the meetings take place. Moreover, discussions proceed in quite a different manner when essential data are "on the table" and do not have to be recited, as they were earlier.

- The proliferation of personal computers and the emergence of the world wide web create entirely new opportunities for making contacts, spreading information, and – the obverse side of the same coin – gaining access to information. Exactly how these opportunities will be exploited remains to be seen, but there is little doubt that both the modalities of democratic systems and the functioning of public administration will be significantly affected.

- The steady flow of images through the visual media, television in particular, has sharpened our perceptions of distant and proximate social conditions and thoroughly transformed the modes of political and administrative communication.

What these examples tell us is that the *physical tools* of governance play an important role in determining the reach and impact of political authorities – the ways in which they can influence and control social, economic and moral conditions and processes. But there are also *mental tools* in the practice of governance, a wide range of assumptions about human nature and organisational behaviour, about goals and means in politics and administration. From the medieval *Fürstenspiegel* to modern handbooks in policy analysis, there is a vast amount of accumulated experience reflecting the lessons drawn from past successes and failures in government. Statecraft has always drawn on the art of creative imitation.

What learning processes are going on in our time? Clearly we are still busy digesting the experience of the 20th century. No very distinct doctrine has as yet emerged from this exercise but some elements or building blocks for future theories may perhaps be discerned, not least in the literature on "reinventing government" and "public entrepreneurialism" (Osborne and Gaebler, 1992). Many recent contributions to the discussion on democratic and administrative control concern the relative merits of what can be called *tight governance* and *loose governance.*

Tight governance stands for a variety of steering methods based on clearly determined objectives, rigorous instructions and meticulous follow-up. Military organisations, totalitarian political systems, and industries organised along the principles of Taylorism and scientific management represent archetypes of tight governance. Many elements of this strategy recur in the wave of proposals and reforms entitled "new public management", in which imitation of the private sector is an important trend. In what has come to be called neo-Taylorism, there is strong emphasis on control through economic and financial information, cost evaluation of everything produced in the public sector, monitoring of individual performance and actively using rewards and incentives (Keraudren and van Mierlo, 1998). In these approaches, a strong goal orientation is combined with a relatively pessimistic or sceptical assessment of human nature. Individuals, if left to themselves, will pursue their own ends and disregard those of the organisation – hence a need for firm frameworks, active efforts to strengthen motivation, and vigilant supervision.

Loose governance, by contrast, is built on a less suspicious view of human behaviour and is linked with more agnostic or empiricist ideas about the choice of organisational means and goals. In management theory this line of thought is represented by the human relations school, with its trust in the creativity and growth potential of employees and in their voluntary participation in joint projects. Political bodies operating on similar assumptions are said to practice "consociational democracy" or "the government of amicable agreement". Loose governance relies on confidence, subtle signals and co-operative environments. It tends to resort to recommendations and "soft law" rather than commands and strict regimes. Key concepts are innovation, adaptability, and learning capacity. Organisations should preferably be flat if not altogether replaced by networks of independent actors.

The search for alternatives to tight governance was linked to the continuing discussion about the limits to a government's capacity to control. In the mid-70s, considerable attention was devoted to the concepts of "governability" and "ungovernability" (country analyses in King *et al.*, 1976, Scheuch, 1977, and Boelsgaard, 1975; overviews in Crozier *et al.*, 1975 and Rose, 1978). A frequent claim was that the bureaucracy had grown to such proportions and complexity that it could no longer be supervised by the political authorities of the state. More recently, a Foucault-inspired line of analysis has begun to address the range and methods of public control in different areas through the notion of "governmentality" (see Smandych, 1999 for a review of this literature).

Is there a long-term trend from tight to loose governance? While some evidence points in that direction, we can also observe a cyclical pattern in the choice of steering methods. Each strategy gives rise to its own discontent. Tight governance generates complaints about overregulation, red tape, government failures and intrusive bureaucracies. With loose governance, on the other hand, there is always a risk that trust turns into gullibility and that flexible arrangements give room to laxity, waste and corruption. In either case, demands for correction might make the pendulum swing back.

But where is the pendulum to go if both reactions coincide? That seems to be the present predicament of the European Commission, which is faced with two vocal criticisms. On the one hand there is widespread alarm about fraud and the diversion of Community funds for illicit purposes, but on the other hand there are persistent complaints about the sluggish payment of Community contributions and the many technical hurdles built into the administrative procedures of the Commission. Attempting to respond to these simultaneous demands for more and less control, Neil Kinnock has presented a report, entitled *Reforming the Commission*, that promises to cut red tape and simplify procedures but is more emphatic in proposing new planning and reporting mechanisms. Although these are intended to increase transparency and facilitate the setting of priorities, they are also likely to generate an additional administrative burden (European Commission, 2000).

Reforming the Commission reflects the continuing influence of trends in public administration that were at their peak in the 1960s and 1970s, the heyday of strategic planning and programme budgeting. It seeks to impose cohesion on an organisation deemed to be too disjointed and incoherent, and it insists on the need for better-co-ordinated evaluation and more systematic reporting of results. It suggests that a "Strategic Planning and Programming Function" should be set up to facilitate the introduction of "Activity Based Management" supported by an "Integrated Resource Management System". At the same time, it says, full use should be made of such techniques as devolution and outsourcing. This is a more recent departure, characteristic of "the new public management" with its emphasis on the strict separation of different public functions (such as regulation, supervision and production) and its reliance on the private sector to take over services previously provided by public agencies.

Much inspiration is also drawn from the private sector in attempts to rationalise and streamline the government machinery. Public authorities have tended to adjust to modern business culture, integrating into their practices a range of methods borrowed from commerce and the private service industry. This convergence of steering techniques has blurred the traditional borderline between the private and public sectors, extended the grey zone of mixed or intermediate activities, and created a seamless web of governmental, quasi-governmental, quasi-non-governmental and non-governmental institutions at different geographical levels – local, regional, national and international. Corporative mechanisms maintain their relevance in this fluid environment and adapt successfully to new functions, such as lobbying at the European level or participation in the regional partnerships established to give guidance to the implementation of the EU's structural policy.

5. Conclusion: The message of Lorenzetti

In the entrance of Palazzo Pubblico on the magnificent shell-shaped central piazza of Siena, we can still admire two 14th century frescoes by Ambrogio Lorenzetti, completed only a few years before the painter perished in the Black Death. On the wall depicting *buon governo*, a combination of allegories and scenes of serene daily life illustrate how concord and diligent work can bring wealth to both town and countryside. On the opposite wall we are shown the misery of *mal governo*, marked by feuds, crime, cruelty and violence.

The message of Lorenzetti still holds: governance matters. Both values and wealth are at stake. The way in which societies are managed affects their mental climate as well as the conditions for economic expansion and social welfare. Good governance remains a requisite for many different forms of growth, whereas the various features of bad governance – corruption, waste, abuse of power and exploitation of public means for private ends – tend to drive unfortunate nations into vicious spirals of decline, disruption and destruction.

With information travelling at the speed of a mouse-click, good practices are not the only things that are now spread more efficiently. New technology gives new powers to governments – but also to the organisations and individuals they endeavour to control. In mobilised societies, group interests are pursued with great vigour and sophistication. This presents new challenges to governance in the next century.

Mitigating group tensions was always a cardinal function of political institutions, but governments also face the subtler task of dealing with our internal contradictions, i.e. the conflicts of interest inherent in every one of us. No single individual is entirely free from ambiguity on central political issues:

- Despite constant criticism of the excesses of big government, electorates in advanced industrial states still strongly support the welfare state and remain addicted to its benefits. Cutbacks meet with strong resistance and those who introduce them are often punished at subsequent elections. Yet in their capacity as taxpayers, the same citizens who insist on preserving the achievements of the welfare state are not so keen on funding it. As demographic changes, the business cycle, and built-in escalator effects conspire to push up costs for established programmes, politicians are frequently confronted with widening gaps in public finance, gaps which to a large extent reflect the ambivalence of the public mind.

- With modern industrial production based on an ever growing number of components and engineering techniques, one alarm follows another and with each come new demands for public intervention to keep the expanding spectrum of risk under control. In a globalised economy, these efforts often require intergovernmental co-ordination and co-operation. In responding to such demands, however, public authorities also incur the wrath of the citizens for being too intrusive and interventionist. Although everybody wants to be protected from threats to health, safety, and the environment, citizens also resent being bossed around, particularly by distant authorities. In this respect, Europeans react to instructions from "Brussels" much as Americans dislike commands or even well-meaning suggestions from "Washington".

Globalisation presents a different dilemma to governments. As Mancur Olson has explained (2000), primitive markets in which commodities are exchanged on the spot in "self-enforced transactions" are not as dependent on institutional frameworks and legal protection as markets in which transactions involve longer time and distance. A globalised economy is therefore in particular need of efficient governance. However, as tax bases become increasingly mobile and elusive, it may also become more difficult to extract the necessary resources for funding such services or to assure compliance with political rules and decisions.

A remarkable growth industry in the postwar period, government remains a crucial determinant of economic expansion and social cohesion. With the sobering experience of the past century behind us, we have learned a great deal about its capacity to do good and evil, and we have become keenly aware of the need to keep it under democratic control. But control is a complex and conflict-intense undertaking with numerous beneficial as well as detrimental effects, and the best way of organising and implementing it is likely to remain a matter of controversy. The 20th century has deprived us of many illusions about possible short cuts towards a better future. But as Lorenzetti demonstrated seven hundred years ago, we will not get very far in that direction without *buon governo*.

Bibliography

BOELSGAARD, K. (1975),
Den ustyrlige stat. Copenhagen.

BRECHT, Arnold (1932),
"Internationaler Vergleich der öffentlichen Ausgaben", Grundfragen der Internationalen Politik II.

BRYCE, James (1921),
Modern Democracies, I-II. London: Macmillan and Co.

BULLOCK, Alan and Maurice SHOCK (1967),
The Liberal Tradition from Fox to Keynes. Oxford: Oxford University Press.

CROZIER, M. et al. (1975),
The Crisis of Democracy: The Trilateral Task Force on the Governability of Democracies. New York: New York University Press.

EUROPEAN COMMISSION (2000),
Reforming the Commission. Communication from Neil Kinnock in agreement with the President and Ms. Schreyer, 18 January 2000.

FORSTHOFF, Ernst (1968),
Rechtstaatlichkeit und Sozialstaatlichkeit. Darmstadt: Wissenschaftliche Buchgesellschaft.

GUPTA, G.S. (1969),
"Public Expenditure and Economic Development – A Cross-Section Analysis", Finanzarchiv XXVIII.

HIRSCHMANN, Albert (1970),
Exit, Voice and Loyalty: Responses to Decline in Firms, Organizations, and States. Cambridge: Harvard University Press.

JOHANSEN, Leif (1968-70),
Den offentliga sektorns ekonomi. Stockholm: Wahström & Widstrand.

KERAUDREN, Philippe and Hans van MIERLO (1998),
"Theories of Public Management: Reform and Their Practical Application" in Tony Verheijen and David Coombes, (eds.), Innovation in Public Management. Cheltenham: Clarendon.

KING Anthony et al. (1976),
Why is Britain Becoming Harder to Govern? London: BBC.

NITTI, F.S. (1904),
Principes de sciences des finances. Paris: Bibliothèque internationale de droit public.

OLSON, Mancur (2000),
Power and Prosperity: Outgrowing Communist and Capitalist Dictatorships. New York: Basic Books.

OSBORNE, D. and T. GAEBLER (1992),
Reinventing Government: How the Entrepreneurial Spirit is Transforming the Public Sector. New York: Plume.

PEACOCK, A.T. and J. WISEMAN (1961),
The Growth of Public Expenditure in the United Kingdom. Princeton: Princeton University Press.

PETERSSON, Olof (1996),
Rättsstaten. Stockholm: Publica.

ROSE, Richard (1978),
Ungovernability: Is There Fire behind the Smoke? Glasgow: Centre for the Study of Public Policy.

SCHEUCH, E. (1977),
Is Germany Becoming Ungovernable? Glasgow: Centre for the Study of Public Policy.

SEN, Amartya (1995),
The Political Control of Hunger. Oxford: Clarendon.

SMANDYCH, Russell, ed. (1999),
Governable Places: Readings in Governmentality and Crime Control. Aldershot: Ashgate.

TARSCHYS, Daniel (1983),
Den offentliga revolutionen (The Public Revolution). Stockholm: Publica.

TROPER, Michel, ed. (1993),
L'Etat du droit. Paris: Presses Universitaires de France.

WAGNER, Adolph (1883),
Finanzwissenschaft. Leipzig: C.F. Winter.

Chapter 3

Long-term Trends in Global Governance: From "Westphalia" to "Seattle"

by
Kimon Valaskakis
University of Montreal, Canada

Introduction

This chapter argues that we are at a dangerous juncture in human history, where the institutions and mechanisms we have set up to govern Planet Earth are in danger of collapsing. This threat is all the more disconcerting because we live in an era of unparalleled affluence and prosperity. What is missing is an updated global governance system to harness the great promise afforded by globalisation and technological change. At stake is not just the redrafting of a trade or investment agreement here and there, or the setting up of a regulatory body to oversee food safety or to prevent pornography on the internet. At stake is the very foundation of the present world order based on the Treaty of Westphalia in 1648. This initially European Treaty, which ended the Thirty Years' War, constructed a framework for global relations based on the inviolability of the concept of sovereignty. This inviolability is now under attack from many sides and yet no convincing alternative has been presented to replace it. As a result we are approaching a major governance vacuum which should be filled in the not too distant future if the gains achieved by humanity since the Industrial Revolution are to be preserved and enhanced.

To support this thesis, the chapter retraces the evolution of global governance from Westphalia, where the present global governance system was born, to Seattle, where in November 1999 the WTO (World Trade Organisation) attempted to launch its vaunted Millennium Round of trade negotiations. That particular conference was unsuccessful, ostensibly because the diplomats around the table could not agree on an agenda. But in a more fundamental sense it was fatally flawed because it was based on "Old Westphalian" assumptions, now obsolescent. Yet the Seattle Approach, with its flawed assumptions, is ported over to other conferences and meetings. These too might fail. The real choice, it would seem, is to either give up the whole Westphalian approach and start from scratch with something completely new – a very dangerous risk at best – or adopt a "New Westphalian" paradigm and design a world order that will be both desirable and feasible.

The chapter is organised in three sections. In the first, the *modus operandi* of the Westphalian World Order (WWO) is examined in the period from 1648 to the end of the Second World War in 1945. The focus is on what the author believes were the five key principles that characterised the Westphalian System: 1) the primacy of national sovereignty; 2) the importance of control of physical territory; 3) the star role played by nation state governments in the global system; 4) the emergence of a body of international law derived from treaties signed by sovereign states; and 5) the recourse to war as an acceptable method of international conflict resolution if all else fails.

The second section examines the global governance systems put in place in the second half of the 20th century from 1945 to 2000, principally characterised by the sea change of globalisation and the emergence of a complex architecture of IGOs (intergovernmental organisations) and NGOs (non-governmental organisations). The author's assessment of these systems is mixed. The belief is that in their present state they will not be successful in meeting the challenges of globalisation.

A short third section indicates possible future directions: bury the Old Westphalian System and replace it with something totally new, or renovate and restructure it into a New Westphalian System better suited for the 21st century. The Road to a New World Order will be long and tortuous. But there is no alternative to taking this road, wherever it leads, because the present road is clearly reaching a dead-end.

1. The *modus operandi* of the Westphalian World Order, 1648-1945

Three systems of global governance

Governance has been variously defined as the exercise of authority or the distribution of power. In essence it is related to the notions of order and decision making. The opposite of governance is anarchy, or the absence of order. In Greek philosophy, Cosmos was opposed to Chaos. An orderly world is one where there are clear rules concerning the legitimate and efficient use of authority.

But "authority" is not a monolithic or homogeneous concept. It can be measured in degrees and is thus closer to the idea of "influence". Absolute authority is a fiction created by legal scholars and embodied in the concept of "sovereignty", described as the ultimate unchallengeable power of the "sovereign." In real life there are very few cases of absolute power, only varying degrees of control. The influence of a legislator to prevent certain types of objectionable behaviour, of a parent attempting to convince his teenage child to do his homework, or even of a general ordering his troops into battle – may be limited by circumstances and is almost never total.

Applying the concept of authority at the continental or planetary level, it can be argued that three major global governance systems have been put to the test.

System 1 – Hegemony by one power or coalition of powers

The model here is that of the *pax*, as in *pax romana* or *pax britannica*. A leading power (or alliance of powers) imposes an *imperium* and dictates a peaceful order on its own terms. The concept of *pax* differs from other words for peace such as the Greek *eirene*, the Arab *salaam*, the Hebrew *shalom* or the Indian *shanti*. These latter each connote a convivial peace arrived at through harmony, friendship and a congruence of goals. *Pax* on the other hand denotes law and order strictly enforced by the dominant power. The instrument of *pax romana* was the Roman legion until it was ultimately defeated, that of the *pax britannica* in the 19th century mastery of the seas, etc. The enforcement mechanism is crucial in a *pax*, while the congruence of goals is the key element in convivial peace.

System 2 – Balance of power

In this approach, power is limited by countervailing forces. There is no universal arbiter. Instead, there are individual players whose power is limited by that of the others. Democracy is an example of a balance-of-power system where the rights of each player stop when they enter into conflict with the rights and prerogatives of the others. In democratic systems conflicts are resolved by majority rule. The market system is another example of balance of power, where the forces of supply and demand achieve equilibrium through confrontation. The price mechanism is the final arbiter and through it, opposing forces achieve balance and the market is cleared. By the same token, it will be shown that the Westphalian World Order set up a balance-of-power system based on sovereignty, which was defined as the irreducible, inalienable power exercised by a number of recognised players within acknowledged jurisdictions. When these sovereignties would clash, conflict resolution would have to be reached either through negotiation or, failing that, war. But in the Westphalian system, the idea of an imposed settlement from above is absent. There are no referees outside the system.

System 3 – Prearranged distribution of power

In this third system, power is distributed through a prearranged set of criteria. A good example is federalism, where the jurisdictions of the central government and the sub-national units (states or provinces) are carefully defined although, as experience shows, there may be numerous overlaps. In principle, the judicial

47

system may then arbitrate and determine the proper distribution of power based on the constitution. The latter becomes the key element in any prearranged distribution of power system. With the advance of globalisation, prearranged distribution of power systems have led to the emergence of intergovernmental organisations such as the European Union and the United Nations. But at this stage there is no such thing as a "world constitution", and global governance initiatives – beyond the sovereignty-based inter-state system of delegated authority – are still in their infancy. In that area we are, as a planet, in the very early muddling-through phase.

It must be noted that the three governance systems above may be mixed and matched, and are not mutually exclusive. Nor is the exercise of authority monolithic, as noted above. There may be rules and exceptions, principal players and mavericks, system loyalists and system rebels. Most human systems are characterised by great fluidity, and governance systems are no exception.

The significance of the Treaty of Westphalia

Pre-Westphalian Europe in the Early Modern Period was a mixture of declining empires, retreating feudal lords and an emerging class of traders and capitalist entrepreneurs. The Church remained very influential and was an instrument of European governance. The Treaty of Westphalia of 1648 brought to an end the Thirty Years' War, the first pan-European war in history. The peace was negotiated from 1644 through 1648 in the Westphalian towns of Münster and Osnabrück. Under the terms of the peace settlement, a number of countries received territories or were confirmed in their sovereignty over territories. They were empowered to contract treaties with one another and with foreign powers, provided that the emperor and the empire suffered no prejudice. The princes of the empire became absolute sovereigns in their own dominions while the Holy Roman Emperor and the Diet were severely weakened. In a nutshell, the central authority of the empire was replaced almost entirely by the sovereignty of about 300 princes.

The treaty brought to an end almost 150 years of continuous struggle in Europe and marked the end of the era of religious wars. It was a turning point in the mutual recognition of sovereignty rights. Although the signatories of the treaty had only the peace of Europe as their ultimate objective, the unintended consequence of their efforts was to create a global order based on a "state system". This global order slowly developed to eventually encompass the whole planet and probably reached its zenith in 1945.

The underlying principles of the Westphalian System

It is important to distinguish between the original elements of the Treaty of Westphalia – i.e. of a European treaty whose goal was to end a regional war – and the evolving "Westphalian Principles" which no one invented but which became the building blocks of the world order from 1648 to 2000. Whereas the former were signed by the plenipotentiary ambassadors then present, the latter developed slowly over three and a half centuries and were periodically validated by additional treaties but never consolidated in one single document. These building blocks are therefore subject to interpretation and may be the object of debate between learned scholars. Observation of the evolution of the Westphalian World Order reveals at least five fundamental characteristics, which may be described as follows.

1. *The primacy of sovereignty*

Originally derived from the Latin term *superanus* through the French term *souveraineté*, sovereignty came to mean the equivalent of supreme power. It was used by Jean Bodin in France to provide legitimacy and strengthen the power of the French king in his battle with rebellious feudal lords. The doctrine of the divine right of kings, according to which they are only answerable to God and cannot be challenged by human beings, is a close cousin of the concept of sovereignty. It led Louis XIV to utter his famous "L'*Etat c'est moi*" boast. The king and the state were indeed indistinguishable in his time. Therefore next to God, the King could exercise absolute power in complete legitimacy.

From its origins as the prerogative of the king, sovereignty slowly evolved, in some countries at least, as the reflection of the unchallengeable will of the people, sometimes referred to as the doctrine of popular sovereignty. The interpretations given by John Locke in the 17th century and Jean-Jacques Rousseau in the 18th linked sovereignty to democracy via the doctrine of the social compact, according to which "The People" are the ultimate owners of sovereignty. They may delegate to governments strong powers to be exercised in their name, but they are the ultimate masters and may withdraw that delegation by voting governments out of office. The French Constitution of 1791 declared that "Sovereignty is one, indivisible, unalienable and imprescriptible." But whether based in the divine right of kings or the unchallengeable will of the people, sovereignty became the absolute reference point in global relations, the ultimate principle upon which all notions of global order should be based. It was to international relations what the speed of light was to Einstein's physics: an absolute.

2. *The importance of control over geographical territory*

In the Westphalian System, the sovereignty of nations expresses itself through the control of geographical territory. This was, in effect, a legacy of the feudal principle "*nul terre sans seigneur*". Land was the principal factor of production in the feudal world, and its control yielded both economic and political power. This "real estate" bias is an essential ingredient of the Westphalian System. Although by the 19th and certainly the 20th century industry became much more important than land, the territorial focus in the exercise of authority remained strong. In the "Scramble for Africa" after the Berlin Congress in the late 19th century, the European Great Powers competed with each other to paint the map of Africa in their own national colours. Thus France obtained the second largest empire after Britain's, although its holdings in Africa (mainly West Africa and the Sahel countries) were resource-poor and not particularly interesting from the economic point of view. However, the territorial imperative was strong enough in political perceptions to make this colonial expansion, even in deficit conditions, highly popular.

3. The star players of the Westphalian System are national governments

The emergence of nation states imbued with absolute power, at least in the legal sense, accelerated the demise of the pre-Westphalian players. The biggest losers were the feudal lords who had lost the invulnerability of their castles after gunpowder became prevalent, and the Holy Roman Emperors who were specifically marginalised by the Westphalian Settlement. Other losers were the Pope and the Catholic Church who lost much of their political influence. By ending the wars of religion the Treaty of Westphalia gradually introduced the concept of secular authority and the separation of Church and State, which became embedded later in democratic constitutions. The threat of excommunication by decision of the Pope used to be a terrifying weapon in feudal Europe. By the 18th century excommunication became a much weaker instrument of influence.

As the pre-Westphalian players receded into the background, the new stars occupying centre stage were the nation state governments themselves. At first these governments were composed only of kings and princes, and the mode of transmission of power was by heredity. But in the 19th and 20th centuries power shifted to the people at large, who elected democratic governments and exercised power by delegation. The principle of separation of power distributed legal influence between the executive, legislative and judiciary branches. Sovereignty was exercised by the government in the name of the nation, and its exercise was submitted to internal checks and balances. In the evolution of British constitutional law, sovereignty became vested not in the people but in Parliament, defined as the King in council with the House of Commons and the House of Lords. In most other countries, however, the ultimate holders of sovereignty were "The People", appointing and dismissing governments through elections.

As European economic development in the 17th, 18th and 19th centuries eventually led to greater international trade and colonial expansion, economic agents such as major corporations became more prominent. But in the mercantilist phase of the Westphalian World Order and probably through most of the 19th and 20th centuries, *economics remained subordinated to politics*, at least in the non-Anglo-Saxon countries. Jean-Baptiste Colbert in Louis XIV's reign developed the techniques of state co-ordination of economic activity into a fine art. Corporations were likened to armies attacking foreign interests and conquering foreign markets in the name of the king. Economics was seen as an extension of policy by other means. Unpatriotic corporations were stripped of their state monopoly.

This subordination of economic interests to national goals remained a dominant feature of international relations for most of the countries of Western Europe in the 18th, 19th and 20th centuries. Napoleon, Bismark, Hitler, Stalin and perhaps even De Gaulle, Mitterand, Adenauer and Kohl all saw the national interest as taking precedence over individual economic interests.

4. *Emergence of a body of international law based on treaties between sovereign countries*

As international relations intensified in the 18th and 19th centuries, a body of international law slowly began to emerge. Two sources of international law were recognised. The first was fully compatible with the principle of sovereignty and centred around the practice of signing treaties which would then have the same power as law for the signatory countries. International law emerging from treaties between countries merely reaffirmed the primacy of sovereignty, since no sovereign country could be forced to accept what it had not consented to. It could of course be coerced into acceptance through defeat in war but only after the capitulation or peace treaty would it be legally bound – not before.

A second source of international law was developed by scholars such as Hugo Grotius and others: so-called *natural law*, presumably based on universal values. This second source was only occasionally acknowledged in the first three centuries of the WWO, but it is gaining momentum today with the emergence of human rights, the revulsion *vis-à-vis* crimes against humanity, the principle of self-determination, etc. More the exception than the rule, universal values as a source of international law, without treaty endorsement, remained outside the mainstream of the Westphalian System since too much emphasis on natural law would contravene the primacy of sovereignty.

5. *War is retained as a recognised instrument of international relations*

One of the surprising features of the Westphalian World Order is its implicit retention of war between sovereign states as a legitimate instrument of external policy. Clausewitz's famous words, "War is an extension of policy by other means", were in retrospect very Westphalian in form and content. The innovation brought by Westphalia to the waging of war was the introduction of the concept of *war with rules*. Although not present in the Treaty itself, the legitimate possibility of war between states was a logical extension of the primacy of sovereignty. If *two sovereign states disagree and there is no power greater than sovereignty, the conflict resolution must come through war*. In the same way that duelling between gentlemen became, in the 18th century, the proper way of settling an aristocratic quarrel, war between states also was considered acceptable, as long as certain rules were followed. There were implicit rules of engagement, limitations on types of weapons, rules of victory and defeat, and a recommendation of gentlemanly behaviour throughout. For instance, in a famous 18th century battle, the French were reputed to have invited their British adversaries to *tirer les premiers* in an emulation of a courteous duel. One 18th century strategist even argued that battles could be decided with practically no bloodshed but by pure manoeuvre. When one army was obviously outmanoeuvred by the other, its general, as a gentleman, should have the courtesy to surrender, in the same way that a chess grandmaster will resign long before the checkmate if it becomes obvious that the game is lost.

In the 19th and 20th century elaborate rules of war were further systematised – proper ways of declaring war, diplomatic immunity, the treatment of prisoners, methods of capitulation, etc. The Geneva Convention is a good example of the Westphalian concept of war, with its precise rules. So is the Charter of the United Nations, which recognises the legitimacy of war in certain circumstances. In a Westphalian War unconditional surrender or capitulation is the proper way of legally transferring sovereignty from the vanquished to the victor.

The principles in action, 1648-1945

The first phase of the Westphalian World Order was dominated by the emergence of mercantilism as a political-economic system. This period lasted, with ups and downs, from 1648 to about 1815. Accompanying the rise of the nation states and the overseas expansion of Europe, mercantilism – especially as designed and implemented by Jean-Baptiste Colbert in the France of Louis XIV – became a tool of advanced statism. The state would intervene in all areas of economic life. It would protect national industry with high tariffs, ensure a favourable balance of payments by subsidising exports, promote population growth, augment the money supply by accumulating gold and silver, and – above all – use corporations, such as the East India Company, La Compagnie des Habitants, Hudson Bay Company, etc., to promote the national interest. The mercantilist corporations were state-created monopolies whose mission was to serve the aggrandisement of the king's power. Under mercantilism the alliance of state and business was to be in the interest of the state first and foremost.

When Adam Smith published his *Wealth of Nations* in 1776, it hardly made a dent in the mercantilist thinking of Continental Europe. Only Britain moved towards free trade and in 1846 symbolically repealed the Corn Laws, putting an end to agricultural protection and relying almost entirely on her comparative advantage. The main instruments of global governance in the period from 1648 to 1815 were a) increased economic sovereignty of the major players through mercantilist policies and

b) periodic but limited wars shifting the balance of power. There was no hegemon, no imperial power able to impose a *pax*. The 18th century conflicts such as the Seven Years' War, the Wars of Spanish and Austrian Successions, etc. did not fundamentally alter the European balance of power, although they did involve a considerable reshuffling of colonial possessions. France, among others, lost Canada and Britain established itself as the pre-eminent imperial power. Napoleon's attempt to unify Europe by force almost succeeded, but by 1815 the battle of Waterloo put an end to those ambitions. The 18th century ended with no *pax* in sight.

Phase 2 of the Westphalian World Order spans the period from 1815 to 1914. The formula for global governance was mixed. A balance-of-power system was put in place through the peace settlement at the Congress of Vienna. The so-called "Congress System" that emerged as a method of conflict resolution was a precursor of the more contemporary IGOs. The Great Powers would periodically meet and settle their differences diplomatically. But what really made the European balance-of-power system work in the 19th century was the fact that it was guaranteed by the pre-eminent colonial power Great Britain, willing to intervene on the weaker side whenever the balance of power was in peril. The *Pax Britannica*, which supported this balance, was subtle and implicit. It manifested itself more by negative interventions than by positive initiatives. The system did not manage to avoid war since Britain and France fought Russia in the Crimea in mid-century and France, Prussia and Austria fought each other in a series of duels. After the Franco-Prussian War of 1870-71 and the cession by France of Alsace Lorraine to Germany, the balance of power was seriously endangered. To restore it an elaborate system of alliances was developed, ultimately opposing in 1914 the Triple Alliance of Germany, Austria and Italy to the Triple Entente of France, Russia and Britain.

In the economic sphere Europe flirted with free trade via reciprocity treaties here and there, but ultimately opted for protectionism coupled with imperial expansion. The late 19th century was marked by a resurgence of mercantilism, protectionism and export subsidies, import restrictions and the use of economic policy for political ends. The French loans to Russia at the end of the 19th century were a case in point. About 25% of French savings went to Russia in the form of state loans. Although the immediate attraction was supposed to be economic (high interest rates), the goal was really political. The French external and finance ministries co-operated with the Russian counterparts to maintain high interest rates for the Russian bonds in order to attract French investors. The object was to secure the Russian military alliance against Germany. The opening of a second front in case of war between France and Germany was important to French generals who were interested in ultimately recapturing Alsace Lorraine. To prevent a quick German victory (as projected in the famous Schlieffen Plan), France needed the Russian steamroller to absorb some of the German forces. If that goal required the manipulation of capital markets, it would be fully acceptable. The political end would justify the economic means.

In the monetary field the most notable achievement of the end of the 19th century was the emergence of a global currency in the form of the gold standard. With Britain acting as the *de facto* world central banker, the gold standard operated quite smoothly in the period immediately prior to the First World War, and facilitated the globalisation of international trade. By 1900 the world had become a unified market for at least some commodities, and portfolio capital movements became more and more widespread although direct foreign investments, multinational company style, were not yet known.

From a Westphalian point of view, the period 1815-1914 was a century of peace in spite of the limited local wars. But this balance broke down in 1914 and the First World War ushered in a third phase of the Westphalian Order, characterised by years of armed military confrontation that ended only in 1945 at the conclusion of the Second World War. In some senses this period marks the apex of the Westphalian System, during which sovereignties reigned supreme and clashed in bloody battles. It was also a period of maximum state intervention in the economy. After the collapse of the stock market in 1929, the free trade and *laissez-faire* assumptions of the 19th century were replaced by forceful state action. In Germany, Italy, Japan, Spain and the USSR, the national government became the leading economic player. Businesses were allied to the government but the latter called the shots and created direct jobs through infrastructure and rearmament programmes. Even in the Western democracies, Keynesianism in Britain, *dirigisme* in France and the New Deal in the United States justified strong state intervention to alleviate the economic disasters brought about by the Depression.

Although the period 1914-45 was dominated by war, the unsuccessful attempt by President Wilson at the end of the First World War to introduce a peaceful and stable global order deserves special mention. He attempted to rally the people of the world in a peace settlement designed to remove the causes of future wars and establish machinery to maintain peace. In an address to the Senate on 22 January 1917, he called for a "peace without victory" to be enforced by a league of nations that the United States would join and strongly support. He reiterated this programme in his war message, adding that the United States wanted above all else to "make the world safe for democracy". And when he failed to persuade the British and French leaders to join him in issuing a common statement of war aims, he went to Congress on 8 January 1918 to demand, in his Fourteen Points address, an end to the old diplomacy that had led to wars in the past and an open diplomacy instead of entangling alliances. He called for freedom of the seas, an impartial settlement of colonial claims, general disarmament, removal of artificial trade barriers, and – again, most importantly – a league of nations to promote peace and protect the territorial integrity and independence of its members: a new international order based upon peace and justice.

The League of Nations did eventually emerge but the United States, its initiator, was unable to participate because of a congressional veto. Deprived of the leading superpower, the League of Nations revealed itself weak and ineffectual, and it did not prevent the deterioration of international relations that eventually led to the Second World War.

2. Global governance, 1945-2000

The impact of globalisation on the Westphalian System

The contemporary phase of the WWO covers the period from 1945 to about 1990. Perhaps the most important aspect of this contemporary phase was the assault on the Westphalian System brought about by globalisation.

Globalisation may be broadly defined as the transposition of human activities from the narrow confines of the nation state to the much larger theatre of Planet Earth itself. ("*All the world's a stage and all the men and women merely players...*") Although in a technical sense globalisation may be traced back to earlier historical periods, the acceleration and sweeping nature of contemporary change was of such a magnitude as to signify a real qualitative shift. The historical antecedents were merely small introductions of things to come. True, by 1900 the world was already a single market for some products and capital moved freely across international borders. True, the voyages of discovery and European expansion between the 13th and 17th century were precursors to modern globalisation. It is equally true that Alexander the Great was one of the first globalists. That said, however, the extent of post-Second World War globalisation dwarfs all these past experiences. The period 1945-2000 witnessed the rise of multinational corporations, which introduced the globalisation of *production* – not of trade, already achieved earlier, but of production itself. The most important aspect of that last trend was the new transborder factor movement – including that of entrepreneurs, unskilled labour through mass migrations, financial capital, real capital, and above all technology. The old theories of fixed comparative advantage based on immobile factors of production had to give way to dynamic competitive advantage – flexible, shifting, and policy-sensitive.

Another important feature of contemporary globalisation has been its *asymmetrical* and uneven character. Had all sectors of human activity globalised at the same pace, the process itself would have been trivial. On the contrary, what happened was globalisation at breakneck speeds in some sectors (finance, technology transfer, skilled labour movements, organised crime, international terrorism) accompanied by agonisingly slow reactions in others (government policies, social attitudes, international regulation, the fight against crime, terrorism and disease). These asymmetries have created winners and losers, and have threatened the social fabric of many countries undergoing rapid and unwanted social change. Huge earnings gaps exist and, according to some authors, are biased in favour of a winner-takes-all outcome, which further complicates the income distribution problems both within and between nations.

In assessing the overall impact of globalisation on governance, attention should be drawn to two points.

1. *Reduction in the policy capacity of national governments*

Originally star players in the Westphalian System, national governments are in the process of becoming the bit players of the new era.

First, the rise of multinational corporations able to elude the jurisdiction of national governments (even their own) has created a lateral shift from political to economic decision making. More and more decisions are now taken by market forces. The corporations can leapfrog past objectionable regulations and pit one government against the other. In addition, the comparative size of corporations (as measured by their annual sales figure or capitalisation versus government budgets) clearly indicates a power shift. If the top 100 economic entities were assembled in, say, a new OECD with both private and public participation, 52 of these major players would be corporations and 48 national governments. If the 200-odd countries in the world were pitted against the 200 top corporations, the result would be even more lopsided. Many members of the United Nations are microstates, sovereign in name only and very vulnerable to international capital flows. They can exert much less power than the major corporations.

Second, while the global private sector creates alliances and mergers, the global public sector is devolving its power downwards. The growth of sub-national governments with competing jurisdictions and shared sovereignty has robbed central governments of much of their clout. In federal states such as the United States and Canada there are literally thousands of governments and quasi-governments empowered to establish regulations, impose taxes and offer subsidies to attract mobile international capital. The intense competition among these sub-national governments gives the footloose corporations and entrepreneurs *l'embarras du choix* in their choice of location even within a given country. States and provinces become humble supplicants offering fiscal incentives and rewards in order to attract the favours of nomadic factors of production.

Third, the creation of IGOs such as the UN, the EU, the OECD, the WTO, etc. has also contributed to a transfer of power away from the original Westphalian players, upwards to these supranational entities. The upward power shift is still in its infancy in most of the IGOs with the exception of the European Union, where supranationality is an acknowledged goal. Even so, the new jurisdictions of these IGOs impose further limits in the policy capacity of individual nation state governments.

In addition to the power shifts, the phenomenon of global interdependence – largely unwanted, real nevertheless – has also reduced the policy capacity of national governments. Today many challenges which could previously be dealt with at the nation state level now have become global. The old adage "Think globally but act locally", eloquent slogan of the futures movement in the early 1980s, is now being replaced in an increasing number of areas with a new one: "Think globally and act globally." Action that is less than global is likely to be ineffective in challenges such as the regulation of the internet, control of climate change, war on terrorism, regulation of genetic engineering, avoidance of financial bubbles, prevention of epidemics, etc. We have become, as one author put it, "One World Ready or Not". This new fact has driven a large nail into the coffin of the Old Westphalian Order, which assumed the world was composed of fully independent sovereign nations with great policy capacity.

2. Reduction in the policy legitimacy of national governments

The process of globalisation has significantly reduced not only the effective policy-making capacity of national governments, but also the very legitimacy of the policy-making process. In the Old Westphalian System there was no second-guessing as to the legitimacy of an act of sovereignty by a recognised government. At most, other countries could declare war if they disagreed and settle the problem by force of arms. But short of war, no other legitimate means of intervention was recognised. National sovereignty was the highest value, by definition.

Today, with the globalisation of media, this is no longer true. The notion of human rights and its corollary, international law, are beginning to emerge as powerful forces in world opinion. There is now a growing belief that certain human values rate higher than sovereignty and must be implemented even if they contravene the latter.

The postwar Nuremberg Trials and the concept of "crimes against humanity", for example, have justified the prosecution of war criminals in spite of their attempted Westphalian defence of "sovereignty". This supranational concept has been used to prosecute and convict Second World War criminals, and more recently those associated with the Yugoslav Wars – Bosnia, Kosovo, etc. It has also been used to attempt the prosecution of General Pinochet for crimes he allegedly committed while the head of a recognised sovereign government. Finally, the possibility of genocide or an ethnic war of extermination has been used to justify the NATO intervention in Kosovo in flagrant violation of the Westphalian principles of sovereign inviolability of territory.

The existence of visual media such as CNN and the internet make indifference to atrocities much more difficult now than in previous times. Although strict interpretation of Westphalian sovereignty allows other countries to merely watch a genocide without intervening, horrific pictures seen on television in fact militate in favour of intervention. The Armenian Genocide was ignored by the Great Powers while the Kosovo War was not. The difference, in the final analysis, may have been television forcing world public opinion either to acquiesce in atrocities by doing nothing or to intervene and by so doing trash the concept of sovereignty.

Multilateralism as a contemporary form of global governance

Faced with growing global interdependence and having witnessed the inability of the Westphalian Order to prevent the Second World War and its 50 million deaths, the community of nations shifted into "multilateral gear," so to speak. Between 1945 and 2000 a host of regional and global organisations were created to help deal with the world's problems. These multilateral organisations generally come in three flavours. The first is the IGO or intergovernmental organisation, where the members are sovereign governments usually represented by plenipotentiary ambassadors. The second is the NGO or non-governmental organisation, where the members are from the private sector but reach across international borders. The third is a hybrid, with private and public elements mixed in varying fashion.

The IGO group was a direct consequence of the Second World War; the principal new IGO was the United Nations and its family of subsidiary bodies. At the top of the hierarchy is the UN General Assembly, the final authority in the UN family. The subsidiary bodies include dozens of agencies, some of which are quite independent such as UNESCO, the World Bank and the IMF. The two latter organisations, although initially born within the UN system, are autonomous agencies.

In addition to the UN family, there are regional and sectoral IGOs. The regional include NAFTA (North American Free Trade Association), APEC (Asia Pacific Economic Community), MERCOSUR, etc. Most of these regional groupings have limited objectives and the IGO itself possesses only a very small secretariat. The European Union is in a class by itself because its final goal is openly political – European unification – while the means to achieve this goal are economic in nature. In the European Union the transfer of sovereignty from national to supranational entities is voluntary and conscious, and not an unintended by-product of the signing of treaties, as is the case in other instances. The creation of a unified currency, the Euro, is another significant step in sovereignty transfer because, as the mercantilists of old claimed: *La souveraineté, c'est le pouvoir de frapper monnaie.* By delegating that power to a politically neutral European Central Bank, the Euroland countries have conceded a good part of their sovereignty.

Another group of regional IGOs exists in the form of military alliances. The principal surviving military alliance is NATO. It assumed direct governance responsibilities in Kosovo in 1999, and less direct ones in Kuwait in 1991 in opposing Iraq's invasion of that country. Not always mandated by the United Nations, NATO has justified its interventions on the basis of principles of human rights, especially in the Kosovo case. In the Kuwait case, the Iraq invasion was a clear violation of Kuwaiti sovereignty, and therefore the intervention much easier to justify on Westphalian grounds. But in the Kosovo intervention, the NATO action was clearly anti-Westphalian.

A small number of IGOs fall into the category of "global" without being "universal" – that is, their reach is global but not their membership. The WTO (World Trade Organisation, a successor to the GATT) sets up global trade rules but does not at the moment count on global membership. Almost three-quarters of the UN member states are also part of the WTO, but a good quarter is still outside. In that missing quarter are very powerful countries who have yet to join. Another global but not universal IGO is the OECD. Composed of 29 Member countries, the OECD has been the club of the advanced industrial nations. Its membership is global, since practically every area of the world is represented, but it is not universal since membership is not open to all countries.

Finally an IGO that exists only in an informal sense but is probably the most powerful is the G8. This gathering of the seven most industrialised nations plus Russia is a powerhouse with considerable clout as long as its members act in unison.

In a parallel course to the IGOs are the NGOs. These are usually voluntary private sector organisations with no profit motive, seeking to realise a goal, redress a wrong, etc. Their very existence is an implicit indictment of governments. If government action within the IGOs were perfect there would be no need for NGOs. In such a case, NGO action would be limited to political interventions *within* member states rather than at the international level. The leading NGOs include ecological organisations such as Greenpeace, Worldwatch, humanitarian groups such as Médecins sans frontières, CARE, etc.

Within the group of NGOs but in a separate class are industrial associations and professional groups which establish rules and regulations within specific sectors. These may set standards and establish performance norms within their area of jurisdiction. Within the nation state these sectoral NGOs have the full support of the national governments, which endorse the norms and apply them as if they were laws. Outside the nation state the enforcement capabilities of these sectoral non-government associations is more limited. The International Olympic Committee, the World Boxing Association, the associations of chiropractors, travel agents, actors or whatever may impose guidelines and rules but have little clout to enforce them against delinquents.

Somewhere between the IGO and the NGO are mixed organisations involving both government and private participation. The UPU (Universal Postal Union) was founded in 1874 and brought later into a relationship with the United Nations in 1948. Uniting member countries into a single postal territory, it fixes international postal rates. The Hague International Tribunal for War Crimes in the former Yugoslavia was created in 1993 to prosecute and punish crimes against humanity committed in that country since 1991. Its official status as an organisation duly created by governments does not necessarily imply that it has coercive powers beyond the will of the leading member countries.

A *global governance vacuum?*

Weaknesses of the intergovernmental multilateral system

The present system of both public and private multilateral organisations appears to be seriously flawed and, in its present configuration, unlikely to meet the challenge of coping with globalisation and its asymmetrical shocks. Here are some of the most obvious weaknesses in the IGOs:

1. A *haphazard architecture*. There are over 500 IGOs officially sanctioned by governments in some form or other and many thousands more with semi-official or consultative status. Some of these IGOs have been created with a definite purpose in mind. Others have emerged from a communiqué at the end of a ministerial with unclear goals. Experience shows that it is much easier to create an IGO than eliminate one. Once created these organisations have their own survival as their principal goal. The abolition of an IGO is a traumatic event which international diplomacy avoids at all costs. What happens instead is that the redundant IGOs continue to exist but with smaller budgets and smaller influence. As a result the constellation of IGOs coexist in somewhat disorderly fashion.

2. *Agenda duplication*. There is no clear division of labour between the IGOs. They often duplicate each other's work, studying the same problems and issues. The same ministers may end up meeting in a number of different venues with different hats but ultimately dealing with the same problems and repeating the same positions over and over again.

3. *Agenda gaps: insufficient attention to linkages*. The opposite is also true. The complexity of modern life has created new important linkages. Some of these are geographic, where decisions in one part of the world affect the rest of the planet. Other linkages are intersectoral (agriculture affecting manufacturing, manufacturing affecting services, etc.) and interdisciplinary (economic decisions having social implications, technological decisions having environmental impacts, etc.) In the failed MAI (Multilateral Agreement on Investment) negotiations at the OECD the negotiators mistakenly believed that an investment code could be agreed upon without reference to its impacts on everything else. This proved to be a costly error since these linkages were noted

by protestors, and the fact that they were ignored in the proposed agreement ultimately brought about the cancelling of the negotiations altogether.

4. *Rigid decision rules.* Most IGOs are governed by the Westphalian principle of sovereign equality, which means one state = one vote. Although at first blush this principle appears "democratic", upon analysis it turns out to be anti-democratic. With the proliferation of statehood as a result of decolonisation and the break-up of empires, many microstates have become members of the IGOs and exert voting power well beyond their true demographic importance. The fact that Togo, Japan, Iceland, the United States, Luxembourg and India all have the same voting weight creates severe distortions in the inter-governmental system. Among other things it gives much greater power to the small number of voters in the microstates who, through the one state = one vote rule, exert more influence per capita than the voters in the more populous states. In other words, one state = one vote negates the principle of one person = one vote. A Luxembourg voter has through the IGOs a much greater voting strength than his American counterpart. In addition, in many IGOs the interpretation of sovereign equality reaches the point where consensus is required for all decisions – in other words, one state = one veto. This author's experience as Canadian Ambassador to the OECD from 1995 to 1999 and his chairmanship of the OECD Council's Committee on the Reform of Decision Making have led him to believe that this is a fatal flaw in the IGOs. The one state = one vote and in extreme versions one state = one veto condemns IGOs to extremely slow decision making that often leads to weak decisions involving bad compromises. In an era of rapid social change, the ponderous and compromise-ridden decision making of the IGOs is not well suited to crisis management. Economic relief packages often come too late and humanitarian interventions finally take place long after hundreds of thousands have been killed, as was the case with Rwanda-Burundi a few years ago.

Weaknesses of the NGO System

The structural weaknesses in the IGOs are matched by equivalent although less visible weaknesses in the NGOs. The general claim of the NGOs is to represent civil society, a laudable goal to be sure. However, that claim cannot easily be validated since there are no established rules concerning the operations of the NGOs. Each sets up its own *modus operandi*. Among the legitimate questions that may be asked are the following.

Who finances the NGOs? Where do they get their money? Is the funding tied to particular positions taken by the NGO, or not? How independent are the NGOs from their funding source?

By what mechanisms do the NGOs receive instructions from the constituencies they are supposed to represent? How is the delegation of power and responsibility effected? In other words, are they as democratic as governments? More so? Less so?

What is the internal decision-making mechanism of the NGO? Is it consensus? Unanimity? Simple democratic majority rule, etc.?

The Seattle Approach

The most recent example of how the present multilateral system operates was the meeting of the WTO in Seattle in November 1999. This meeting was supposed to kick off the so-called Millennium Round, a further stage in trade liberalisation to be achieved in the early years of the 21st century. The meeting was unsuccessful ostensibly because its formal participants, the 140-odd trade ministers from member states, could not agree on an agenda. In the author's view the meeting failed because of the fundamental flaws in the multilateral process itself.

First, the participants were trade ministers with jurisdiction limited to trade matters. Given global interdependence and interdisciplinary linkages between economics, politics, social affairs and the environment, the agenda of issues should have been much larger. But a wider agenda would have required the presence of other ministers and perhaps even the heads of government of the member states, who alone could have dealt with the breadth of challenges occasioned by further trade liberalisation. Given the complexity of international relations in era of globalisation, anything less than a summit conference would not be adequate. On the other hand, it is clear that a summit conference of 140-odd heads of government operating under Westphalian rules of sovereign equality and consensus decision making is likely to be an exercise in futility unless carefully prepared.

Second, only the Old Westphalian actors, i.e. nation state governments, were officially at the table. The new emerging nonstate actors were in the wings and in the streets demonstrating loudly against the WTO. These were the self-appointed representatives of civil society, consumer groups, special interest groups, etc., all genuinely concerned with the direction that globalisation is taking and yet without a clear negotiating mandate from their various constituencies. Should they have been at the table, and if so, how? Do they have the same legitimacy as elected governments?

Third, the underlying theme of Seattle and similar conferences seems to have been the *elimination* of the existing rules created by sovereign nation states to regulate international trade, not their replacement by new international rules. The focus was and is on liberalisation, on reducing the role of the state and moving more and more towards free markets. The indiscriminate and accelerated migration of decision making from the one-person = one-vote democratic formula to the one-dollar = one-vote market formula creates a danger of serious democratic deficits, increasingly deplored by many.

What we call the Seattle Approach (narrow sectoral agendas; trying to deal with each issue, one at a time without regard to linkages; formal representation only by national governments; and decision-rules based on consensus) is likely to lead to further failure in future conferences, not just of the WTO but of other IGOs as well – the IMF, the World Bank, etc. The severe backlash against globalisation evident at Seattle should give pause to national governments and lead to new approaches in international negotiation.

Is anyone in charge?

The net result of the structural weaknesses of the global governance system currently in place creates in our view a very dangerous situation. As globalisation proceeds in asymmetrical fashion, creating winners and losers and introducing major distortions in the world system, there is an uneasy feeling that *no one is in charge*. A number of areas of human endeavour are in danger of spinning out of control. There is no rule of law at the international level, enforced by a neutral legislator and referee. There are sectoral guidelines here and there, and the unilateral imposition of regulations by one or two superpowers within their territorial jurisdiction. Among the areas likely to experience strong turbulence in the near future are the following:

The global financial system. Currently unregulated worldwide, the global financial system is vulnerable to speculative attacks by large investors who can use market momentum and volume to realise self-fulfilling prophecies. There are no global financial regulators and the two institutions that have some claim to that title, the IMF and the World Bank, are under severe criticism for worsening the problems they have set out to cure.

The internet. At this stage no one regulates the global internet, although legislation exists in specific countries that is necessarily limited by the territorial jurisdiction of the legislators. Some international agreements exist but they tend to be guidelines and rules of thumb. There are no universal laws that are fully enforceable. The possibility of rogue players, hackers, saboteurs or whatever remains real. In the face of this delinquent behaviour there is possible action by one superpower, the United States, but its extra-territorial reach is neither simple nor considered legitimate by other countries.

The global environment. If the dangers associated with possible climate change are in any way real, they will have to be dealt with at the global level. At present the Kyoto Agreements and other similar initiatives are tentative, not really enforceable, and even if enforced judged to be insufficient by many experts. The

63

climate change issue is far from a consensus in either its diagnostics or the remedies to be brought forth. Yet if the magnitude of the problem is as high as some experts believe, we may be in for real trouble.

Genetic engineering. Biotechnology is probably the scientific discipline that is the closest to allowing Man to play God. The potential for genetic engineering, both good and bad, is enormous. Yet it is totally unregulated worldwide and there are no institutions likely to change this situation in the near future. Legislation by individual states is quite meaningless since their jurisdictions can be circumvented by going elsewhere.

The spread of epidemics. The world is at the mercy of the spread of disease, much more so than during the outbursts of bubonic plague in the 14th century. There are very few global instruments to prevent or control such epidemics beyond some special-purpose IGOs with limited jurisdiction and enforcement powers.

International terrorism and weapons of mass destruction. The success of the suspected terrorist Osama Bin Laden in operating globally from a base in Afghanistan underscores the difficulty in trying to find national responses to global problems. The continued existence of states either tolerating or sponsoring terrorism creates a Westphalian dilemma: respect the sovereignty of these states and do nothing, or intervene unilaterally against all principles of international law as the United States has done in the past.

3. Future directions: Bury Westphalia or reinvent it?

In looking ahead at the next ten years, the first decade of the New Millennium, one thing appears clear. The Old Westphalian Order, based on the assumption of strong policy capacity by nation states acting individually, is dying. Their policy capacity is now quite weak and in fact almost every one of the five principles of the Old Order appear to be negated by globalisation.

First, sovereignty is no longer what it used to be. National governments cannot exert the imperative power they used to, through legislation and regulation. National rules can be avoided by moving to competing jurisdictions. In addition, the legitimacy of sovereign acts is increasingly challenged by invoking higher principles such as human rights.

Second, unlike the classical Westphalian Order emphasis on the control of physical territory, the competitive arena today is *virtual* rather than *geographic*. Distance, trivialised by the jet age and the internet, has become a much less meaningful economic variable, and no longer affords natural protection against foreign competition. In addition, the community of internet-surfers has shown that affinity groups are no longer territorial. They exist in the ether and ignore physical distance.

The Old Westphalian Order is ill-equipped to deal with virtual reality and therefore finds itself increasingly marginalised.

Third, the nation state star of the old system is becoming the bit player of the new. Corporations, special interest groups, NGOs and other ad hoc players are now seizing the limelight. These new players – especially corporations, to a lesser extent industry associations – are now called upon to exercise governance functions without clear legitimacy or democratic mandate. Yet their presence and power cannot be ignored. They must, as players, be factored into the system.

Fourth, the idea that the only sources of international law are treaties between sovereign nations applicable only to the signatories is losing ground. Considerations that take precedence over sovereignty are now invoked to create international law, beyond treaties. In addition, the applicability of that law no longer depends on the acquiescence of all parties. The UN Charter is theoretically applicable even to non-members, and armed intervention in the internal affairs of another country no longer requires the acceptance of that intervention by the country in question, as the Kosovo case demonstrated.

Fifth, although war still remains an option in dealing with international conflict, it does not have the respectability it enjoyed in the Old Westphalian Order. Even when armed action is taken, war is no longer formally declared. In fact there have been very few formal declarations of war between sovereign states since 1945. Instead, armed conflict is seen as temporary police action or self-defence, not a legitimate instrument of policy.

For all intents and purposes practically every assumption of the Old Order is now invalidated. But as it limps into obsolescence there is nothing to replace it. Currently the only candidate is the "Market System". According to its advocates, all or almost all decisions could be taken by free markets through the interplay of supply and demand. The role of the state would be minimised to almost nothing. It would continue its retreat through further trade liberalisation, privatisation, deregulation and budget cuts. Market forces would take up the slack and ensure governance services, which could be treated like any other commodity.

Is this scenario sustainable? Probably not, for at least three reasons.

First, the asymmetrical shocks created by globalisation will have to be alleviated by an actor or actors *outside* the market mechanism. If the gap between winners and losers is allowed to increase without control, social cohesion is likely to suffer. The resulting social fracture may create very dangerous situations as the new malcontents with nothing to lose may resort to violence and to weapons of mass destruction.

65

Second, the efficiency of market systems depends on the existence of competition. If there are no antitrust or anti-combine rules, competitors are tempted to unite rather than compete. The trend towards mergers and acquisitions seems to vindicate that view. As one CEO put it, Why beat them if you can buy them? As markets become more concentrated and oligopolistic, competition diminishes. New monopolies may assume governance roles with no democratic legitimacy whatsoever. Is it better to submit to the rules of a private monopoly which no one controls or to those of a public one which, theoretically at least, could be controlled through the democratic process? Since there are no globally enforceable antitrust rules, given present trends, the absence of competition is more likely to prevail in global markets than its presence.

Third, market systems have always depended on the rule of law to function properly. Without such rule of law, they tend to become *mafia* systems since, in the absence of a policeman, taking by force is cheaper than selling and intimidating more effective than marketing. The collapse of the rule of law in the former Soviet Union and the emergence of a mafia-dominated market system there could be a precursor of things to come at the global level. The assumption that markets will discipline themselves spontaneously appears overly optimistic and has not so far been vindicated in those instances where the rule of law does not prevail.

If governance by markets is not a suitable alternative to the Old Westphalian System, what is? We believe in the desirability of a Westphalia II – a full reinvention of the concept and its applications. "Westphalia II" would retain some of the elements of the Old System and update them for use in the 21st century. It would most likely involve a fundamental rethink of the idea of sovereignty itself. Because of its link with democracy, sovereignty cannot be discarded altogether. But its home base in nation states may have to be shifted elsewhere. More direct forms of global governance may have to be devised. Principles of shared sovereignty along federal or confederal lines could be explored and, in some form or other, all relevant actors should be at the negotiating table.

The road to Westphalia II is likely to be arduous, with pitfalls and barricades along the way. But in our view this is the true Millennium Challenge in international relations and should be taken up within the next few years while the Old Westphalian System is still capable of maintaining some order in the world. Let us hope that we will not need another Thirty Years' War to goad us into action.

Chapter 4

Governing by Technique: Judgement and the Prospects for Governance of and with Technology

by
Perri 6
Senior Research Fellow, Department of Government,
University of Strathclyde
United Kingdom

1. Governing by technique – Introduction*

The oldest problem

The skilled use of machines and techniques has always been at the centre of what it is to govern. For long centuries, the power of states, and hence their capabilities of exercising governance, rested in large part on their greater capacity than their rivals, both internal and external, to own and skilfully deploy machines of war (Tilly, 1992). But direct skilled use of military machinery has never been enough. From the most ancient times, the control of skills and machinery for construction has been critical to governance, both in the most instrumental uses for building roads and in the eternally important ritual uses of technology for, among other things, public buildings and shared spaces of civic life.

At least as important has always been the capabilities of those charged with government to encourage their citizens to develop and deploy new techniques with which to develop economic life. The offer that governments have always made

* The author is grateful to Professor Paul Frissen of the Catholic University of Brabant's Centre for Law, Public Administration and Informatisation, and to Steve Ney of the Interdisciplinary Centre for Comparative Research in the Social Sciences - International in Vienna, for comments on an earlier draft of this chapter. Neither of them should be held responsible for the author's errors, nor necessarily be thought to share his views. The second part of the chapter, which examines governance with technology, is based partly on work that the author is currently conducting on "e-governance" which has been grant-aided by Cisco Systems Ltd.

to populations in exchange for being granted the right to govern has been protection from certain kinds of risk – natural disasters, hostility from others in the form of crime or war, and in more recent times ignorance, poverty and sickness. Whether that protection takes the form of deterrence, prevention, cure or palliation, it has always been delivered through the skilled use of machines by government and the regulation of their use by their populations.

From earliest times, territorial governments could achieve these goals of governing technique only by some combination of competition and collaboration with other governments. From military alliances between Greek city-states through diplomatic co-ordination between Carthage and other enemies of Rome, from Prussian emulation and surpassing of Western military and governmental statistical techniques to joint physical projects in riverine flood management to deal with risks shared between pre-Pharaonic Nilotic proto-states or mediaeval Chinese warlords, governing by technique has always been an intensely trans-state and latterly transnational affair.

Skills in the use and management of machines – rather than the machines themselves – have always constituted, directly and indirectly, the real wealth on which great economies have rested. The raw materials assembled by ancient empires were as worthless before the capabilities of their engineers, generals and factors were invested in them, as the iron and coal that were the raw materials of the 19th century before Brunel and his contemporaries worked upon them, or the metal, fuel and silicon that are the dominant raw materials of today's economies without the investment of the knowledge and skills of today's applied scientists and entrepreneurs. We have always been "knowledge economies", for there are no other kinds (*contra* e.g. Leadbeater, 1999).

Contrary to many fashionable views, therefore, the basic problems of governance of technique that we face in the 21st century are not particularly new, and the resources needed to rise to them are not new either. Neither the rationalist intellectual movements of the European 18th century, nor the Industrial Revolution, nor yet the coming of the joint stock company, nor the advent of digital computers nor the global hyper-productivity of media – called by the fashion-conscious, respectively, modernity, industrialism, capitalism, the information age and postmodernity – represent quite the great discontinuities and ruptures they are so often claimed to. Neither contemporary problems nor the available governance strategies for managing them are so very different from those of human history that we cannot learn as much from our past as from the meticulous analysis of today's skills and machines.

The genuinely significant historical changes in human social organisation are not the kind that admit of sharp discontinuities and neat periodization. As Durkheim argued just over a century ago, the most important change in social organisation has been the steadily increasing ramification of the division of labour

(Durkheim, 1984). The division of labour, Durkheim saw clearly, is both a technical and an institutional feature. Technically, its growing depth and complexity both reflects and produces a wider range of techniques – skills and artefacts and implements – that work as systems. That is to say, no individual artefact or skill is of much use without all the others available to the society as a whole, and failures, disasters, problems and the cultural significance of design choices represented by the ways in which artefacts and skills are developed have consequences for the whole society. Institutionally, increasing the division of labour increases our dependence upon everyone else for services that we do not perform for ourselves. That is to say, increasing the ramification of the division of labour both requires as its precondition – and when successfully prosecuted, itself reinforces – institutions that enable people in different specialisms and walks of life to be able to trust one another. At the same time, it makes the institutional solving of trust problems more complex – not more difficult, and indeed often easier (Douglas, 1994a, b), but certainly more ramified and complex. For as we work in different fields, with different patterns of social organisation, we become committed to different styles of solidarity and different thought styles, using different basic categories and classifications. Creating trust and agency and exchange relationships between institutional organisations of technique is essential to the cohesion of societies characterised by steadily growing pluralism – what Durkheim called "organic solidarity" – but also very demanding. What Durkheim did not do was to develop the implications of this recognition for what can be called governing by technique. That challenge has been taken up by a number of writers and thinkers working within the penumbra of Durkheim's inspiration, and much of the argument that follows draws on and develops this argument (6, 1999a).

In this chapter, therefore, it will be argued that the effective governance of the technological possibilities of the 21st century will call, above all else, for the refinement, institutionalisation and commitment of some very old capabilities of governance.

Why is it important to make this point today? One reason is that these very old capabilities are in danger of being neglected, if we allow some common ways of thinking about technology to dominate. Specifically, the author argues against those who consider technology the greatest threat to humane living and good governance (e.g. Winner, 1977), as well as those who think it the cornucopia from which those things will flow: neither Jeremiah nor Dr Pangloss is of any use. There is no denying that there have been important innovations in technique, or that much of our political and social context is fresh, and it shall be positively argued that the capabilities of governance commanded by contemporary states and supranational institutions are indeed greatly enhanced if compared with those of their forebears. Indeed, the next section discusses some of the principal technical innovations, and places some stress on their technical novelty. But the chapter attempts to show that the basic challenges of governing by technique are ones best addressed by better appreciation of lessons from enduring features of both technical development and governance.

The second reason for the urgent concern with the most ancient capabilities is that societies that fail to cultivate them tend to respond poorly to major technological change, because they fail to manage conflict well; they suffer from polarisation and an inability to reconcile rival solidarities. As the division of labour advances with technological development, the importance and complexity of this reconciliation become greater, but it becomes easier for some people to imagine that it will be achieved automatically, either by a kind of invisible social hand or else by some technological fix. It is against this prevalent error that the argument here is directed. Specifically, one of the most important ancient features of good governance to be nurtured is *judgement*. For the fears and worries about technological risks that lie behind major social and political conflicts over technology present major challenges to judgement as well as opportunities for its exercise.

The central argument for this proposition will be threefold, as follows. First, in securing the appropriate development of technologies in the wider society and acceptable distributions of their benefits and risks, the capability among policy makers that ought to be at the greatest premium is that of good judgement. In this context, an account is offered of what in the author's view judgement really is, in policy making contexts such as those of managing technological risk. Secondly, as policy makers make more and more complex use of new technologies in the course of their own work of exercising governance, the key challenge is to commission, select, use, manage and shape those technologies in such a way that they sustain and cultivate the skills of judgement among policy makers, and to ensure that they do not undermine or substitute for it. Judgement – to offer only a preliminary characterisation to be refined later – is the central skill of making decisions under conditions of uncertainty. Thirdly, the wider social consequences of the use of technologies and of making decisions using technological aids are themselves uncertain; anticipation and foresight, necessary as they are to judgement, often prove limited, and not infrequently wrong. The chapter concludes that a key goal not only for policy makers but also for publics of citizens for governing by technique is to shape technological development and use so as to cultivate and spread capabilities of judgement among citizens – the better to equip them to cope with all the unanticipated consequences of the deployment of particular technologies.

Governance of and governance with

First, it is necessary to make an elementary distinction between the two fundamental challenges addressed in this chapter. Governing by technique may be divided into (governmental – a qualification hereafter assumed) governance *of* technology and governance *with* technology. Broadly, governance *of* is outward-looking, focused on the regulation of private activity, while governance *with* is internally focused, concerned with augmenting the technical capabilities of public agencies.

Governance *of* technology refers to the work of the public executive to:

- Encourage the invention, development and deployment of existing and new technologies (technology refers to both physical artefacts and the skills required for their effective use).

- Assist producers and consumers in identifying opportunities for the use of existing and new technologies and those that are expected in the near future.

- Identify, and help producers and consumers to identify, risks (as perceived by experts) potentially associated with the development and deployment of existing and new technologies, and identify and develop strategies (themselves often both skills and artefacts) to manage those risks.

- Identify patterns of and conflict between different lay public perceptions of risks associated with the development and deployment of new technologies, and develop strategies for managing those conflicts.

Governance *with* technology refers to the:

- Development, deployment and use of existing and new technologies to enhance the governing capabilities of executive, legislative and judicial public agencies and authorities.

- Identification of opportunities for the use in governance of existing and new technologies, and those expected in the near future.

- Identification of risks (as perceived by experts) potentially associated with the development and deployment in governance of existing and new technologies, and identification and development of strategies (themselves often both skills and artefacts) to manage those risks.

- Identification of patterns of and conflict between different lay public perceptions of risks associated with the development and deployment of new technologies in governance, and development of strategies for managing those conflicts.

Strategies for both governance of and governance with technology have a wide range of intended and unintended – and sometimes, unforeseeable longer-term – consequences for societies, economies and polities, and these are not confined within the formal jurisdictions of the particular agencies of governance deploying those strategies. In turn, these consequences create new challenges, opportunities, risks and technologies for governance. They include actual harm and benefits; changing patterns of public acceptance or fear of governance agencies or particular strategies; reorganisation in the mobilisation of social movements (such as green activism); different patterns of investment and economic activity (such as those for privacy-enhancing or low-emission technologies); altered social structures of ties and networks (such as those emerging between new materials-based industries and green movement organisations); and cultural effects ranging from new systems of classification (e.g. what is counted as "acceptable" risk or what is deemed to be "irreversible") to the adoption or abandonment of cultural rituals [e.g. new types of litigation, audit (Power, 1997), public enquiry], capabilities (e.g. new practices of environmental or social audit), metaphors, recognitions, commitments and practices.

The remainder of Section 1 sets out the framework for thinking about governance and technology in the coming century. With governance now characterised, we can proceed to an understanding of the toolkit for it, the capabilities of governance, and a brief listing of the kinds of technologies that are likely as the century progresses to present interesting and important challenges to systems of local, regional, national or federal, continental and global systems of governance. Section 2 will discuss governance of technology and Section 3, governance with technology. Each part will deepen the argument about the nature of judgement.

The tools of governance

Governments have a specific set of tools available to them with which to exercise governance. Figure 1 presents a classification of the tools of government that synthesises the understanding of the toolkit for governance within the mainstream of political science (Hood, 1983; Salamon and Lund, 1989; Bemelmans-Videc *et al.*, 1998; 6, 1997*a*; Margetts, 1998). Within each category (row), tools are ranked in decreasing order of coerciveness of the degree to which they leave those upon whom the tools are used with discretion about whether and how to behave in the way desired by the agency of government that deploys the tool.

Figure 1. **The power tools of governance**

Types of power tool	Tools, ranked strong to weak
Effectors (for producing changes in culture or behaviour)	1. *Organisational capacity*: direct government provision, government-owned corporations 2. *Authority*: regulation, mandation, permission, prohibition, rights and systems of redress 3. *Treasure*: contract purchasing, loan guarantees, grants-in-aid, matching grants, tax expenditures 4. *Situation in information networks*: information delivery: persuasion, propaganda, example, demonstration projects, education, training

Figure 1. **The power tools of governance** (continued)

Types of power tool	Tools, ranked strong to weak
Collectors (for obtaining money and other resources)	taxation, direct or indirect levies service fees and charges appeals
Detectors (for acquiring information)	requisition inspection purchasing, barter appeals (including rewards for information)
Selectors (for managing, selecting, analysing, presenting information)	audit cost-benefit analysis performance indicators and measurement cost measurement, resource budgeting management review scenario-building, risk assessment

Strategy consists in applying the arts of political judgement – a subject to which we will return later – the combinations and concatenations of tools. For example, in negotiation with, bargaining with, or requesting of actors outside government, typically governments will combine persuasion with the threat of coercive regulation and the offer of incentive (or, when combined, "throffers"; see Dowding, 1991, p. 68ff).

In recent years, and especially since the major recent change of policy by the World Bank (International Bank for Reconstruction and Development and World Bank, 1997), there has been much discussion of the concept of the "institutional" capabilities, capacities and effectiveness of governance. These phrases are often used rather loosely (Weiss, 1998 is an exception) to encompass certain kinds of economic and regulatory policies, avoiding excessive intervention, providing a basic welfare state, having certain general priorities about sustainable development, checking governmental corruption and arbitrariness, providing basic goods such as the rule of law and constitutionality.

However, as the term "capacities of governance" will be used in this chapter, what is intended is the following narrower and more precise meaning of the abilities within the appropriate parts of government for the skilled exercise of the *policy* activities and the selection and management of tools in the *programme* activities of government:

- *Decision-making*: the possession by policy makers (elected politicians in office, senior civil servants and local government officers, etc.) of the skills of

  - appreciation of risks as perceived by experts and by lay members of the public, and of the key problems and challenges for governance;

73

> – judgement about the appropriate range of possible goals, priorities, choices, tools and strategies for action, and the plausible and probable consequences of those choices (Vickers, 1995).

- *Oversight*: the possession by the entire apparatus of legislative, senior political and managerial executive and judicial government to discover and appraise the quality of priority, performance, property, probity of the executive operations of government.

- *Programme*: the possession by the executive of skills of selecting, managing, deploying and controlling the appropriate tools of governance in programme delivery, whether in regulation, service delivery or otherwise.

In this sense, then, capabilities of using effectors in governance depend on the effective deployment of capabilities in the use of collectors, detectors and selectors.

Having set out this framework, it is now possible to make clearer the distinction between governance of technology and governance with technology.

- *Governance of technology* requires the capabilities of decision making, oversight and programme delivery and the selection and deployment of tools appropriate and sufficient to secure publicly accepted goals – about which there will inevitably be some conflict – that have to do with the reaping and the distribution of the benefits, and the control and distribution of the risks, that arise from the deployment of technologies.

- *Governance with technology* requires the intelligent use of technologies to enhance the capabilities of decision making, oversight and programme delivery throughout government.

In the body of the chapter, this framework for thinking about governance will be applied to the technologies that are expected to be of particular significance in the coming century. First, we consider what those might be.

Transformative technologies

Some technologies seem to be more important than others in human history. Everyone agrees that fire-making and the wheel were important. There would probably be general agreement that the propelling pencil, although useful and not to be despised, did not cause fundamental changes in how we organise our social life. Thus, some technologies appear to be transformative – that is, involved in large-scale discontinuous change to societies.

Of course, technologies by themselves do not transform societies: people do. People invest in research and development, regulate, buy, and so on – all for social, cultural, ritual, religious, financial and political reasons. These actions transform the ways in which societies organise, look and work. Technologies are implements by which people transform societies.

On the other hand, there are as many unintended as intended consequences of deploying and using new technologies: some can have large consequences. However, when science and technology, used or developed in response to these pressures, deliver new opportunities to do things very differently rather than merely incrementally differently, it is not unreasonable to talk of transformative technologies. Although technology is not the sole or fundamental cause of social change, it is a proximate and mediating force that has social and political consequences.

Some key transformative technologies of the 18th century were automation in agriculture and textiles and the utilisation of steam power. In the 1950s, arguably, antibiotics and television were among the most important transformative technologies. In the past twenty years, digital and electronic information and communications technologies surely fall into this category.

Social transformation here refers to change in some of the most fundamental social practices – for example, the pattern of social networks (think of the effects of new communications on the nature of work, friendship, acquaintance and kinship relations over vast distances); the experience of time and geographical mobility (think of air transport's influence on our sense of time); the scope of individuals' aspirations (think of the effects on longevity and aspirations for retirement of antibiotics, and of the transition in public health from a society in which most people died of infectious diseases to one in which most people die much later from degenerative ones); or social organisation (think of the multifarious causal linkages, often mediated in complex ways, between the emergence of industrial technologies and the new organisational forms in the 19th century of the joint stock company, the co-operative, the modern mutual, modern civil service and local government: 6, 1998a). Technology is not the unmoved prime mover, but can be used or reacted to in powerfully transformative ways.

Once conceived, technologies take a long time to develop to the point where they are offered on a large scale as solutions to one kind of problem, before finally becoming transformative – often by being used for problems different from the ones to which they were first applied. The typical lag is one of decades. Some commentators speculate that the lag is becoming shorter.

This chapter is concerned with technologies that are not yet mature, that do not yet have many commercial applications and that, in some cases, are perhaps as much as a decade or two away from reaching that stage. It is not concerned with technologies that are promising and valuable but basically incremental developments of present technologies, such as further use of miniaturisation. We already have a reasonably good idea of what the transformative technologies of the 2010s, 2020s and 2030s are likely to be. It is widely thought some of the main ones are likely to be those listed in Figure 2.

Figure 2. **Transformative technologies of the 21st century**

- *Distributed intelligence network engineering* – the technology of more or less loose networks of intelligent artefacts capable of communicating with one another to manipulate environments; today, systems of barcodes and smart tags do this daily, but in the next ten years, "smart homes" will emerge in which many ordinary objects communicate for a variety of purposes (Kelly, 1994).

- *Nano-engineering* – the technology of using enzymes as assemblers for building or disassembling almost anything from the molecular level or even the subatomic level (Drexler, 1991); at present, the commercially applicable achievements of nano-engineering have been unimpressive, not least because nano-engineering represents a high cost for very low volumes of output (Kaku, 1998, pp. 266-273).

- *Quantum computing* – the application of nano-engineering at the subatomic level to increase the speed and range of computing capacity to many orders of magnitude over anything that can be achieved with micro-silicon systems, because at some level of miniaturisation, quantum effects begin to cut in (Drexler, 1991; Kaku, 1998; Gershenfeld, 1999, pp. 176-191; Singh, 1999, Chapter 8).

- *Bio-computing* – the application of biological techniques to use enzymes for computing, also with improvements by orders of magnitude in capacity; because biotic matter is relatively cheap to reduce to a useful format, many commentators believe this to be a more promising investment than quantum computing (Drexler, 1991; Kurzweil, 1999).

- *The new robotics* – the development of networks of kinetically intelligent, learning, self-directed, self-replicating, self-repairing, fault-tolerant artefacts and systems capable of making decisions as well as executing prescribed tasks (Warwick, 1998).

- *Genetic engineering* – the manipulation of the genetic code of almost any biotic material to repair, enhance or transform plant or animal life, including human characteristics (Reiss and Straughan, 1996; Kitcher, 1996; Burley, 1999; Silver, 1998).

- *Neuro-engineering* – simulating and modelling neural functions in order to apply genetic, chemical, surgical and eventually prosthetic engineering techniques to repair, enhance, or change the characteristics of human brains, including eventually integrating biotic brain activity with artefactual memory and processing capacity (bio-engineered, quantum engineered or, in the shorter term, using silicon-based technology) (Blank, 1999).

- *Sustainable, non-polluting, resource-efficient production technologies* – the substitution of a wide range of less polluting, less resource-intensive technologies for present ones in every area of production; these may include, for particular purposes, the application of nano-engineering and distributed intelligence engineering as well as genetic engineering. In this category, we can include low-emission energy systems such as photovoltaic cells, hydrogen fuel cells, wind turbines and biofuel systems, systems that either produce no waste or else reuse products traditionally treated as waste. In addition, there is scope for bio-engineering to clean up contamination after it has occurred (von Weizsäcker *et al.*, 1998; Christie and Rolfe, 1995; Hawken *et al.*, 1999).

- *New space transport technologies* to support the commercial exploitation of nearby asteroids etc. – such as solar sailing (Kaku, 1998, Chapter 14).

Although this list is not necessarily exhaustive, it is important to select some important technologies of the next wave that will mature in the 21st century, in order to give an account of the technological context in which the particular technologies will be used. These technologies have a number of important characteristics, listed below. There are good reasons to think that all are likely candidates for fulfilling the criteria listed above for being transformative.

- All are developed drawing on cutting-edge – as defined by whatever scientific consensus there exists – basic as well as applied science.

- Although they build on previous work in biology, selective breeding, silicon-based computing, etc., all of them nevertheless do appear to many commentators to represent step-changes in the scale and in some cases the direction of development of human capabilities, rather than simply incremental enhancements of existing capabilities (by contrast with, for example, many new technologies in the chemicals industry or biomass energy sources).

- All will have consequences distributed very widely across many areas of life, not only in particular industries (by contrast with, for example, many new technologies developed in the materials sciences).

- All are likely to be sufficiently high profile to attract the attention, interest and risk perception of social movements, citizens, politicians and regulators.

- All are already the subject of extensive public debate and attention by futurists, journalists, ethicists and technologists.

- None of these seem today so far from development that little can be expected for at least fifty years, nor in any of these cases does basic feasibility remain uncertain (which is why, for example, nuclear fusion has been omitted: Kaku, 1998, Chapter 13).

These technologies will have applications in every area of human endeavour – medicine, manufacturing, food production, environmental clean-up, political decision modelling...the list is endless. The social effects of these technologies will probably be neither discrete nor simply cumulative. Experience suggests that we can expect convergence and interaction between these technologies. There are already experiments in combining biotechnology applications with informatics; nano-engineering is likely to be undertaken using bio-computing; genetic therapies may in time be best accomplished using nano-level assembly; distributed intelligence engineering may merge with the new robotics; and so on.

However, it should be stressed that as the initially soaring expectations – and fears – associated with any new technology begin to fade, disappointments set in and claims and fears become more modest; moreover, lead times between inventions and discoveries and the occasions of use in social transformations can be stubbornly long – although they may be shortening slightly.

These transformative technologies, individually and together, present policy makers and their systems of governance with important challenges.

2. Governance of technology

Governance of technology, as defined in Section 1, can best be considered under three headings of related and interdependent types of activity. These are:

- The promotion of technique, which encompasses the promotion of innovation and competition addressed briefly below.

- The identification of technological risks as perceived by experts, which will not be explored here for reasons of space and because it raises no major issues of governance separately from the third element, which is:

- The process of reconciling rival perceptions of technological risks from different publics, to which the bulk of this section is devoted.

Promoting technique

It is perhaps helpful to begin by presenting the available "effector" tools of governance for the promotion of technique. Figure 3 lists these under the major categories identified above. (Buchanan, 1992, Chapter 12 provides a review of European states' balance between these tools in use.)

The record of governments in the successful use of some of these tools is, at best, mixed. While for many years Japan successfully exploited a highly *dirigiste* strategy of government-co-ordinated consortia of major companies combined with very limited use of competition policy, with some direct subsidy, it is not clear that in recent years this method has been as successful as it appeared to be up to the end of the 1980s. Moreover, with the partial exception of France, it has not been tried with the same vigour in many other OECD countries, and where it has been tried the results have generally been less impressive than in the Japanese case prior to the 1990s. The argument is sometimes made that the early years of the Japanese experiment were more successful because the programme was focused on technology catch-up. But when Japan had achieved this goal, the institutional arrangement proved much less effective in pushing Japanese commercial research and development effectively into the most promising new areas of invention.

In general, therefore, the trend in OECD Member countries has been to shift away from directly managed research and development and away from government officials trying to "pick winners", at least in the sense of identifying for state support

---

Figure 3. **Tools for the promotion of techniques**

Organisation

- Direct undertaking of research and development in government laboratories.

Regulation

- Disincentive side-constraint regulation for techniques and applications: health and safety, environmental impact, data protection, etc.
- Competition policy and in particular the treatment co-operation between firms in research and development.
- Universal service regulation.
- Grants of monopoly status to professional institutes of technology.

Incentive

- Patents, i.e. temporary rights to monopoly rents from technical innovations.
- Publicly funded university-based research.
- Direct subsidy or tax incentives for private sector research and development – including regional policy to promote urban or regional investment, collaboration in research and development, clustering and networking in particular industries.
- Tax incentives for business users and end-consumers to adopt technologies.
- Export promotion and underwriting.
- Purchasing policies to encourage development of cutting-edge technologies, e.g. defence *matériel*.

Persuasion

- Foresight exercises.
- Technology assessment programmes.
- Technology-related education.

---

particular companies from among those working with new technologies. Many governments have also scaled back their technology export credit guarantee commitments, and even their appraisal systems. Indeed, the United States has recently closed its Office of Technology Assessment. Instead, governments have moved toward the regulation of "bads" in order to stimulate innovation in and take up of, for example, environmentally cleaner or privacy-enhancing technologies. There has also been growing government interest in and expenditure on technology foresight exercises (*Foresight*, 1999). However, governments have recently invested heavily in incentives for households and small business to adopt a wide range of information and communication technologies. In the name of combating the "digital divide" (6 and Jupp, forthcoming), governments around the world are continuing to expand their spending on persuading households and small companies to purchase computers, encouraging access to the internet and also to proprietary networks, and so

79

on. The US Government has just proposed to Congress a new tranche of measures in this regard (Office of the Press Secretary, 2000), as has the British government (Policy Action Team 15, 2000). It remains to be seen how successful these kinds of initiatives will be.

However, it should be noted that, for good or ill, this promotion of the take-up of certain technologies demonstrates that governments have not entirely stopped "picking winners": rather, they have tended to shift from picking firms for long-term protection and subsidy to more short-term efforts to press the use of particular technologies that are seen already to have "won" or are believed likely to "win" in the near future, or toward the greater use of regional policy to identify "loser" areas and to try to reverse those dynamics. Targeting of policy remains central, but the nature of the targets and the character of the tools used have changed (Cowling *et al.*, 1999).

This raises one of the key challenges for governance of technology, namely the relationship between competition policy and regulatory goals for universal service. In large countries such as the United States, it is possible to find ways to avoid conflicts between them, for example by requiring companies that offer services in an affluent area also to accept responsibilities in poorer ones, as US utility regulators do. This enables a measure of competition, but secures the provision of new technology-based services in poorer communities. In smaller countries, it is much harder in any case to secure competition, and universal service requirements have tended in practice to reinforce national monopoly. This will be a debate of particular importance in relation to the provision of broadband services in rural areas. As the global economy increasingly favours cities, contrary to the proponents of the "death of distance" hypothesis (see Castells, 1989, 1996), the incentives for investment in broadband infrastructure in rural areas remain low or may even fall (Wilhelm, 2000, pp. 113-116) – yet this may be essential to any rural economic development strategy, for diversification out of agriculture will increasingly depend on the presence of this infrastructure.

Indeed, there seem to be cycles in the culture of policy making from which different styles of promotion of technique stem. In some periods, such as the late 1960s and the late 1990s up to the present, anticipation, foresight, future studies and contingency planning have been regarded as essential commitments of governance. In others, such as the 1970s and 1980s, they were rejected in favour of strategies based on resilience, or focusing on institutionalising capacities of governance to respond to whatever opportunities technological innovation may deliver. For the governance of opportunity is only the obverse of the governance of risk, and there are similar cycles (6, 1999b) between anticipation and resilience (Hood and Jones, 1996; Wildavsky, 1988) in cultures of risk perception, which shape the judgement of policy makers in much the same way.

Conciliating risk as spoken by publics

Understanding how lay publics perceive technological risk

The risks that people worry about or fear, and the risks they dismiss or regard as acceptable are the basic shaping factors for conflicts over technologies, and the most important factors in shaping patterns of trust and distrust between government, business and social movements in striking settlements over how technologies are to be regulated and managed (Krimsky and Golding, 1992; Löfstedt and Frewer, 1998; Cvetkovich and Löfstedt, 1999).

The first challenge to governance capacity is to understand how lay publics perceive technological risk. [It is not suggested that "experts" are necessarily or always very different, much as they – and some academics (e.g. Viscusi, 1998, Margolis, 1996) – often insist that they are. For they are exposed to at least some of the same cultural pressures as publics are. Indeed, some commentators complain of exactly this: e.g. Breyer, 1993.] When confronted with new transformative technologies, people typically work with a surprisingly limited repertoire – which persists over time and gets applied to many different technologies – of concerns, or perceptions of risk, that inform their political responses to the availability, desirability and acceptability of those technologies, and therefore, their demand for political action or inaction. Some people – or rather, some cultures – are not particularly preoccupied with risks but only with opportunities. For others, some technologies are inherently risky and others not. Figure 4 offers a way to classify the standard repertoire of "alarmed" risk perceptions.

The selection of technologies to which perception of risk applies does not generally reflect ideally rational calculation and comparison of technical features or of human uses. Rather, the conflicts over aesthetics, ethics and governance that shape how a transformative technology is received are intimately connected with the patterns of perception of risk.

The neo-Durkheimian approach

There are various ways in which public perception of risks associated with technologies may be understood (Krimsky and Golding, 1992; Löfstedt and Frewer, 1998). Some key findings of the conventional psychological and psychometric research traditions (as reviewed in Renn, 1998) are that

- The more salient a risk is, the more likely people typically believe it to be.

- Singular events are believed more probable than the frequencies suggest.

- People adjust their perceptions of likelihood and acceptability to their setting.

81

Figure 4. **A taxonomy of alarm: risk perceptions hostile to new technologies**

1. *Loss of control*. Loss of human control over the products and applications of technology through the growing autonomy of self-directed learning systems, and the loss of accountability to humans of artefacts and machines. In particular, the fear of the "irreversibility" of transformative technologies is a fear of loss of control.

2. *Incompetence*. Accidents, disasters, shocks, fiascos and more chronic failures in the implementation of the governance of technologies.

3. *Tyranny*. Control of technology by an élite, profession, class or sect acting in their members' interests only.

4. *Danger and loss of safety*. Uncertainty and risk of unanticipated side-effects, errors in use; this especially influences environmental sustainability.

5. *Evil*. Increased human capacity will be used for evil, including violence, abuse of technology by malevolent groups of humans (criminals, dictators, imperialist or aggressive states).

6. *Redundancy*. Reduced requirement for humans in economic production and consumption.

7. *Injustice*. Increased inequality, exclusion and stigma from differential access to technologies and related skills.

8. *Indignity*. Invasiveness of applications of technology; reduced cultural commitment to humane emotion and solidarity; and excessive cultural commitment to functionality, instrumentalism and utilitarianism.

9. *Irresponsibility*. Erosion of personal responsibility by increased knowledge of the means, capacities and determination of individual decision making, and increased capacity for manipulation of determination of individual decision making.

10. *Loss of protection*. Changing scope of the insurability of life-event risks and increased life-event risks as a result of the introduction of technologies.

11. *Revulsion*. Aesthetic rather than moral disgust at certain applications of technologies.

12. *Loss of integrity*. Anxiety at the perceived implications of technologies for what is believed to be distinctive about human nature, or the integrity of the body, or the natural order; for example, the determinacy of a legal condition of death or of personhood or responsibility.

- People avoid cognitive dissonance – they can reject information that does not fit their world view.

The key factors that seem, from the findings in this tradition, to explain variance in public perception of, and therefore acceptability of, technological risk are the following (Renn, 1998):

- Perceptions of acceptance of responsibility for the creation and management of risk by those in charge of the development and deployment of the technology.

- Perceptions of competence of the regulators, technology users and controllers.

- Perceptions of the degree of care, commitment and effort that regulators and technology users put into managing risk.

- Perceptions of the fairness of the distribution of risk between categories of people.

- Perceptions of the fairness of procedures in place to make decisions about how risks should be managed, including – where appropriate – their openness.

- Perceptions of the degree to which the risk is seen to be under control.

- Perceptions of the degree to which the risk is seen to be one that is voluntarily chosen or at least accepted by those most affected.

- Perceptions of the degree to which individuals and organisations affected can secure information about scale of risk and have some choice over actions they themselves can take to manage their own exposure to risk.

Renn (1998) distinguishes four images of risk that people resort to in connection with different technologies or other sources of potential harm:

- *Pending danger* – random, catastrophic, inequitable, seek flight.

- *Slow killer* – delayed, non-catastrophic, seek blame, seek deterministic risk management.

- *Cost-benefit calculation* – balance quantifiable asymmetric gains and losses, probabilistic thinking.

- *Thrill* – voluntary, personal control and skill, non-catastrophic.

But this is rather limited. It tells us very little about who might have which perceptions, or in what circumstances any of us might have these perceptions. The variables are so proximate and so loosely related to one another, so lacking in clustering, that as an explanation, the psychological work is very unsatisfying and of limited use to policy makers concerned with the governance of technological risk (Douglas, 1985, 1997).

Fears and worries about risks are not simply inaccuracies and errors that have crept into a process that should "normally" operate to protect individuals from the "correct" subset of all conceivable dangers that people should be worrying about, nor simply noise and confusion that cloud an individual-level process that connects real interests miraculously provided in advance with calculations of what threatens them (*contra* economists such as Viscusi, 1998). It is misguided therefore to imagine – as some in the "public understanding of science" movement still do – that if publics are provided with better scientific education or greater understanding of probability theory, their

83

perceptions of risk will converge with those of experts or that they will come to "trust" in or defer to experts more readily. Risk perception is much more political than this.

In the author's view, the most fruitful way forward is to look to the neo-Durkheimian tradition (Douglas, 1982, 1994a, Douglas and Wildavsky, 1982; Gross and Rayner, 1985; Rayner, 1992; Adams, 1995; Ellis and Thompson, 1997; Thompson *et al.*, 1990; Schwarz and Thompson, 1990; Thompson *et al.*, 1999; Thompson, 1992; Lupton, 1999, Chapter 3). The neo-Durkheimian view is that the selection of particular technological risks to worry about, the kind of affect attached to different risks, the determination of what information is counted as relevant in thinking about risk all reflect people's commitments to particular forms of social organisation or "solidarity", for those shape perceptions that people have of the forms of social organisation in which technologies are developed, used, deployed and consumed (Douglas, 1994a). Acceptability is not necessarily a matter of probabilities, costs and benefits – save in particular institutional settings for those solidarities that work with those commitments. The argument is that those technologies about which someone has few fears but sees only opportunities and benefits tend to be those that are deployed in patterns of social organisation which that person recognises, is shaped within, understands, has some commitment to (perhaps unwillingly or stoically). This is one reason why formal education, official communications and propaganda about risk, probability and magnitudes of harm have limited impact on patterns of risk perception. The view that there is a single correct way to calculate "objective" risk, commonly held in engineering circles, misses the point that people have different priorities between risks and that magnitudes of harm matter differently to different risk cultures, irrespective of probabilities. How, then, can we understand the links between commitments to certain types of social organisation and biases about risk?

Humans are not endlessly inventive in social organisation: they reproduce certain basic patterns. Therefore we need a taxonomy, a heuristic device with which to capture some of the plurality. The neo-Durkheimian tradition offers exactly this, in the form of a two-dimensional matrix. The first dimension is the degree to which institutions render salient understandings of fixed roles, rules, and facts of life taken to be given, self-evident, or fixed. This dimension is usually called "grid", and might be defined as follows:

- *grid*: the degree to which social relations are conceived as if they were normally, naturally, properly, desirably or unavoidably, but principally *involuntary*.

The high grid end of the dimension, then, represents a tragic view of society, and the low grid end offers a heroic view of society. If the conditions that shape life are not under voluntary control, then the scope is tragically limited for individuals to transform those conditions. By contrast, if social relations are subject to human choice, then either bold or heroic individuals or groups can hope to overcome the limitations of their inheritance and refashion the conditions of their lives.

The second dimension is usually known as "group" and can be defined as follows:

- *group*: the degree to which social relations are conceived as if the norm, the natural situation, the desirable condition or else the unavoidable situation is one in which individual autonomy is always held *accountable* to a larger group.[1]

Cross-tabulating these two dimensions yields a two-by-two matrix (Figure 5), which in turn yields four basic biases about social organisation – or lenses through which people try to make sense of the world.

Neither dimension can be derived from the other. For, as is clear from Figure 5, there is no logical incoherence in the idea of accountability to a voluntarily chosen order (the egalitarian enclave, the sect) or, for that matter, in the idea of an unaccountable life in an order of involuntary relations (isolates, fatalism). In fact, these two positions turn out to be very important.

It is important to stress that this is not a classification of psychological types. No one individual is an egalitarian or a hierarchist, *tout court*.[2] Most of us have all four biases, that are called forth, elicited, activated (passive), and which we shape, strike settlements between (active) in particular institutional contexts, according to the conflicts involved (Rayner, 1992).

The theory argues that people select and prioritise risks according to the particular balance of forms of social organisation to which they are committed, not according to some (of course impossible) probability ranking of all conceivable risks and all conceivable resources against some once-and-for-all settlement of priorities. While some moderate forms of hierarchy and individualism may attach great importance to the calculation of probabilities and the balance of costs of benefits, the selection of risks for this technical, economic, epidemiological or engineering treatment reflects their fundamental institutional commitments. Hierarchy is anxious about technologies that enable people to behave in less rule-bound ways. For example, much of the anxiety about the allegedly unregulated character of content on the world wide web reflects this hierarchical commitment.

Individualism sees most risk in those technologies that empower monopoly companies or overweening government, such as supercomputing, or those that promote collectivist forms of organisation.

By contrast, the egalitarian solidarity worries most about technological risks that are perceived as coming from those technologies that require either unconstrained markets or very large organisations to manage, or that are seen to tread very heavily on the earth. Hence the egalitarian anxiety about, for example, the alleged dangers of civil nuclear power. Egalitarianism rejects the calculative, probability-based, balance-of-harm-and-benefit approach to risk in favour of precaution (O'Riordan and Cameron, 1994).

85

Figure 5.   **The varieties of perceptions of social organisation and institutional co-ordination that shape cognition**

Group ⇧	Social relations are conceived as if they were principally involuntary Tragic view of society ⇧		
⇦ Individual autonomy should not always be held accountable	**Fatalism / isolate** *Co-ordination*: None: all systems are capricious *Social network structure*: Isolate; casual, shallow ties, occasion-bound networks *Value stance*: Personal withdrawal (e.g. from others, social order, institutions), eclectic values *Institutions*: Suspicious of the efficacy of any institutional design *World views*: Fatalism at the bottom of society and despotism at the top of society *Blame strategy for power*: "No point" *Weakness*: Tends to be poor in predicting and responding strategically to new situations, shocks, etc. (this may not be seen as a problem since the basic belief is that there is little one can do about change)	**Hierarchy / central community** *Co-ordination*: Regulated systems are necessary: unregulated systems need management and deliberate action to give them stability and structure *Social network structure*: Central community, controlled and managed network *Value stance*: Affirmation (e.g. of social values, social order institutions) by rule-following and strong incorporation of individuals in social order *Institutions*: Rational, steerage capacity, rule-dominant *World view*: Hierarchy *Blame strategy for power*: Violation of rule and role *Weakness*: Tends to produce brittle systems and networks, vulnerable to unexpected shocks from other solidarities (this may not be seen as a problem since the basic belief is that other solidarities are essentially reactive, and the task is to keep systems within bounds where vulnerability can be minimised)	⇨ Individual autonomy should be held accountable
	Individualism / openness *Co-ordination*: Spontaneous, hidden hand: regulated systems are unnecessary or harmful: effective system emerges spontaneously from individual action *Social network structure*: Individualism, markets: open, configurations characterised by weak ties *Value stance*: Affirmation (e.g. of social values, social order institutions) by personal entrepreneurial initiative *Institutions*: Self-restricting, transparent, non-intrusive, guaranteeing basic property rights etc. *World view*: Libertarianism *Blame strategy for power*: Intrusion, disturbance of spontaneous process *Weakness*: Tends to be poor in solving collective action problems (this may not be seen as a problem since collective action problems are not recognised as problems worth solving)	**Egalitarianism / enclave / sect** *Co-ordination*: Charismatic, mutual: regulated systems are oppressive – except when they protect *Social network structure*: Enclave, sect, inward-looking *Value stance*: Collective withdrawal (e.g. from perceived "mainstream"), dissidence, principled dissent *Institutions*: Charismatic, value-dominant, solidaristic *World view*: Egalitarianism *Blame strategy for power*: Failure to protect, violation and pollution of fragile order *Weakness*: Tends to schism in network structures (this may not be seen as a problem because the basic egalitarian belief is in small, tightly cohesive, transparent community)	
	⇩ Heroic view of society *Social relations are conceived as if they were principally voluntary*		⇨ Grid

The danger with assessments of risk that are led by experts is that they tend to be biased in favour of hierarchy or individualism, or some bilateral treaty between them. Whatever the technical accuracy of such assessments – and experts make errors too, as the BSE story in the United Kingdom suggests – the problem is that they forget the difficulties of securing public legitimacy in a democracy for any strategy that makes no concessions to other solidarities and their preferred forms of social organisation. This was very clear in the case of Shell's problems with the disposal of the Brent Spar oil platform in the mid 1990s. To protest, as technology experts tend to,[3] that this makes the debates about something other than risk as they understand it, may be literally correct, but it is beside the point. It would be surprising if, in democracies, where life is sufficiently complex that there are too many risks to count and everyone must make some selection of what to worry about and why, debates about risk were ever purely about disagreements over the technical probabilities of particular harms. Those who cannot or will not engage in debates about what kinds of social power, social organisa-tion and governance are or can be made acceptable should not expect to prevail in conflicts over risk. Making settlements does indeed require trade-offs between differ-ent risks (Graham and Wiener, 1995), as perceived by different solidarities: but the governance of technological risk is not itself essentially a technical exercise. Not least, this means that technology policy cannot and must not be left to engineers and econ-omists alone. Trust – which usually means deference here – is not the product of pro-viding information that reflects the commitments of one or more solidarities to people who work with others. Rather, it is the result of a political process of negotiation for the construction of settlements (6, 1998*b*, Parts III and IV). In more successful settlements there is a process of institutional development, by which forms of organisation around risks are developed in which several solidarities can see some representation of their own commitments – in short, what are sometimes called "clumsy institutions" (Thompson, 1997*a*, *b*, *c*). While attention to procedures of settlement making is vital, a tendency in recent conflict management has been to focus exclusively on this (for a review of techniques and innovations see Dukes, 1996, Part II), rather than on issues of substance that divide solidarities or on ways of striking settlements (6, 2000*a*).

The neo-Durkheimian theory offers not so much another tool for policy makers as an approach, a style, a provisional heuristic with which to cultivate their appreci-ation of the nature of the conflict-ridden institutional contexts within which they must exercise judgement.

Judgement

For these solidarities are in permanent tension, and all settlements between them are shifting, unstable affairs that break down sooner or later. Therefore, the key challenge for governance is to help people to strike fresh settlements as old ones collapse in any field of technological risk perception. This indeed requires at-tention to the technical issues of technology design and the calculations of experts

87

about probabilities of harm. But it also calls for much more than this. Governance requires judgement, or what Aristotle (1925, 142ff) called *phronesis* or practical intelligence (Annas, 1993, pp. 73-84). The contribution the author wishes to make here to the debate about judgement in governance of technique is to suggest that it consists in intelligent appreciation in order to engage in four-way rebalancing between the basic solidarities that make up any society.[4]

The important judgement skills and capacities of governance, then, are those of making more rather than less viable settlements between solidarities. Durkheim argued that societies with complex divisions of labour are viable only when settlements between each of these four "mechanical" solidarities [that is, solidarities that would, if they had their way, insist on a single form of social organisation being reproduced throughout the society – what Durkheim (1984) called "similarity" or Douglas (1966) called "purity"] are able to produce "organic" solidarity, or a more or less viable settlement.

It has been helpfully argued (by the late Hannah Arendt: see D'Entrèves, 1994, Chapter 3) that judgement, in political and in other contexts, consists in two activities, which are in essential tension with one another even though each is incomplete without the other:

- Passing a balanced judgement on the situation in which we find ourselves – this is backward-looking: evaluative, responsibility-based, blame- and praise-focused, sanction- and reward-focused.

- Striking a balance between the forces that make up the situation in order to make a decision about what is to be done next – this is forward-looking, decision-focused, outcome- and constraint-based.

In judgement, policy makers cannot and do not follow a crudely ideal model of rationality, setting goals first and then identifying means. Rather, as the late Sir Geoffrey Vickers (1995) argued, they exercise and thereby cultivate the craft skill of "appreciation", which combines the "reality judgement" of selecting and organising from the complex balance of forces and identifying some of their responsibility for it, tracking potential future trends, with the "instrumental judgement" of ingenuity and innovation in rebalancing those forces (or solidarities) for a "valuation" that strikes some settlement between the rival normative commitments that turn a condition into a problem for the policy system.

But we can perhaps offer a slightly richer account of the two central activities of judgement by synthesising a number of strands of thought.

First, to exercise judgement is to be willing to take *responsibility for one's decision*, to own up to it and be willing to be held to account for it: that is, policy makers and citizens alike must independently judge but in a social context of interdependence

(Fleischacker, 1999, pp. 132, 135-6). Second, there is an initial phase of judgement which involves the short-circuiting of deliberation, by simply exercising prior knowledge, understanding and sensitivity to the concerns regarded as important by all those with an interest, as well as one's own priorities, in order first to *allocate attention to priority problems*. A third element is *appreciation*, both backward and forward-looking. Crucial to both is, as Adam Smith stressed (Fleischacker, 1999, pp. 138-9), a certain *astuteness* about one's own and others' interests, character and commitments, and a capacity to *project* the insights taken from that astuteness forward into possible futures. Fourth, there is a dimension of *normativity*, in which one selects the contextually appropriate principles or norms, strategies and styles of argument for the social context of the decision to be made. The fifth element is a moment of *distancing*: judgement calls for a capacity to distance oneself from one's own short-term interests, from the pressures placed upon one by others, from one's own and others' emotions. Sixth, judgement consists essentially and perhaps most vitally in *balancing*, in striking trade-offs between different risks, in balancing rival norms and rival solidarities, constraints and commitments: the recognition of and sensitivity to the value of each of these is contributed by the moment of appreciation. Balancing should elicit at least a provisional priority ordering. Seventh, judgement requires a willingness to *come to closure*, to reach a decision and be firm about it. However, a person with the virtue of judgement does not, as we commonly say, "rush to judgement", but in fact, where appropriate (again, to follow common parlance taken from the courtroom), "reserves judgement". Coming to closure should, at least in the ideal case where sufficient time is available (a kind of "stages model" perhaps?), follow astute allocation of attention, appreciation, normativity, distancing and balancing. Eighth – and here we come full circle back to responsibility – judgement requires that the decision maker accept the consequences of his or her decision, including those of the trade-offs and the opportunity costs, accepting the foreseeable but unwelcome consequences as the price for the values or priorities adhered to: we might call this a kind of *gravitas* (Yankelovich, 1991). Because judgement has these eight quite distinct and complex moments, it often requires rituals, or as Arendt saw it, *performance*, for its exercise and cultivation. Clearly, there is no necessarily correct sequence of these eight moments, nor does good judgement require ideally rational "synoptic" decision making of the theoretical kind that, it has long been recognised, policy makers cannot achieve. But certainly, the possibility of good judgement does require the falsehood of some of the most fatalistic theories about human decision making capabilities – for example, that humans can only mindlessly follow implicit scripts, make incremental mutual adjustments to existing or inherited systems, engage in purely zero-sum behaviour, or randomly attach pre-given solutions to randomly generated or identified opportunities. All of these famous theories are powerful critiques of actual decision making, but they do not need to be read as implying fatalistically that nothing else is ever possible.

In however modest a way, policy makers always exercise judgement of some kind. But good judgement is subject to a law of requisite variety – the sophistication of its reality and instrumental judgements in appreciation must be adequate to the ramifications in structure of the problems to which appreciation is directed (the law of requisite variety, as formulated within the cybernetic tradition, is the thesis that an effective control system corresponds in complexity to the complexity of the system under its control: Ashby, 1947 cited and discussed in Dyson, 1997 at pp. 174-178). The criterion of adequacy proposed here is the neo-Durkheimian one – that an appreciation is adequate to the degree that it recognises the dynamics of the full set of solidarities engaged. The cultivation of better judgement both among policy makers and among publics consists in the cultivation of capability for adequate complexity in appreciation for the problems to which attention is directed (March and Olsen, 1976) – accepting that the allocation of attention to problems is itself a matter that requires judgement, and is obviously shaped implicitly by the pressures of particular solidarities and their biases.

Finally, it must be stressed that if social science has anything to offer to normative understandings of what judgement is and how it can be cultivated, then the most important finding is that judgement is not an individual endowment or achievement (as Adam Smith thought: Fleischacker, 1999, p. 132ff). Rather, it is a collective practice, institutionally sustained, and a collective capability of policy makers at any and every level charged with particular kinds of decision making. The learning of judgement is social, and essentially about decisions made in the midst of conflict, and the content of what is learned is also social, in that no individual policy maker "possesses" a complete set judgement capabilities, any more than an individual can "possess" an institution's memory (Sabatier and Jenkins-Smith, 1993; Goody, 1995).

Managing technological risk fundamentally is simply brokering between the conflicting solidarities that organise perceptions of technological risk among different publics. Of course, those who do this cannot be neutral any more than any of the activist parties. But they can work to establish institutions and roles that will give them a provisional distance from at least some of the activists, to secure some leverage. That may require formal institutions of conciliation and the formation of difficult and tension-ridden "clumsy" institutional settlements (Thompson, 1997a, b, c) that inconsistently give something to each solidarity. Examples of innovations in this field in recent years are well known. They include consensus conferences, citizens' juries, stakeholder negotiation systems, conciliation and mediation, and a wide range of innovations in public consultation (Dukes, 1996, Part II). Traditional styles include face-to-face bargaining or simply debates in legislatures. Alternatively, it may call for much more informal mutual adjustment without extensive dialogue. In either case, judgement, on this understanding, is about the intimate dependence of policy activity upon democratic, political and oversight activity. From oversight, the means of passing judgement and making what Vickers' called the reality judgement are taken; from political action comes the skill of institutional building for organic solidarity; from democratic activity comes the basis of viability for those settlements.

These are among the most ancient skills of governance. Indeed, the writings of Marcus Aurelius are as good a statement on them as any. But their cultivation remains the central challenge for the governance of technology in the 21st century.

Challenges to governance capabilities from technologies

Do new technologies raise new issues?

It is sometimes argued that some of the transformative technologies of the 21st century will present challenges to governance that previous technologies have not.

With one partial exception that will be addressed in a moment, this argument is overstated. Certainly, every new technology presents a different challenge to governance. But for the most part, technologies present variants of traditional challenges, differences of degree rather than differences in kind. For example, the transformative technologies listed above present the following challenges to governance – we already face all of them with today's technologies:

- *Jurisdiction*: many applications of new technologies will exacerbate already difficult problems of identifying the appropriate jurisdiction for regulation, and the related problems of making regulation effective (more on this below).

- *Definition of property rights*: for example, commercial exploitation of space will require international law to define the allocation of real estate property on asteroids, the moon, other planets, comets, etc.; to define extraction rights, leasehold and other rights for the lawful organisation of commercial tourism; and to set in place constraints on ownership arising from environmental duties and so on.

- *Prevention of terrorism*: for example, nanotechnology and genetic engineering could, like many of today's technologies, be used by terrorists; it will be necessary to find ways to ensure control internationally of the applications of these capabilities.

- *Data protection and privacy*: for example, neuro-engineering could be abused to collect data directly from human brains without the consent of the subjects, and it will be necessary to apply data protection laws and privacy rights in international human rights law to prevent and sanction such abuses.

- *Health and safety and environmental regulation*: many of the new technologies will raise issues of health and safety and environmental impacts, to be dealt with by existing regulatory authorities.

91

None of these are new problems, although the applications we can expect of new technologies will provide new contexts for them, to which institutions of governance will have to adapt. In the last three cases, existing institutions are in place with capabilities for this work. In the case of the definition of property rights, we face challenges not fundamentally different from those to which the development of the international law of the sea, the treaties governing the Antarctic, and – in a different mode – the allocation of domain names on the internet have been creative institutional responses.

The key challenge remains the enduring one of ensuring that our institutions, our rituals, our settlements between rival solidarities sustain practices of social organisation that enable us to avoid dangerous stand-offs and polarisation over perceived technological risk, and that enable us to generate intelligence and deliberation at every level about actual hazards. For this, we shall need highly adaptive institutions of governance, committed to deliberation, conciliation and settlement between mechanical solidarities, and specifically, institutions that cultivate judgement among decision makers and among wider publics.

There is a partial exception to this generalisation that we are facing new contexts for, exacerbations of, differences of degree in existing problems for governance. This arises in connection with innovations in the field of artificial intelligence that are only now coming to fruition and which we can expect to be of growing and enormous importance through the 21st century. For artificial intelligence applications in the fields of digital agents and robotics promise machines and virtual systems that operate much more autonomously from the decisions of human operators, users, owners and commissioners than artefacts have previously done. Indeed, the trend of innovation in machinery and artificial systems has been toward steadily greater autonomy for some centuries, but the cognitive capacities for autonomous learning and decision making that are promised by the new generations of neural net-based systems, and the possibility of *general* learning capabilities, represent a step change (6, 1999c, Chapter 2). While some of the issues that this raises for governance are indeed changes of context or incremental changes in the severity of existing challenges – for example, data protection issues in the handling of personal information by autonomous intelligent digital agents, or health and safety issues of graceful degradation in safety-critical systems, environmental impacts of electro-magnetic emissions from large-scale use of certain types of physical realisation and embedded systems — the new artificial intelligence does raise some problems for governance that, while not wholly new, nevertheless represent significantly greater difficulties. In particular, first, some difficulties may be raised for the law of liability and the doctrine of remoteness of effect in respect of decisions made by systems on the basis of learning autonomously undertaken in environments not under the control of identifiable individual humans or collectively acting groups. Second, because autonomous artificially intelligent systems develop their own systems of communications and "dialects" with each other over time that are not necessarily immediately intelligible even to their original pro-grammers (Warwick, 1998, pp. 251-2), this raises issues of supervision, accountability, transparency to human owners, users and, where appropriate, regulators. There are design solutions available for this, as for the privacy, environmental and health and safety issues, but there are problems too in persuading people – and in future auton-omous self-replicating systems – to adopt them. Moreover, some designs of such so-lutions that allow for human intervention may further complicate the liability and data protection issues (6, 1999c).

Transnationalisation and jurisdiction

It is by now a commonplace in discussions of governance to point out the difficulties facing nation states attempting to regulate problems that run across national borders, including those of technological risk spill-over and those that arise from the transnational flow of communications.

Contrary to the hyperbole of some of the hyperglobalists of a few years ago (e.g. Ohmae, 1995), it is not true that the increasing transnationalisation of economic and financial markets and environmental impacts have rendered even national govern-ments impotent, let alone all forms of governance. Indeed, a rapid survey of the growth of legislation during the period from, say, the early 1970s when the Bretton Woods system broke down to the present day would show a huge increase not only in the formal powers granted by legislatures to national and supranational execu-tives, but also in the organisational capabilities assembled to exercise them. Indeed, with the advent of data protection and environmental protection law and with the huge increase in health and safety and product liability law in the same period, this could be said to be particularly true of the governance of technology risk. The great age of globalisation has *also* been the age of vast increase in the governance capabil-ities of nation states: far from being alternatives, the two have been complements. In-deed, it has been powerfully argued on empirical grounds that nation states have at least retained and in many cases actually increased *choices* of regulatory strategies in order to respond to economic globalisation (Weiss, 1998; Hirst and Thompson, 1999).

But too often this point is presented as though these challenges to governance were something entirely new that systems of governance had not had to deal with in living memory. The point is not that nothing is new in globalisation, but rather that what is new is often best understood and judged by analogy with previous ex-perience, using the ancient craft skills of policy judgement. But there never was a golden age of nation states that could operate wholly autonomously, expecting to be able to run domestic policies that could control everything they needed to in their own legal jurisdictions. Despite the rhetoric of nationalism or the "realist" myth of the "Westphalian" nation state as an autonomous sovereign, nation states have always been interdependent in most regulatory matters, and especially in

93

respect of the governance of technology. International treaties over water extraction are found in the earliest civilisations. The supposed heyday of the nation state in the late 19th century saw the emergence of the international law of the sea to govern the use of maritime technology, and the international postal and telegraphy unions, and then a plethora of other global treaty-based organisations for transnational regulation (Held *et al.*, 1999, pp. 44-45). It has been argued that much of the pooling of sovereignty in the postwar period was done to further the vital interests of nation states. The attempt at Bretton Woods to create international systems of governance for monetary flows and exchanges – global money is a technology, after all – was a major commitment of nations. The creation and development of the European Union is best explained in this way (Milward, 1992; Milward *et al.*, 1993). The skills and capacities of interdependent governance are among the oldest in the armamentarium of policy makers.

To be sure, there are difficulties in making transnational governance effective. It has long been the conventional wisdom of scholars of regulation (e.g. Majone, 1994, at pp. 204-205) that it is costly to negotiate, strike, monitor and enforce international agreements, and therefore, other mechanisms are sought. Indeed, in any system of collective action, there will be some incentives for at least some to defect. There are always risks that the least scrupulous users of technology will gravitate, with their investment, to the least regulated states, and use free trade rules and technological capacities to reach anywhere and to operate with impunity in countries that attempt tighter regulation.

However, it is not necessarily the case that this is in the interests of businesses generally. Business influence over – or even "capture" of – regulatory rule-making processes has been used to explain both deregulation and reregulation, to explain both "races to the bottom" and "to the top", and agreements to avoid competitive deregulation becoming an unstoppable process (Sun and Pelkman, 1995 at pp. 460-461). For valued business investment may avoid states that offer inadequate regulation, since underregulation is a form of sovereign political risk (Moran, 1998) as much as overregulation where it is of a more long-term nature that requires institutions and infrastructure of trust.

Moreover, those states that want to secure a baseline of regulation do not have to accept a "race to the bottom". For states that choose to defect also face costs in lost investment of certain kinds, for which others may well not compensate. The importance of mass market consumer pressure in developed and better regulated states also puts some pressure on companies' location decisions. Moreover, despite the apparent vulnerability to competition from others, much can be achieved in joint international action in regulation through "coalitions of the willing", if the willing countries collectively represent large, important, developed markets.

In the transnational governance of technological risk today, there is a spectrum of strategies – listed in Figure 6 – open to countries wishing to collaborate in regulation.[5]

Figure 6. **A spectrum of types of international collaboration in regulation**

1. *Encouragement of markets in insurance against regulatory failure.* Just as commercial international political risk insurance has grown up to protect private investors in countries where regulation is believed to be potentially arbitrary or excessive (Moran, 1998), so it may be possible to envisage other forms of international insurance for businesses, but not for end-consumers, against inadequate regulation. However, because this can create moral hazard, it is a potentially unreliable strategy.

2. *Encouragement of transnational self-regulation.* For example, the encouragement of voluntary standards bodies in internet domain names control, or quasi-voluntary systems of alternative dispute resolution (Perritt, 1997).

3. *Syndication of regulation.* National regulators engaging in mutual adjustment, dialogue, co-ordination on timing of enforcement, sharing information about violators and new technologies to be promoted, taking each other into account, agreeing joint priorities, creating international colleges of regulators to conduct joint training, policy development and advice.

4. *Catchment area regulation.* Agreement separately to regulate, either through executive regulatory agencies or in the courts, transnational flows in their domestic manifestations, on either the destination or course principle, but agreeing to eschew attempts to enforce national laws extraterritorially.

5. *Mutual recognition, mutual adjustment and toleration of some jurisdiction shopping.* Here, within a span of broadly similar national laws, there is some discretion accorded both regulators and regulated about where enforcement is done.

6. *Comity, or permitted extraterritoriality in case of recognised greater interest.* A right for regulators from one state to enforce in another if they can show the greater interest than that of the state in the jurisdiction of which they seek to enforce (Johnson and Post, 1997); this is not unlike the principle behind extradition in criminal matters.

7. *Nested regulation.* Harmonisation of regulatory standards through international agreement, enforced nationally, within which national systems operate (Aggarwal, 1998).

8. *Delegated regulation.* Creation of supranational regulatory bodies with independent enforcement powers and authority.

9. *Harmonisation of laws.* Either through gradual mutual convergence and adoption of model codes developed by international private and professional bodies, or by direct negotiation.

In general, syndication appears to be the way in which health and safety, data protection (6, 1998b) and some environmental regulation systems are moving. In many areas of court-administered law, catchment area regulation is settling down. For example, it seems likely that following the limited success of early attempts to enforce obscenity and hate speech laws on the world wide web extraterritorially, these forms of content regulation are now tending toward respecting catchment areas or accepting comity-based regulation. Jurisdiction shopping is tolerated, for example, to some extent in war crimes and human rights abuse trials, where many nations are accepted by others as having rights to prosecute and where laws are regarded by others as meeting basic standards. This is possible on the basis that, where guilt is proven, penalties are accepted as being broadly similar, principally because they will be very severe in any country in any case. Nested global regulation is now commonplace in many policy fields within the European Union, and its use is increasing globally in the field of international trade following the establishment of the World Trade Organisation. The establishment of the International Conference on Harmonisation of Technical Requirements for the Registration of Pharmaceutical Products has developed a global momentum in that industry for nested regulation, and in some cases for harmonisation (Vogel, 1998). This is powerful testimony to the limitations of the conventional wisdom about the impossibility of international agreements, particularly where there are important transnational business interests at stake in securing orderly regulation. In banking, similarly, a system of encouragement of transnational self-regulation has begun to develop, and this has led prominent national governments to adjust laws toward one another (Wiener, 1999). Similarly, the work of the European and national standards bodies within the International Standards Organisation is increasingly nested. The same story is emerging in international control of money laundering (Reinicke, 1998; Wiener, 1999), and many other fields. In some areas of commercial law, model codes have been developed by professional bodies of lawyers that have been the basis of transnational convergence in property rights, disputes jurisdiction settlement, etc. (Wiener, 1999). In many fields of policy, it is possible and sensible to combine strategies at several points on the spectrum – this amounts to what has been called "multi-layered governance" (Held *et al.*, 1999, pp. 63-86).

How should policy makers make their decisions about which of these strategic options for regulatory governance of technological risk to follow? There can be no specific answer that is generally applicable. This is a matter for political judgement. That judgement must be made on the basis of the balance of solidarities and their mobilisation in any given field of technological risk, the technicalities of legal feasibility and treaty-basis, the public legitimacy of particular strategies of pooled sovereignty, the distribution of existing regulatory capabilities at national and international levels, and so on. The challenge for transnational governance, then, is centrally the cultivation of judgement capabilities.

The organisational legacy – toward holistic regulation

Finally, reform of the regulation of technological risk will have to take into account the changing direction of policy action more generally in the post-reinvention era of governance. In the reinvention era of the mid-1980s to mid-1990s, the focus of public management was upon the dedicated agency paradigm, in which agency roles were defined functionally and performance measured in input, activity (throughput) or, at most, output terms. In the period that has followed, as it has become clear that this model is running out of problems that it is well equipped to solve, the watchwords across all OECD Member countries have been integration, holistic governance, joined-up working, collaboration, inter-agency working, and outcome- or problem-shaped government (6, 1997b, 6 et al., 1999; Bardach, 1999; for a critique, see Challis et al., 1988). This calls for accountability structures that force agencies working in the same country in different fields but contributing to the same outcome to think about what degree of collaboration they need to be undertaking. A spectrum of types of relationships for this has been developed that is analogous to that offered above for international collaboration in regulation (6 et al., 1999).

A process is beginning with regulation similar to that which has been taking place within the provision of services in which there is a public interest (6, 1998a). First of all, there are movements toward very basic integration of regulation at the input level. Where technologies converge, as is the case with telephony, television and computing, regulators are increasingly working together to respond to this. Secondly, at the activity level, regulators of different problems are combining forces to conduct, for example, joint inspection visits of physical sites and joint requisitions of information from companies and organisations regulated. Thirdly and most importantly, where several regulatory bodies make a contribution to the same overarching outcome – human safety, environmental protection, etc. – they are increasingly working together and redesigning systems to take into account each other's contribution and stimulate activity in the gaps between their own work. All of this requires much greater co-ordination of policy objectives and stances on risk management between different regulators (Better Regulation Task Force, 1999).

The organisational inheritance from the reinvention era will need to be adapted to respond to these new demands. There is no single blueprint for the kinds of collaboration required. However, many of the lessons drawn from the early initiatives in holistic service provision are applicable here (6 et al., 1999). But, at bottom, only with sound judgement and appreciation of both the conflicts of goals and the balance of forces constraining available and legitimate means can policy makers identify workable strategies. Fundamentally, judgement here means striking settlements between the basic rival solidarities that shape conflicts over regulation – the hierarchical imperative for rule, the individualist commitment to liberty, the egalitarian fear of risk, the fatalist resignation to random harm and luck.

3. Governance with technology

Technologies to support decision making

The work that goes on in the offices of policy makers – and in those of the people who communicate with them – probably looks, at least at first sight today, as though

---

Figure 7. **The toolkit of e-governance: electronic tools to support policy making**

Democratic activity   (6, 2000c; Wilhelm, 2000)

- electronic voting using digital signatures, for example on smart cards, to control the electoral process

- web and email-based petitioning using digital signatures

- on-line consultation through websites, email, etc.

- email surveys of public or consumers on trust, satisfaction, other attitudes, etc.

- email complaints

Political activity

- email listserv networks of activists

- email contact and video-conferencing for communication between policy makers

- chat rooms for policy makers to offer contact to members of the public

- searching out political opponents and critics in Usenet or listserv networks, combating or in-filtrating them

Policy activity

- problem-structuring tools such as electronic whiteboards

- intranets and extranets to share banks of policy-relevant information between networks of policy makers

- graphical front-ends for database interrogation, as in the very widespread investment by governments in geographical information systems (GIS)

- digital agents as detectors and selectors for a wide range of purposes

- content analysis software for managing policy-relevant information

- simulation and modelling of problems and impacts of policy tools, assessing risks and opportunities, estimating some conditional probabilities, and developing scenarios – some using classical rule-based inference engines (such as the simpler economic and land use planning models), some using neural nets, some using hybrid "artificial life" technologies (for example, in public health epidemiology policy work)

- expert systems and neural nets to provide analysis of decision values, goals and principles, and to allow changed relative weightings of principles while showing inconsistencies, especially in political ethics or for other discretionary activity

Programme activity

- on-line submission and reporting

- "push" system selection for policy makers of key information from submissions and reports; eventually, real-time updating of "dashboards" of selected key income and expenditure, balance sheet, activity, performance and outcome information for policy makers

- video-conferencing for scrutiny commissions to interrogate executive members

it differs more from what went on in, say, 1970, than the visible work of the policy makers of 1970s differed from that of their predecessors of 1870. In the last few years, a plethora of new information and communication technologies have been introduced to support each of the four dimensions of governance identified in Section 1, and investment in their use is surely set to grow, although for a variety of reasons growth in take-up has been slower than might have been expected a few years ago (6, 2000*b*).

Figure 7 identifies some of the most important information and communication technologies that together make up the promise of "e-governance" – and this, it must be stressed, is quite separate from the burgeoning investment in the electronic delivery of public services.

It can sometimes be difficult for policy makers to justify to their voters this kind of expenditure on supporting their own work, particularly when they must exercise restraint in spending on services to the public. Nevertheless, there seems to be a steady rise in interest and real investment in these systems, and it seems reasonable to expect that over the course of the next decade, their use by policy makers, their researchers, advisors and other staff will become as routine as the use of word processing software for producing reports, or the use of spreadsheet software for conducting budget analysis had both become at every level of government in most OECD Member countries by the mid-1980s.

Rival views of "raison du gouvernance"

What will these developments mean? What will they lead to? Will they sustain better governance or not? It is fair to say that there is no consensus among political and administrative scientists about this. Broadly, there are four types of theory on offer about the potential impact of the use of these systems. Each theory can be treated as one possible future scenario for understanding the potential impact of e-governance.

First, there are those who argue uncompromisingly that the use of these technologies represents a major once-and-for-all improvement in the capabilities of governance and in at least the possibility of rationality in decision making (Tapscott, 1997). The only price that this improvement comes at is the cost of investment and the running costs. Indeed, in this view, these systems reduce the costs of acquiring, ordering, coding, organising, selecting, managing and using information steadily over time. Therefore, the initial investment costs will more than pay for themselves over the lifetime of the systems. This optimistic view is based on the classical cybernetic theory (Wiener, 1948; Reschenthaler and Thompson, 1996) that information is control, or more exactly (in the summary provided by Overman and Loraine, 1994) that:

- Information decreases uncertainty.

- Information slows entropy.

- Information increases system control (decrease variance) by feedback and deviation correction, and in general that more information enables more control (or at least up to a point that we have not yet reached, if the relationship between information and control is conceived as curvilinear).

It is fair to say that, at least in its canonical form, this cybernetic assumption is basically still an article of faith, and all of the rival accounts either qualify it or reject it outright.

The second group of theories are those that accept at least the possibility of greater control, quality and rationality in decision making, but insist that this comes at a price. The main theories in this group accept that there will or may be modest increases in policy maker control and grounded decisions but, at least without a great deal of effort to put safeguards in place, this control will or may be achieved at the expense of, and in some cases, that improvement in decision making will or may be itself compromised by damage to:

- Citizens' individual liberty and privacy (Raab, 1997).

- Citizens' collective (democratic) influence over governmental decisions.

- Politicians' control over decision-making agendas in favour of civil servants' or officers' "infocracy" (Zuurmond, 1998) or an oligopoly of private contractors (Margetts and Dunleavy, 1995).

- Civil servants' capability to exercise constraint upon populism of politicians.

A variant of this tradition acknowledges the possibility of increased short-term technical rationality of decision making but at the expense of long-term substantive rationality and the humaneness of decision making that admits a place for affect. On this view, e-governance is the final arrival of Max Weber's "iron cage of rationality" (Weber, 1976; van de Donk, 1998). These theories fear, for example, that due to mechanical rule-following as suggested by overly simple data interpretations, overly simple modelling, and by overly simple expert system flows from analysis to recommendation, the cultivation and the exercise of judgement in decision making will be crowded out. These theories essentially share the cybernetic theorists' conception of information as control, but want to stress the darker sides of control.

The third view is the most pessimistic, for it argues that e-governance will actually reduce the quality of decision making. It points to the pathologies of excessive demand for policy analysis thus delaying action – "paralysis by analysis" – the bloating out of the policy advice industries among think tanks and consultancy firms, the problems of sheer information overload, the allegedly lesser ability of the public sector to manage information than private citizens or businesses, and the obsession with the already measured that distracts policy makers' attention away from tacit, implicit, qualitative, unstructured factors and toward formal, explicit, quantitatively measured, structured factors and information. In this view, the burgeoning of information in governance simply leads to fragmentation, not better co-ordination (Frissen, 1999). This theory wholly rejects the cybernetic faith that information is control, and prefers the trope of information as noise.

The fourth and final cluster of theories argue that there will be no very fundamental and independent impact of technology itself on technical or political rationality of decision making. In this view, both continuities and changes in governance are driven socially and politically, not by technology itself. Technologies are means by which styles of governance are changed or preserved, and there are broadly two styles of the social shaping of technology (Mackenzie and Wacjman, 1985; Bijker, 1997; Bijker and Law, 1994):

- *"Conservative" social and political shaping*: political systems (decision-making units may be whole national governments, departments, agencies, authorities, etc.) select technologies, use technologies, innovate with use of technologies, to preserve their existing patterns of governance, leadership and decision-making; and

- *"Radical" social and political shaping*: political systems (decision-making units may be whole national governments, departments, agencies, authorities, etc.) use opportunities for investment in technologies, select technologies, use technologies, innovate with the use of technologies, to make changes they would want to make anyway to their existing patterns of governance, leadership and decision making.

For example, it could be argued that the Dutch research on e-governance (Frissen, 1999), which shows that it has promoted horizontal network co-ordination styles of policy making and public management, combined with modest experimentation in public consultation, in fact shows more conservative than radical social and political shaping at work. While the rigidities of the traditional pillars may be almost dismantled by now, the Dutch tradition is perpetuated: creating and relying upon relatively autonomous networks of organisations engaged in both implementation and rule-making, which are not dominated hierarchically by politicians exercising authority and leadership (Frissen, 1999, p. 204). By contrast, the British case shows conservative social shaping of the opposite kind: technologies of e-governance are selected and used to perpetuate the British commitment to the dominance of the executive, and secondly to continue the role of elected politicians as story-tellers and leaders in public. Therefore, we find British politicians committed to seeing the development of digital television and to chat rooms – mass media for which politicians already possess the requisite communication skills – and to more leadership-centred technologies of e-governance for decision making. However, the prospect that most citizens might access digital services using mobile phones, which provide far fewer opportunities for the kinds of political communication that politicians need to engage in, rather than digital television, is one that politicians find disconcerting. All this reflects the prior political culture, at least at national level, that characterises the Westminster system.

Crucial to the shaping of technology in the exercise of governance in this view are the rituals that policy makers perform that legitimate their decisions (Kertzer, 1988). New intellectual technologies can provide an array of ritual resources for demonstrating to wider publics the grounding and authority of their decision-making practices, but in fact, the underlying style or rationale of decision making remains fundamentally politically driven. Information, in this view, is neither control nor noise. Rather, it is a totem – not in any derogatory sense, but rather in the vitally important political sense that all societies depend for their cohesion on symbols and rituals of their collective decision making and the judgement of their policy makers, and the real, indeed vast, importance of information is to be found here.

If the first theory starts from Norbert Wiener and Alvin Toffler, the second from Max Weber and the third from the more nostalgic postmodernists, then the last stems from Émile Durkheim. Precisely because the third and fourth differ on their basic conception of information from the qualified cybernetic consensus of the first two, it is possible for them to come to quite the opposite conclusions about the impacts of new intellectual technologies on leadership and collective action from their conclusions about the impacts on decision making. For the very characteristics of being either noise or totem that can undermine the quality of decision making may in fact *increase* the capabilities of politicians to engage in leadership and collective action, for the cover of fog and the power of symbolism are powerful tools in the pursuit of these activities of governance. Figure 8 summarises some of the key differences between the theories.

Figure 8. **Theories of e-governance at a glance**

Theory / *Specific view*	*Rationalisation*	*Rationalisation at a price*	*Loss of rationality*	*Social shaping*
Information as:	control (positive)	control (negative)	noise	totem
Impact upon organisation of public management	integration	integration	fragmentation	either, depending on balance of solidarities
Planning style	anticipation	anticipation	resilience	either, depending on balance of solidarities
Power shift	to policy makers	captured by special interests	undermining power	open, depending on political forces

Each theory has some empirical support (for rationality, Hasan and Hasan, 1997; for iron cage, see van de Donk, 1998; for totem, see Overman and Loraine, 1994; for rationality at the price of personal benefits for decision makers, see Nedovic-Budic and Godschalk, 1996, Berry *et al.*, 1998: for a thorough review of the empirical evidence, see 6, 2000*d*). Most empirical studies, however, have been rather limited in scope and generally not designed to test, let alone falsify, these rival theories. Moreover, if one sets the standards of what counts as "control", "noise" and "totem" sufficiently high or low, then almost any empirical work one could design can be read as confirming any of the theories. Equally misguided is any attempt to reconcile them. All of them describe real and fundamentally different processes at work in the business of governance. Each describes entirely possible scenarios, and together they serve the functions that sets of scenarios should – to pick out trends, to help identify risks, to structure thinking about both choices and constraints. No doubt whatever the future of governance, it will display features of each of these theories in some combination.

The first conclusion to draw from the fact that each of the theories, even when pointing to some of the less morally admirable but still unavoidable and necessary features of governance, is that their usefulness is, rather, in helping policy makers to exercise judgement about the risks they run as they plan their e-governance strategies, and in assisting policy makers who are aware of them to be more self-conscious and self-critical about solidarities behind, the reasons for, and the consequences of the selections they make of available technologies for governance. However, the final section will present some key arguments for the "social shaping" theory, which is the concomitant of the argument offered above about the challenges for governance of technological risk.

Technologies to support judgement and appreciation in e-governance

Judgement and appreciation are the craft skills of governance. One way to tell the history of technology is to describe the mechanisation and then the automation and finally the replacement of craft skills generally and skills of thought in particular. The argument is made that the modelling of decisions in automation has removed arbitrariness and particularism by representing decision grounds on objective, general abstract rules. On this account, European societies moved from the automation of work in the 18th century, beginning the process that leads to a global process of the automation of skill and finally of thought in ever more universal forms at the end of the 20th and the beginning of the 21st century. This version is widely shared among the many people who believe that technology, far from providing human beings with more control as the cyberneticists thought, is out of control, and among those who believe in technological determinist theories of the scope for and capacity for governance (e.g. Gray, 1999, pp. 19-20).

But the evidence for this account of history is not particularly compelling. On the contrary, new craft skills have emerged in many high-technology fields, and some of the highest-paid people in the private sector are those who exercise craft skills of judgement, especially in decisions about investment but also in the design and use of technologies. The move toward the reduction of arbitrary administrative discretion by street-level bureaucrats in public service decision making about individual entitlements such as cash benefits (Snellen, 1998) has not been the thin end of the wedge for the substitution of automated decision-making in policy judgement, or the final coming of Weber's (1958) "iron cage" of bureaucratic rationality. Despite the burgeoning investment by governments in the technologies listed above, there is little evidence of policy makers in finance ministries or land use planning departments following wholesale and mechanically the recommendations that are cranked out casually for them by junior staff from crude software models.

To be sure, the software industries that offer new tools for e-governance should be asked to devote more attention to what might be called Policy Maker-Computer Interaction (PMCI, perhaps), which is not necessarily much the same as anything else in the Human-Computer Interaction (HCI) field. Similarly, rather little of the work on Computer Assisted Learning has been specifically addressed to the on-the-job learning context and culture of practical policy makers, or their needs for support tools to sustain the long-term learning of judgement skills. An important ethical responsibility incumbent upon the designers of simulation systems and models of policy problems and the impacts of policy choices, is that they should provide appropriate health warnings, lest neophyte policy researchers and advisors mistake digital signs for governance wonders, or too readily follow the outputs of a single model. As political ethics become more codified and ramified throughout the world (Jupp, 1995, Frederickson, 1993; Chapman, 1993), there is a need for more and more sophisticated tools that enable policy makers to think through the ethics of their decisions and their own situations (Whitby, 1996, pp. 68-92 and Seville and Field, 2000 describe some experimental tools for assisting with moral choice). For his part, the author would welcome the direct use of the neo-Durkheimian heuristic within the design of simulation tools for policy choice.

But there is something much more significant in ensuring that e-governance sustains and cultivates judgement. The more important challenge is for policy makers themselves to develop norms, customs and rituals for the appropriate use of these technologies. For the study of the social shaping of technology suggests that in fields far removed from politics, public administration and policy making, it is these social practices that enable people to make sense of new techniques, to domesticate them to the point that they no longer think of them as "technology" but as tools of their trade, appropriate for some things and not for others, and under their control. It is common in policy studies to be rather dismissive of ritual, on the grounds that ritual behaviours are supposedly sub-optimal, less than rational if not

104

outright irrational: in mainstream policy sciences, it is often a debunking strategy to suggest that something is "mere" ritual or is "symbolic", or irrational (*contra* March and Olsen, 1989, 1995). This is absolutely not the author's view. Ritual is not insincerely and cynically conducted public ceremonial, as the Puritan tradition has misled us into thinking (*contra* Edelman, 1988; Kertzer, 1988). Rather, it is the repeated enactment of social organisation and of settlement between rival and conflicting forms (Bell, 1992; Douglas, 1970, 1986; Turner, 1974, 1982). Anthropologists have long known that ritual is never empty, never formalistic, but endlessly inventive (Turner, 1982), and essential to the ways in which cultures, habits, expectation and solidarities are developed and judgement is practised, and to the social shaping and impact of technologies.

In particular, institutions, customs and norms in the use of technologies govern expectations of speed and time. Many policy makers report that the impact of global media scrutiny and interviewing after events, of the culture of email that has grown up on the internet, and the customs of responsiveness associated with on-line voting press them to make decisions and respond at greater speed than permits the exercise of judgement. The effect can be to reinforce the sensibility that treats information as noise.

One of the customs and norms that we ought increasingly to expect in democratic societies is that the electronic tools of e-governance will increasingly be put into the public domain and be tested by experts and by ordinary citizens against a variety of assumptions, and against rival systems. Freedom of information should extend to public availability for all the models, simulations, problem-structuring tools, geographical information systems and content analytic agents that policy makers themselves use (recommended by Performance and Innovation Unit, 2000). For the aim, in a democratic society, of the cultivation of judgement in governance should not be the empowering of a political élite, but the strengthening of the competence, maturity and self-governing capabilities of the citizenry (Elkin and Soltan, 1999). Indeed, every democrat must hold that in the medium to long run, only the robustness of the judgement capabilities of citizens can guarantee that those of policy makers will be similarly stout.

Developing alternative customs requires more than simply assertion and effort: it requires work on institutionalised expectations and solidarities among wider publics.

In any society, as Durkheim (1995) showed, this is a process that is achieved essentially through ritual, in which technologies – including technologies of judgement – are used as totems by which solidarities are mobilised. For example, in the 18th and 19th centuries, the rich rituals of early democratic life were much more important than were, for example, the technicalities of the aggregation of votes under different systems of representation, in managing conflict and in cultivating deliberation and judgement. Similarly today, it is often the richness of the rituals involved in participative and deliberative programmes, including those using e-governance tools, for coming to judgement that sustains the ability and willingness of participants to develop judgement and to come to settlements. When we speak casually of improving "capacity" among decision makers and publics, we mislead ourselves if we imagine that this can be achieved by providing more computers, more models. Durkheim's (1995; Durkheim and Mauss, 1902) insight, which is developed in the tradition that sees technologies as totems in social shaping, was that certain kinds of ritual provide the means by which societies can enable individuals to enrich or accept challenge to their hitherto dogmatically accepted systems of classification, to their ideas about what counts as relevant to making a decision, and to their thought styles generally. Why is this point of particular urgency today? The key reason is that when policy makers recognise the importance of ritual, they tend to think principally about formal, rigid public ceremonial, and they are often creative in developing new forms of this. But this is only the most hierarchical form of ritual, and it is important to help citizens develop new forms of ritual that cultivate and sustain judgement of quite informal kinds that are not necessarily for public broadcast. For only through the wider ritual development of all the solidarities that make up a polity can trust be sustained, on the basis of which settlements can be achieved between solidarities that otherwise pull apart and threaten the viability of the society.

E-governance and conflict over social organisation

Debates about the provision of more and new kinds of technical support to policy work are not new. The development of bureaucracies for the management of governmental statistics in the 18th and 19th centuries raised many of the issues that are being debated about e-governance today – perceived risks of technocracy crowding out politics, erosion of the exercise of policy judgement in favour of the mechanical application of algorithms, disproportionate effort for limited benefit, wider social impacts from the use of governmental authority to embed systems of categorisation of people and behaviours (Hacking, 1990). The same kinds of debate attended the mid-19th century reforms across Europe and North America to create professional civil service systems (Silberman 1993). In the fifty years since the Second World War, these debates have become particularly poignant because of the successive waves of enhancement in computing capacity.

In general, risk perception reflects less a process of calculation of probabilities than a working out of commitments to certain types of social organisation that select for attention the risks they feel most threatening to those commitments (Douglas, 1994a). So it is with perceptions of risk that might arise from e-governance. Those whose basic outlook is hierarchical see only noise, disorderly fragmentation of authority; those with a more libertarian outlook fear the greater capacities for control in the most negative sense, including social engineering, surveillance and intrusion; those of a more egalitarian persuasion worry about inhumane and rigid governance by algorithm. The specific technologies – double-entry accounting, governmental statistics, merit-based independence civil service or, in the last fifty years, e-governance systems – are the occasions, the arenas, the foils for the conflict between these basic forms of social organisation, rather than the real subjects of the conflict.

The uses to which technologies such as second wave e-governance can be acceptably put reflect the settlements, treaties and trade-offs that are struck between these rival forms of social organisation. For the inputs to second wave e-governance – the knowledge bases captured and analysed, the understandings of the causation of policy problems, the models of public willingness to accept measures and of other constraints, even the styles of inference from evidence to trend to recommendation that are embodied in simulations and scenarios – all articulate particular political and institutional commitments of forms of social organisation. If we fear "rationalisation at a price" or "loss of rationality" from the use of such systems, what we typically fear is the rationality of forms of social organisation other than our preferred form. When people feel anxious about the possibilities of excessive power being shifted to politicians and out of the control of the balance of powers, or toward an "infocracy" of salaried officials skilled in the use of e-governance tools, or when we fear the tidal wave of data overwhelming judgement, what is really feared is usually not the consequences of a technology, but its use by a particular group or institutional form of technology as an occasion for assertion of its peculiar commitments. To the extent that these fears must be acted upon, the more effective form of action is usually to act to limit the power of particular groups, rather than to hobble the technology that all groups with a stake in governance would share.

The point here is precisely not that e-governance technologies are "neutral" and that the real conflicts are elsewhere. Rather, the point is that we need to attend to the forms of social organisation that are more or (ideally) less implicit in the technologies that we encourage policy makers to adopt or eschew.

Similarly, the challenge to make e-governance tools serve the cultivation of policy judgement requires not only better-designed software systems, but the institutional buttressing of the practice of political settlement between rival forms of social organisation.

All this has several major implications for strategies for e-governance. The first is that it would, at least in the author's view, be helpful to develop e-governance systems that explicitly modelled conflicts over policies as conflicts over forms of social organisation, and that related rival claims explicitly to the particular styles of organisation that they typically reflect (in 6, 1999a, the author defends the particular account of social organisation that seems to him most worth modelling).

107

Secondly, it should be a key element in the professional ethics of solution designers and system developers that their systems should make palpable to the policy makers who use them just what the political presuppositions of the systems under development are.

Thirdly, as politicians explain to their electorates why these systems justify the expense of investment, they need to make clear the central political virtues of judgement, as settlement between rival forms of social organisation are being cultivated through the use of such tools.

For the scope for the exercise of judgement, which is and always has been the key capability of governance, is heavily dependent upon the prevailing patterns of political trust. Those patterns are shaped by the balance of the four basic solidarities. Appreciation of these structures, and achieving settlements between them, together constitute the central task for governing by technique in the 21st century, just as it always has been. In short, governing by technique is about building organic solidarity.

Notes

1. The source of the two dimensions is Durkheim, 1951, Chapter 5. He argued there that anomic suicide was partly explained by the disconnection from "social regulation", whereas fatalistic suicide is explained by excessive social regulation – in short, opposite ends of the "grid" spectrum. In Book Two, Chapters 3-4, he argued that egoistic suicide could be explained in part by "excessive individuation", whereas altruistic suicide is the product of excessively strong "social integration" – alternate poles of the "group" dimension. However, he did not explore the relationship between the two dimensions of regulation and integration, as the neo-Durkheimians have done (Thompson *et al.*, 1990, p. 138), and he did not always draw the distinction as clearly as they have done (see Durkheim, 1951, p. 258ff). Moreover, he was insufficiently sensitive to the fact that these dimensions may not be experienced directly, but rather may work by shaping what counts as having been experienced: this crucial shift in theoretical focus is achieved in Douglas' work.

2. The late Aaron Wildavsky sometimes used to write as if such stock characters in fact described real people: see, e.g., Wildavsky, 1987. This is a misunderstanding, and in his more careful writing, e.g. Thompson *et al.*, 1990, he did acknowledge this.

3. In the United Kingdom, for example, there were bitter and still not forgotten set-piece battles within the Royal Society in the 1980s and early 1990s over exactly this issue, leading at first to a stand-off between some social scientists on the one hand and technology and natural scientists on the other at the time of the first Royal Society report on risk management in 1983 (Royal Society, 1983), and later to a kind of apartheid in which each side produced their own material under their own names in the 1991 report (Royal Society, 1991). By the later 1990s, an uneasy truce was brokered. But there remain many technology experts who still fiercely resent the idea that, in a democracy, risk management strategies should be justified on the basis of any criteria other than those that the institutional commitments of expertise themselves dictate. For a report on a recent encounter, see 6, 1999d.

4. This is both a definitional and a normative claim. The author is not suggesting that all politics, empirically, is already judgement between solidarities. On the contrary, many political tragedies are best explained by its absence, and the pressure exerted by particular mechanical solidarities to crowd out judgement and what Durkheim called organic solidarity, or settlements between the four mechanical solidarities.

5. For an alternative and, in the author's view, coarser classification, see Reinicke, 1998. Reinicke there tries to suggest that there is a general tendency toward delegated regulation: in my view, this is a generalisation from too small a number of cases.

Bibliography

ADAMS, J. (1995),
  Risk. London: UCL Press.

AGGARWAL, V.K., ed. (1998),
  Institutional Designs for a Complex World: Bargaining, Linkages and Nesting. Ithaca, New York: Cornell University Press.

ANNAS, J. (1993),
  The Morality of Happiness. New York: Oxford University Press.

ARISTOTLE (1925),
  The Nicomachean Ethics. Oxford: Oxford University Press.

ASHBY, W.R. (1947),
  "Principles of the Self-Organising Dynamic System", *Journal of General Psychology*, 37.

BARDACH, E. (1999),
  Getting Agencies to Work Together: The Practice and Theory of Managerial Craftsmanship. Washington, DC: Brookings Institution.

BELL, C. (1992),
  Ritual Theory, Ritual Practice. Oxford: Oxford University Press.

BEMELMANS-VIDEC, M.-L., R.C. RIST and E. VEDUNG, eds. (1998),
  Carrots, Sticks and Sermons: Policy Instruments and Their Evaluation. New Brunswick: Transaction Press.

BERRY, F.S., J.D. BERRY and S.K. FOSTER (1998),
  "The Determinants of Success in Implementing an Expert System in State Government", *Public Administration Review*, July/August, Vol. 58, 4, pp. 293-305.

BETTER REGULATION TASK FORCE (1999),
  Second Annual Report, Cabinet Office, London. Available at http://www.cabinet-office.gov.uk/regulation/index/publications.htm.

BIJKER, W.E. (1997),
  Of Bicycles, Bakelites and Bulbs: Toward a Theory of Sociotechnical Change (Inside Technology). Cambridge, Massachusetts: Massachusetts Institute of Technology Press.

BIJKER, W.E. and J. LAW, eds. (1994),
  Shaping Technology/Building Society. Cambridge, Massachusetts: Massachusetts Institute of Technology Press.

BLANK, R (1999),
Brain Policy: How the New Neuroscience Will Change Our Lives and Our Politics. Washington, DC: Georgetown University Press.

BREYER, S (1993),
Breaking the Vicious Circle: Toward Effective Risk Regulation. Cambridge, Massachusetts: Harvard University Press.

BUCHANAN, R.A. (1992),
The Power of the Machine: The Impact of Technology from 1700 to the Present. Harmondsworth: Penguin.

BURLEY, J., ed. (1999),
The Genetic Revolution and Human Rights. Oxford: Oxford University Press.

CASTELLS, M (1989),
The Informational City: Information Technology, Economic Restructuring and the Urban-Regional Process. Oxford: Blackwell.

CASTELLS, M (1996),
The Rise of the Network Society – Volume 1 of The Information Age: Economy, Society and Culture. Oxford: Blackwell.

CHALLIS, L., S. FULLER, M. HENWOOD, R. KLEIN, W. PLOWDEN, A. WEBB, P. WHITTINGHAM and G. WISTOW (1988),
Joint Approaches to Social Policy: Rationality and Practice. Cambridge: Cambridge University Press.

CHAPMAN, R.A., ed. (1993),
Ethics in Public Service. Edinburgh: Edinburgh University Press.

CHRISTIE, I. and H. ROLFE (1995),
Cleaner Production in Industry. London: Policy Studies Institute.

COWLING, K. C. OUGHTON and R. SUGDEN (1999),
"A Reorientation of Industrial Policy? Horizontal Policies and Targeting" in K. Cowling (ed.), Industrial Policy in Europe. London: Routledge, pp. 17-31.

CVETKOVICH, G. and R. LÖFSTEDT, eds. (1999),
Social Trust and the Management of Risk. London: Earthscan.

D'ENTRÈVES, M.P. (1994),
The Political Philosophy of Hannah Arendt. London: Routledge.

DOUGLAS, M. (1966),
Purity and Danger: An Analysis of the Concepts of Pollution and Taboo. London: Routledge.

DOUGLAS, M. (1970),
Natural Symbols: Explorations in Cosmology. London: Routledge.

DOUGLAS, M., ed. (1982),
Essays in the Sociology of Perception. London: Routledge and Kegan Paul.

DOUGLAS, M. (1985),
Risk Acceptability According to the Social Sciences. New York: Russell Sage Foundation.

DOUGLAS, M. (1986),
How Institutions Think. London: Routledge and Kegan Paul.

DOUGLAS, M. (1994a),
Risk and Blame: Essays in Cultural Theory. London: Routledge.

DOUGLAS, M. (1994b),
"Institutions", Italian Encyclopaedia.

DOUGLAS, M. (1994c),
"Institutions Are the Product", paper presented at the Conference of the Society for the Advancement of Socio-Economics, Paris, July.

DOUGLAS, M. (1997),
"The Depoliticisation of Risk", in R.J. Ellis and M. Thompson (eds.), Culture Matters: Essays in Honour of Aaron Wildavsky. Boulder, Colorado: Westview Press, pp. 121-132.

DOUGLAS, M. and A. WILDAVSKY (1982),
Risk and Culture: An Essay on the Selection of Technological and Environmental Dangers. Berkeley: University of California Press.

DOWDING, K.M. (1991),
Rational Choice and Political Power. Aldershot: Edward Elgar.

DREXLER, K.E. (1991),
Engines of Creation: The Coming Era of Nanotechnology. London: Fourth Estate.

DUKES, E.F. (1996),
Resolving Public Conflict: Transforming Community and Governance. Manchester: University of Manchester Press.

DURKHEIM, É. (1951) [1897],
Suicide: A Study in Sociology, tr. J.A. Spaulding and G. Simpson. London: Routledge.

DURKHEIM, É. (1984) [1893],
The Division of Labour in Society, tr. W.D. Halls. L. Coser, intro. Basingstoke: MacMillan.

DURKHEIM, É., (1995) [1912],
Elementary Forms of the Religious Life, tr. K.E. Fields. New York: Free Press.

DURKHEIM, É. and M. MAUSS (1963) [1902],
Primitive Classification, ed. R. Needham. Chicago: University of Chicago Press. Originally published as É. Durkheim and M. Mauss, 1903, "De quelques formes primitives de classification: contribution à l'étude des répresentations collectives", Année sociologique, Vol. VI, 1901-2, pp. 1-72.

DYSON, G. (1997),
Darwin Among the Machines. Harmondsworth: Penguin, at pp. 174-178.

EDELMAN, M. (1988),
Constructing the Political Spectacle. Chicago: University of Chicago Press.

ELKIN, S.L. and K.E. SOLTAN, eds. (1999),
Citizen Competence and Democratic Institutions. University Park, Pennsylvania: Pennsylvania State University Press.

ELLIS, R.J. and M. THOMPSON, eds. (1997),
Culture Matters: Essays in Honour of Aaron Wildavsky. Boulder, Colorado: Westview Press.

FLEISCHACKER, S. (1999),
A Third Concept of Liberty: Judgement and Freedom in Kant and Adam Smith. Princeton, New Jersey: Princeton University Press.

Foresight: The Journal of Futures Studies, Strategic Thinking and Policy (1999),
Special Issue, December.

FREDERICKSON, H.G., ed. (1993),
Ethics and Public Administration. Armonk, New York: M.E. Sharpe & Co.

FRISSEN, P.H.A. (1999),
Politics, Governance and Technology: A Postmodern Narrative on the Virtual State. Cheltenham: Edward Elgar.

GERSHENFELD, N. (1999),
When Things Start to Think. London: Hodder and Stoughton.

GOODY, E.M., ed. (1995),
Social Intelligence and Interaction: Expressions and Implications of the Social Bias in Human Intelligence. Cambridge: Cambridge University Press.

GRAHAM, J.D. and J.B. WIENER, eds. (1995),
Risk vs Risk: Tradeoffs in Protecting Health and the Environment. Cambridge, Massachusetts: Harvard University Press.

GRAY, J. (1999) [1998],
False Dawn: The Delusions of Global Capitalism, 2nd edn. London: Granta.

GROSS, J.L. and S. RAYNER (1985),
Measuring Culture: A Paradigm for the Analysis of Social Organisation. New York: Columbia University Press.

HACKING, I. (1990),
The Taming of Chance. Cambridge: Cambridge University Press.

HASAN, H. and S. HASAN (1997),
"Computer-based Performance Information for Executives in Local Government", Australian Journal of Public Administration, Vol. 56, 3, pp. 24-29.

HAWKEN, P., A.B. LOVINS and L.H. LOVINS (1999),
Natural Capitalism. London: Earthscan.

HELD, D., A. MCGREW, D. GOLDBLATT and J. PERRATON (1999),
Global Transformations: Politics, Economics and Culture. Cambridge: Polity Press.

HIRST, P. and G. THOMPSON (1999) [1996],
Globalisation in Question: The International Economy and the Possibilities of Governance, 2nd edn. Cambridge: Polity Press.

HOOD, C.C. (1983),
The Tools of Government. Basingstoke: MacMillan.

HOOD, C.C. and D.K.C. JONES, eds. (1996),
Accident and Design: Contemporary Debates in Risk Management. London: UCL Press.

INTERNATIONAL BANK FOR RECONSTRUCTION AND DEVELOPMENT and the WORLD BANK (1997),
World Development Report 1997: The State in a Changing World. Oxford: Oxford University Press.

JACKSON, T. (1996),
Material Concerns: Pollution Profit and the Quality of Life. London: Routledge.

JOHNSON, D.R. and D.G. POST (1997),
"The Rise of Law on the Global Network" in B. Kahin and C. Nesson (eds.), Borders in Cyberspace: Information Policy and the Global Information Infrastructure. Cambridge, Massachusetts: Massachusetts Institute of Technology Press, pp. 3-47.

JUPP, B. (1995),
"The Grey and the Good: Government Ethics Around the World" in Missionary Government, Demos Collection 7, pp. 50-52.

KAKU, M. (1998),
Visions: How Science Will Revolutionise the Twenty First Century. Oxford: Oxford University Press.

KELLY, K. (1994),
Out of Control: The New Biology of Machines. London: Fourth Estate.

KERTZER, D.I. (1988),
Ritual, Politics and Power. New Haven: Yale University Press.

KITCHER, P. (1996),
The Lives to Come: The Genetic Revolution and Human Possibilities. Harmondsworth: Penguin.

KRIMSKY, S. and D. GOLDING, eds. (1992),
Social Theories of Risk. Westport, Connecticut: Praeger.

KURZWEIL, R.. (1999),
The Age of Spiritual Machines: How We Will Live, Work and Think in the New Age of Intelligent Machines. London: Orion Business Books.

LEADBEATER, C. (1999), Living on Thin Air: The New Economy. London: Viking.

LÖFSTEDT, R. and L. FREWER, eds. (1998),
The Earthscan Reader in Risk and Modern Society. London: Earthscan.

LUPTON, D. (1999),
Risk. London: Routledge.

MACKENZIE, D. and J. WACJMAN, eds. (1985),
The Social Shaping of Technology: How the Refrigerator Got Its Hum. Buckingham: Open University Press.

MAJONE, G. (1994),
"The Rise of the Regulatory State in Europe", West European Politics, 17, pp. 77-101, reprinted in slightly abridged form in R. Baldwin, C. Scott and C. Hood, eds. (1998), A Reader of Regulation, Oxford: Oxford University Press, pp. 192-215.

MARCH, J.G. and J.-P. OLSEN (1976),
Ambiguity and Choice in Organisation. Oslo: Norwegian University Press.

MARCH, J.G. and J.-P. OLSEN (1989),
  Rediscovering Institutions: The Organisational Basis of Politics. New York: Free Press.

MARCH, J.G. and J.-P. OLSEN (1995),
  Democratic Governance. New York: Free Press.

MARGETTS, H. (1998),
  "Computerising the Tools of Government?" in I.Th.M. Snellen and W.B.H.J. van de Donk
  (eds.), *Public Administration in An Information Age: A Handbook*. Amsterdam: IOS Press, pp. 440-459.

MARGETTS, H. and P. DUNLEAVY (1995),
  "Public Services on the World Markets" in *Missionary Government, Demos Collection 7*, pp. 30-32.

MARGOLIS, H. (1996),
  Dealing with Risk: Why the Public and the Experts Disagree on Environmental Issues. Chicago: University of Chicago Press.

MILWARD, A.S. (1992),
  The European Rescue of the Nation State. London: Routledge.

MILWARD, A., F.M.N. LYNCH, F. ROMERO, R. RANIERI and V. SØRENSEN, eds. (1993),
  The Frontier of National Sovereignty: 1945-1992. London: Routledge.

MORAN, T.H., ed. (1998),
  Managing International Political Risk. Oxford: Blackwell.

NEDOVIC-BUDIC, Z. and D.R. GODSCHALK (1996),
  "Human Factors in the Adoption of Geographic Information Systems: A Local Government
  Case Study", *Public Administration Review*, Vol. 56, 6, pp. 554-567.

OFFICE OF THE PRESS SECRETARY, WHITE HOUSE (2000),
  The Clinton-Gore Administration: from Digital Divide to Digital Opportunity. White House, Washington DC. Available at <http://www.digitaldivide.gov/2000-02-02.html>.

OHMAE, K. (1995),
  The End of the Nation-State: The Rise of Regional Economies – How New Engines of Prosperity Are Reshaping Global Markets. New York: Free Press.

O'RIORDAN, T. and J. CAMERON, eds. (1994),
  Interpreting the Precautionary Principle. London: Earthscan.

OVERMAN, E.S. and D.T. LORAINE (1994),
  "Information for Control: Another Management Proverb?", *Public Administration Review*,
  Vol. 54, 2, pp. 193-196.

PERFORMANCE AND INNOVATION UNIT (2000),
  Adding It Up: Improving Analysis and Modelling in Central Government. London: Cabinet Office.

PERRITT, H.H., Jr. (1997),
  "Jurisdiction in Cyberspace: The Role of Intermediaries" in B. Kahin and C. Nesson (eds.),
  Borders in Cyberspace: Information Policy and the Global Information Infrastructure. Cambridge, Massachusetts: Massachusetts Institute of Technology Press, pp. 164-202.

POLICY ACTION TEAM 15 (Social Exclusion Unit) (2000),
  Closing the Digital Divide: Information and Communication Technologies in Deprived Areas. London:
  Department of Trade and Industry.

POWER, M. (1997),
The Audit Society: Rituals of Verification. Oxford: Oxford University Press.

RAAB, C. (1997),
"Privacy, Democracy, Information" in B.D. Loader (ed.), The Governance of Cyberspace: Politics, Technology and Global Restructuring. London: Routledge, pp. 155-174.

RAYNER, S. (1992),
"Cultural Theory and Risk Analysis" in S. Krimsky and D. Golding (eds.), Social Theories of Risk. Westport, Connecticut: Praeger, pp. 83–116.

REINICKE, W.H. (1998),
Global Public Policy: Governing Without Government? Washington, DC: Brookings Institution.

REISS, M.J. and R. STRAUGHAN (1996),
Improving Nature: The Science and Ethics of Genetic Engineering. Cambridge: Cambridge University Press.

RENN, O. (1998),
"Three Decades of Risk Research", Journal of Risk Research, 1,1, pp. 49-72.

RESCHENTHALER, G.B. and F. THOMPSON (1996),
"The Information Revolution and the New Public Management", Journal of Public Administration Research and Theory, 6, 1, pp. 125-143.

ROYAL SOCIETY (1983),
Risk Assessment: A Study Group Report. London: Royal Society.

ROYAL SOCIETY (1991),
Risk: Analysis, Perception and Management. London: Royal Society.

SABATIER, P. and H. JENKINS-SMITH, eds. (1993),
Policy Change and Learning: An Advocacy Coalition Approach. Boulder, Colorado: Westview Press.

SALAMON, L.M., assisted by M.S. LUND, eds. (1989),
Beyond Privatisation: The Tools of Government Action. Washington, DC: Urban Institute Press.

SCHWARZ, M. and M. THOMPSON (1990),
Divided We Stand: Redefining Politics, Technology and Social Choice. Philadelphia, Pennsylvania: University of Pennsylvania.

SEVILLE, H. and D.G. FIELD (2000),
"What Can AI Do for Ethics?" – paper presented at the Symposium on Artificial Intelligence, Ethics and (Quasi-)Human Rights at "Time for AI and Society", the 2000 Convention of the Society for the Study of Artificial Intelligence and the Simulation of Behaviour, University of Birmingham, 17-20 April 2000.

SILBERMAN, B.S. (1993),
Cages of Reason: The Rise of the Rational State in France, Japan, the United States and Great Britain. Chicago: University of Chicago Press.

SILVER, L.M. (1998),
Remaking Eden: Cloning, Genetic Engineering and the Future of Humankind. London: Phoenix.

SINGH, S. (1999),
The Code Book: The Science of Secrecy from Ancient Egypt to Quantum Cryptography. London: Fourth Estate.

SNELLEN, I.Th.M. (1998),
"Street Level Bureaucracy in An Information Age" in I.Th.M. Snellen and W.B.H.J. van de Donk (eds.), Public Administration in An Information Age: A Handbook. Amsterdam: IOS Press, pp. 497-508.

SUN, J.-M. and J. PELKMAN (1995),
"Regulatory Competition in the Single Market", Journal of Common Market Studies, 33, pp. 67-89, reprinted in slightly abridged form in R. Baldwin, C. Scott and C. Hood, eds. (1998), A Reader of Regulation. Oxford: Oxford University Press, pp. 443-467.

TAPSCOTT, D. (1997),
"The Digital Media and the Reinvention of Government", Canadian Public Administration, Vol. 40, Summer, pp. 328-345.

THOMPSON, M. (1992),
"The Dynamics of Cultural Theory and Implications for the Enterprise Culture" in S. Hargreaves Heap and A. Ross (eds.), Understanding the Enterprise Culture: Themes in the Work of Mary Douglas. Edinburgh: Edinburgh University Press, pp. 182–202.

THOMPSON, M. (1997a),
"Rewriting the Precepts of Policy Analysis" in R.J. Ellis and M. Thompson (eds.), Culture Matters: Essays in Honour of Aaron Wildavsky. Boulder, Colorado: Westview Press.

THOMPSON, M. (1997b),
"Cultural Theory and Technology Assessment" in F. Fischer and M. Hajer (eds.), Living with Nature: Environmental Discourse as Cultural Politics. Oxford: Oxford University Press.

THOMPSON, M. (1997c),
"Cultural Theory and Integrated Assessment", Environmental Modelling and Assessment, 2, pp. 139-150.

THOMPSON, M., R.J. ELLIS and A. WILDAVSKY (1990),
Cultural Theory. Boulder, Colorado: Westview Press.

THOMPSON, M., G. GRENDSTAD and P. SELLE, eds. (1999),
Cultural Theory as Political Science. London: Routledge.

TILLY, C. (1992) [1990],
Coercion, Capital and European States, AD 990-1992, 2nd edn. Oxford: Blackwell.

TURNER, V. (1974),
Dramas, Fields and Metaphors: Symbolic Action in Human Society. Ithaca, New York: Cornell University Press.

TURNER, V. (1982),
From Ritual to Theatre: The Human Seriousness of Play. New York: PAJ Publications.

van de DONK, W.B.H.J. (1998),
"Beyond Incrementalism? Redistributive Policy Making, Information Systems and the Revival of Synopticism" in I.Th.M. Snellen and W.B.H.J. van de Donk (eds.), Public Administration in An Information Age: A Handbook. Amsterdam: IOS Press, pp. 381-404.

VICKERS, Sir G. (1995) [1963],
The Art of Judgement: A Study of Policy Making, Centenary Edition. London: Sage.

VISCUSI, V.K. (1998),
Rational Risk Policy. Oxford: Oxford University Press.

VOGEL, D. (1998),
"The Globalisation of Pharmaceutical Regulation", Governance, 11, 1, pp. 1-22.

von WEIZSÄCKER, E., A.B. LOVINS and L.H. LOVINS (1998),
Factor Four: Doubling Wealth, Halving Resources Use. London: Earthscan.

WARWICK, K. (1998),
In the Mind of the Machine: The Breakthrough in Artificial Intelligence. London: Arrow.

WEBER, M. (1958),
"Bureaucracy" from Economy and Society, in H.H. Gerth and C.W. Mills, eds. (1958) [1946],
From Max Weber: Essays in Sociology. New York: Galaxy/Oxford University Press, pp. 196-245.

WEBER, M. (1976),
The Protestant Ethic and the Spirit of Capitalism, tr. T. Parsons. London: Allen and Unwin, pp. 181-1.

WEISS, L. (1998),
The Myth of the Powerless State: Governing the Economy in the Global Era. Cambridge: Polity Press.

WHITBY, B. (1996),
Reflections on Artificial Intelligence: The Legal, Moral and Ethical Dimensions. Exeter: Intellect Books.

WIENER, J. (1999),
Globalisation and the Harmonisation of Law. London: Pinter.

WIENER, N. (1948),
Cybernetics: The Emerging Science at the Edge of Order and Chaos. New York: Simon and Schuster.

WILDAVSKY, A. (1987),
"Cultural Theory of Responsibility" in J.-E. Lane (ed.), Bureaucracy and Public Choice. London: Sage, pp. 283-293.

WILDAVSKY, A. (1988),
Searching for Safety. New Brunswick: Transaction Publishers.

WILHELM, A.G. (2000),
Democracy in the Digital Age: Challenges to Political Life in Cyberspace. London: Routledge.

WINNER, L. (1977),
Autonomous Technology: Technics-out-of-control as a Theme in Political Thought. Cambridge, Massachusetts: Massachusetts Institute of Technology Press.

YANKELOVICH, D. (1991),
Coming to Public Judgement: Making Democracy Work in a Complex World. Syracuse, New York: Syracuse University Press.

ZUURMOND, A. (1998),
"From Bureaucracy to Infocracy: Are Democratic Institutions Lagging Behind?" in I.Th.M. Snellen and W.B.H.J. van de Donk (eds.), Public Administration in An Information Age: A Handbook. Amsterdam: IOS Press, pp. 259-272.

6, P. (1997*a*),
  "Governing by Cultures" in G.J. Mulgan (ed.), *Life after Politics: New Thinking for the Twenty First Century*. London: HarperCollins, pp. 260-285.

6, P. (1997*b*),
  Holistic Government. London: Demos.

6, P. (1998*a*),
  "Ownership and the New Politics of the Public Interest Services", *Political Quarterly*, 69, 4, October-December, pp. 404–414.

6, P. (1998*b*),
  The Future of Privacy – Volume 1: Private Life and Public Policy. London: Demos.

6, P. (1999*a*),
  "Neo-Durkheimian Institutional Theory", paper presented to the University of Strathclyde conference, "Institutional Theory in Political Science", Ross Priory, Loch Lomond, 18-19 October 1999.

6, P. (1999*b*),
  "A Culture of Constitutionalism for More Participation: What Would It Look Like?" in N.D. Lewis and D. Campbell (eds.), *Promoting Participation: Law or Politics?* London: Cavendish, pp. 75-100.

6, P. (1999*c*),
  Morals for Robots and Cyborgs: Ethics, Society and Public Policy in the Age of Autonomous Intelligent Machines. Brentford: Bull Information Systems.

6, P. (1999*d*),
  "Understanding, Presenting and Managing Risk", report of a Ditchley Foundation Conference, Ditchley Foundation, Oxfordshire, May 1999.

6, P. (2000*a*),
  "The Morality of Managing Risk: Paternalism, Prevention, Precaution and the Limits of Proceduralism", *Journal of Risk Research*, 3,2, pp. 135-165.

6, P. (2000*b*),
  "E-governance: Issues, Prospects, Theories", manuscript, Department of Government, University of Strathclyde.

6, P. (2000*c*),
  London_Mayor@Your_Service: *The Prospects for Digital Democracy in the Capital City*. London: A New Voice for London.

6, P. (2000*d*),
  "E-governance: Weber's Revenge?" – paper given at the Political Studies Association annual conference, London School of Economics, London, 10-13 April.

6, P., D. LEAT, K. SELTZER and G. STOKER (1999),
  Governing in the Round: Strategies for Holistic Government. London: Demos.

6, P. and B. JUPP (forthcoming),
  Divided by Information? The "Digital Divide" That Really Matters and the Implications of the New Meritocracy. London: Demos.

119

Chapter 5

A Quiet Revolution of Democratic Governance: Towards Democratic Experimentalism

by
Charles F. Sabel
Columbia Law School
United States

1. The quiet stirring of democratic governance

Democracy is stirring.[1] The economic turmoil and political revolts of the 70s and 80s, together with the globalisation of world markets that continues today, have brought renewal as well as disruption. At the local level, citizens in many countries are directly participating with government in solving problems of economic development, schooling, policing, the management of complex ecosystems and drug abuse. The successes are fragile. But they already suggest possibilities of public co-ordination that even recently seemed beyond reach. The exhaustion of the party politics of Left and Right, together with assaults on central governments and spasmodic efforts to reform them, encouraged these developments. National governments of nearly all colours, embarrassed by responsibilities they cannot or will not discharge, are devolving authority to lower levels and loosening the grip of public bureaucracies on the provision of some services. Others are wholly privatised. At times central government abets these changes simply by tolerating local experimentation, waiving formally – or through inaction – their statutory rights to specify how programmes are administered. Viewed from the centre today, government seems reformable (surprisingly so, given recurrent fears that the modern state would prove a new feudal overlord), but more in its capacities for self-limitation and dis-entrenchment than its positive abilities to co-ordinate and construct. Viewed from the local problem-solving units, the central government seems indispensable as an ally in the consolidation of nascent innovations, but capriciously unreliable in its ignorance of local circumstance and its own potential to foster development. Both perspectives take government as disjointed and fragmentary, not formative and framing.

In this they invite questions about the practicality and legitimacy of representative democracy, centred in a national legislature, in a world where the centre devolves more than it directs. Where the rich democracies were once diagnosed as suffering a crisis of governability (Huntington, Crozier and Watanuki, 1975), today they are more likely to be diagnosed as suffering a deficit of democracy.[2] More exactly, there is fear of parallel government, *imperium in imperio*: new structures of public action, outside the old ones, whose efficacy undermines the legitimacy of traditional democracy without offering an equivalent form of accountability of its own.

In the United States this confusion is largely masked, and the questions it raises are muted. Because of its malleable federalism, its proud tradition of domesticating government by setting its branches to war among themselves, and the validation of US institutions – whatever their actual coherence – by the current successes of the American economy, America revels for now in its disjoint state.

But the United States is an exception. The European Union (EU) is more representative. There the transformation of the regulatory law of the member states into an EU regime – harmonisation is the anodyne but inaccurate term of art – occurs by an obscure process of committee consultation far beyond the supervision of the European Parliament. Excepting a few experts in comitology (who anyway disagree sharply among themselves in claiming some democratic justification for the harmonising consultation), the common view is that this law-making itself is an important instance of a larger democratic deficit in the constitution of the EU, and hence a threat to the Union's material successes (Joerges and Voss, 1999). Further scrutiny heightens the doubts: regional policy, again largely beyond the ambit of parliamentary control, transfers vast sums from some areas within the EU to others. At the least the transfers stir up local politics, giving emergent economic and political groups new possibilities to challenge local élites.[3] But the effects can be transformative, or nearly so. In the Republic of Ireland, EU regional funds helped finance construction of a national system of local public-private partnerships creating problem-solving, participatory local governments of the kind referred to above, and like those, paralleling and competing with the constitutionally provided ones (Sabel, 1996).

The Whitehall countries – Great Britain, New Zealand, Australia and Canada – are most actively and self-consciously at work on their democracies. Menaced by insolvency at some point in the 1970s and 80s, each has torn the fabric of its traditional constitutional order, distancing itself from much of its past while struggling to the legacy of its identity. The Whitehall countries went farther than others in applying familiar models of corporate governance, based on clear distinctions between conception and execution, to the reform of government. They learned, in consequence, more than others about the limits of these principal-agent models, and the need to correct them by forms of governance that take means and ends to be mutually determining.

Beyond all this there is the matter of regional devolution. Great Britain is managing the (mostly) orderly devolution of quasi-sovereign powers to Wales, Scotland and Northern Ireland, according them qualities of post- or para-nationality while maintaining the integrity of the existing union. Canada is arguably doing the same with Québec, and with aboriginal peoples. The Crown in New Zealand is in permanent negotiation with the Maori (Durie, 1998; Coates and McHugh, 1998). These efforts recall, but surely will do more than simply recreate, the forms of sovereignty and nationality that prevailed in composite states such as Switzerland, the Netherlands and the British Isles themselves in the period before Westphalian nationalism. The suspicion of irrevocable change that troubles the rich democracies is thus almost an open secret in the Whitehall countries.[4]

The aim of this chapter is to suggest that the emergent changes in governance may cohere into a new, participatory form of democracy that can be called democratic experimentalism. The role of the administrative centre in this experimentalist democracy is not to set rules and police compliance. Rather, with local units, it defines broad projects and fixes provisional general standards. In addition, it provides infrastructure by which local units can achieve their own goals, and pools measurements of performance to allow refinement of the general standards as well as the particular local strategies in the light of results. The resulting organisation is neither a formal bureaucracy nor an informal network, yet it combines the capacities for super-local learning characteristic of the former with the access to local knowledge characteristic of the latter. It affords forms of public accountability consistent with the Madisonian traditions of the United States and central strands of European constitutionalism (Dorf and Sabel, 1998).

To convey this suggestion of emergent coherence, the chapter resorts to a method – more often deployed than noted – that might be called counter-intuitive illustration. Limits of current public problem-solving are traced to theoretically fundamental limits of our capacities to solve problems. Repeated efforts to extend our capacities fail, fortifying the conviction that the theory has indeed identified tragic limits to our abilities. This result is then juxtaposed to a detailed account of a new institution, based on assumptions contrary to current intuitions, that manages feats of co-ordination that are on conventional accounts theoretically impossible. Most of the work of thinking through the implications of the new assumptions and, especially, imagining the present world recast in the light of the counter-intuitive success are left to the reader. The aim of juxtaposing the familiar and the surprising is to give some plausibility to the hope that fumbling forward we may indeed be enriching the capacities for public action rather than re-enacting the tragedy of our imperfections.

The body of the chapter is in five parts. Section 2 briefly reviews the common features and the common limits of the constitutional settlements defining democracy in the advanced countries since mid-century, when not before. Using the

Whitehall countries – and Great Britain in particular – as a kind of natural laboratory, it shows how the response to those limits, and especially the use of principal-agent governance as the template for a reformed democracy, in turn created new problems of effective co-ordination and accountability. Section 3 details thoughtful, closely related proposals currently advanced in Great Britain, Scotland, and the United States to address these limits in order to respond to the "wicked problems" of co-ordination: for example, drug abuse, economic development, schooling and others whose solution requires local provision of differentiated, complex bundles of services. The manifest shortcomings of these proposals suggest that the principal-agent model, however modified, can transpose the familiar problems of democracy but not resolve them.

The rest of the chapter develops the counter-intuitive alternative. Section 4 argues that modern firms operate on pragmatist, not principal-agent principles. Instead of trying to resolve ambiguity by creating clear goals (the province of the principal) and clear roles for achieving them (the responsibilities of the agents), these firms accept that ends and means are mutually defining. Hence initial choices of each must be corrected, and corrected again, in the very effort to realise the projects they embody. The differences between conventional and pragmatist firms are illustrated by comparing their respective methods of design and the relations they establish between customers and suppliers. Section 5 presents democratic experimentalism and illustrates its operation by looking in detail at governance reform in the Chicago public schools. Section 6 returns to the problem of democratic deficit and shows how democratic experimentalism provides in a new way the kind of accountability that the constitutional traditions of the United States and Europe demand.

2. The administrative state, delegation, and the aftermath: The short story of Whitehall from beginning to end

The problems agitating representative democracy today are rooted in an antinomy that has bedevilled self-government since the end of the 19th century. Formally, democracy requires that all citizens be treated alike, regardless of differences in their life circumstances. But practically effective co-ordination under modern conditions requires attention to just these differences. Reconciling these demands has required institutional innovations as well as changes in the understanding, if not the explicit constitutional design, of representative democracy.

The great institutional innovation, and the one that forms the context for the problems under discussion here, is of course the administrative state: the rules and institutions that together regulate economic exchange, and provide services and security to citizens most vulnerable to it. The doctrinal innovation that legitimated the administrative state is the theory of delegation. That theory reaffirms the formal sovereignty of the legislature as the authoritative source of law. But it also recognises that no assembly can itself competently address the complexity of modern society. Hence the legislature is allowed to delegate some of its sovereign authority to other entities more proximate to civil society and so able to specify rules suited to particular contexts beyond the ken of a central lawmaker. In electing parliament, citizens manifest their equality; in delegating authority to administrative bodies, parliament takes account of their distinctiveness (Friedrich, 1940).

Delegation of legislative authority took two main forms. In the Whitehall system, parliament entrusted civil servants with responsibility for translating general laws into precise rules in distinct policy areas, and co-ordinating activities across areas. Expertise, exercised collegially and informed by dedication to the public good, enabled officials to do both. In the neo-corporatist states of continental Europe – Germany, Italy, the Nordic countries – authority was delegated not to the civil service, but to the affected interests in civil society themselves: trade unions, employers' associations and the like. These organisations were presumed to represent the natural and mutually complementary constituents of industrial society – labour and capital first and foremost. Because the groups depended on each other, and society depended on their co-operation, they could be entrusted to make law in the name of democracy by negotiating among themselves (Schmitter, 1977).

Most countries are in fact, of course, a combination of the two. Trade unions have a place in the British polity as surely as civil servants have a place in the German one. But nowhere is the mixture more evident than in the United States. The constitutional battles of the New Deal were fought precisely to delegate congressional authority to expert agencies on the one hand, and to interest associations such as trade unions and employers' associations on the other, who were to resolve differences through collective bargaining.

In the long term these forms of delegation produced neither accountability nor effective co-ordination. The reasons are clear in retrospect. The jurisdictions of interest groups do not naturally conform to the boundaries of the problems they need to solve – not, unless by sheer luck, at first, when problems and groups are initially defined; and surely not when problems begin to change (perhaps in response to the groups' own actions). This is true if only because interest groups have interests of their own, which grow out of and reinforce initial institutional boundaries. This sedimentation makes adjustment to new circumstances increasingly difficult. The less adapted the organisation of interest groups is to its environment, the more partial and self-interested the interest group representation. Exactly the same can be said of bureaucracies, their jurisdictions, and the self-interest of bureaucrats. Combining delegation to interest groups, as neo-corporatism does, with delegation to the civil service in the fashion of Whitehall compounds error by obstinacy. At least, that has been the increasingly vehement sentiment in almost all the advanced countries since the late 1960s.

125

The first measures to issue from the growing concern about the accountability and efficacy of the administrative state were in the way of palliatives and correctives. The United States was among the first to react. It lacked both the tradition of the tutelary state and the tradition of government by estates of the realm upon which Whitehall and neo-corporatism could build. In addition, it was well armed against any possible aggrandisement of government by the separation of powers. Federal judges tried to pry open the collusive iron triangles of interest groups, expert agencies regulating their behaviour, and congressional committees with oversight responsibility for the regulatory agency. Courts also created regimes for the vindication of rights by groups (minorities, prison inmates, women in the workforce) whose interests are not well protected either by interest groups or administrative agencies. On occasion the judges simply acted as regulatory bodies themselves – as, for example, in the break-up AT&T (long the equivalent of a European PTT). Congress tried to limit the authority delegated to regulatory agencies by writing detailed legislation (the Clean Air and Water Acts, for example) that substantially reduced the scope for agency discretion. The president tried to limit congressional interference in the agencies to protect the executive branch, then tried to limit the agencies' discretion to reassert the presidency, and so on.

While the branches of government squabbled over accountability, moreover, each level of government – federal, state, municipal – was devolving responsibility for formulating or implementing policy to a lower one, or to NGOs, in recognition of the impossibility of asserting effective control on its own. Periodically this devolution was interrupted by hapless efforts at bureaucratic re-centralisation (imposition of strict rules on NGOs; "recategorisation" into distinct accounts of funds initially dedicated to separate programmes and then pooled into block grants) to limit the exercise of discretion made possible by decentralisation. The Reagan Administration's overt attack on the New Deal State was thus in many ways as much continuity as change, and debates about its significance remain accordingly murky (Sunstein, 1990).

The new public management and its limits

In the Whitehall countries, reactions to the problems of administrative delegation came later rather than sooner, but were all the more vehement and thoroughgoing for the delay. The tardiness had to do with the absence of dis-entrenching mechanisms such as the US courts and the separation of powers. Without them, interest groups and bureaucracies could fortify their positions. Political traditions valuing social consensus and deference to an administrative élite gave a patina of legitimacy to the bulwarks of the state. The vehemence of the reaction was a response to the backlog of unsolved problems. But it was also a consequence of the first-past-the-post electoral systems and unitary governments of countries like New Zealand and Great Britain. Such systems produced big winners: narrow parliamentary majorities with a free hand to implement radical programmes.

The driving idea of the New Public Management (NPM), taken directly and openly from US economics of the 1980s, was to re-establish the control of the democratic principal – the sovereign people acting through elections – over its agents in government by reducing insofar as possible the ambiguities of delega-tion.[5] Just as shareholders were to wrest control over the corporation from man-agers, perhaps in collusion with the workforce, so the citizens were to retake control of their state from public officials and interest groups.

This assertion of "straight-line" accountability required a profound transforma-tion in the organisation and scope of government. Conception was to be separated from execution: if self-interested agents can effectively set tasks for themselves as they collaborate in the setting of goals, then they recommend goals that provide them with rewarding tasks, regardless of whether those goals are in the interest of the public. Instead, politically appointed ministers, supported by expert staffs and hired consultants, were to determine strategy, and civil service managers were to execute it. By the same logic the scope of responsibility of individual ministries, and the pro-grammes within them, was reduced. Asked to pursue multiple goals simultaneously, agents will naturally have to make trade-offs among them, and will favour trades that serve their interests first, and the public interest accidentally if at all. The narrower the scope of the ministerial portfolio or individual programme, the less the danger that self-interest can use competing purposes as a lever for its own ends. These changes led to a decentralisation of authority within administrative units, and an in-creased emphasis on measuring, and increasing, the satisfaction of the citizens (now recast as customers) who were the beneficiaries of particular services. The clearer the goals, and the less the chances for conflict among them, the smaller the need for mid-dle managers to break complex tasks into simpler ones, adjudicate differences of opinion about the priority of competing programmes, or rate the performance of sub-ordinates in the face of further ambiguities. Instead, given the narrower, flatter struc-ture of administration, front-line managers with a clear understanding of their purpose would determine how best to achieve it. Customer satisfaction would be the measure of their success. All these changes went hand in hand with an emphasis on global performance measures: (improvements in) crime rates, numbers of unem-ployed persons placed in jobs, test scores (of the competence of students at various grade levels and their teachers), and so on. Performance of tasks sufficiently simpli-fied to admit of straight-line accountability could be captured by such metrics; con-versely, the definition of the performance metrics helped encourage the necessary simplification of tasks. Instead of trusting co-ordination of public policy to unreliable self-interested negotiation among interests or collegial consultation among civil serv-ants, management of public affairs could be by results.

A consequence – for some reformers the very purpose – of these reforms was a reduction in the scope of government itself. The clearer the purposes of govern-ment, and the more measurable the results of its actions, of course, the easier it is to translate the tasks of public administration into contracts, and to hold contractual partners to account if they fail to meet their obligations. This made it easier for government, first, to contract with private parties, instead of its internal units, for the provision of service: what mattered to the public as citizens and consumers, after all, was the contractual terms and the respect accorded them. Straight-line accountability thus made the monopoly of public administration on service provision contestable in theory. (Making it contestable in fact took an endless series of battles that are already becoming hard to recall now that they have been mostly won.) Second, contractability and contestability made it easier to privatise wholly some government functions such as the provision of water or electric power. This transfer of formal ownership turned the analogy between private and public governance advanced by the principal-agent reforms into an identity.

The successes of the NPM in establishing the contestability of public administration and devolving authority are indisputable, and largely taken for granted by the vast middle of the modern democratic polities. At the most general level, leaving particular victories over inertia and self-dealing aside, they have shown that the public can prevail against the interests and experts. We made the state; learning from our mistakes we can remake it. This realisation distresses on the one side advocates of the traditional administrative state, who often treated modern government as a kind of natural organism evolved in the primordial broth of contemporary society and destined to flourish with it. But it also, perhaps paradoxically, discomforts those partisans of NPM for whom the advance of privatisation and contestability were vindications of the truly natural form of co-operation – the market – against unnatural co-operation by means of politics and the state. It is easy to understand their baffled outrage at the ability of governments like those of President Clinton and Prime Minister Blair to absorb key lessons of the NPM – and go on with governing.

But measured by its own standard – as a movement to restore accountability and effectiveness to government – the results of the principal-agent movement are equivocal at best. Government in the Whitehall countries, Great Britain in particular, is arguably less accountable and on balance no more effective than before, for two reasons connected to the principal-agent underpinnings of the reform movement itself.

First, it has proved impossible to separate strategy from implementation, or more generally, conception from execution. Those who carried out orders learned not only how to refine the execution of tasks, but also which tasks might be worth pursuing. Nor was it just public or private-sector service providers who acquired knowledge relevant to goal-setting in this way. Citizen-users of the services provided also turned out to have knowledge relevant to choosing public purpose. Put another way, the principal/agent distinction was untenable in practice. At the limit, citizens proved to be in some measure the co-producers of services as well as consumers of them and, ultimately, their principal authors.

The upshot, as Rhodes shows in *Understanding Governance* (1997), is that in Great Britain government agencies – responsible in the NPM scheme of things for the operational implementation of strategy – in fact develop a near-monopoly of expertise in their policy area, notwithstanding efforts to outfit the politically responsible minister with capacities for strategic surveillance. Policy therefore emerges from innumerable small decisions, such that "the agency tail will wag the departmental dog". To increase the confusion, the department, emboldened by official encouragement to assert its directive powers, often uses its oversight responsibility to meddle in the details of agency decision-making. If results disappoint, the minister can play on the ambiguities in the distinction between policy (the responsibility of the minister) and management (the domain of the operating agency) to avoid accountability. Civil servants are no longer in charge; but no one else is, either. Rhodes for one concludes that "British government has undergone a significant decrease in political accountability" (1997, pp. 102-103).

Second, narrowing programmes in the interest of accountability had the unintended consequence of the making it difficult to co-ordinate the narrower entities. While a certain local clarity was achieved, at least within the limits just described, its price was an increase in general confusion. Given specific tasks, and encouraged by new incentive systems to focus exclusively on them, and contract with others to provide collateral services, what was to induce the agencies to co-operate among themselves to solve problems requiring their joint action?

As Rhodes observes, the resulting problems are most conspicuous at the level of local government. There are few efforts at government reform as vigorous and protracted as that aimed at local government by successive British governments. From 1979 to the early 1990s, central government acted to control expenditure, limit taxing capacity, alter management, increase accountability, and redefine the legislative base: in short, to attain "straight-line" accountability by applying all the devices of NPM to the public, private and voluntary sectors. But Rhodes found, in the wake of the reforms,

> services are…delivered through a combination of local government, special purpose bodies, the voluntary sector and the private sector. Service delivery depends, therefore, on linking organisations. Policy implementation becomes more difficult because policy has to be negotiated with more and more organizations. Organizational interdependence is ubiquitous and the government faces the increasingly difficult task of steering several distinct organizations (1997, p. 100).

Both of these problems – the impossibility of maintaining the principal/agent distinction and the need for broad co-ordination to correct the effects of narrow steering – are manifest in the sudden salience of what the British call "cross-cutting" or "wicked problems": problems like the reform of schools or the provision of treatment to substance abusers that both draw on the local knowledge of service providers and service users *and* require co-ordination of service provision across a wide range of formal jurisdictions. These two problems have prompted a set of thoughtful proposals that aim to make use of the new plasticity of government created by NPM while attending to the movement's shortcomings. These are discussed next.

3.   Whitehall redux? Reforming the reforms

The current British Government, through the Cabinet Office and other departments, has been among the most relentless critics of the shortcomings of the old administrative state, even as corrected by NPM, and among the most determined proponents of reforms to address the wicked problems – thought to be particularly acute with regard to social exclusion, small business development and environmental protection. In a series of innovative papers, it develops proposals for policy co-ordination (Performance and Innovation Unit, 2000*a*), new relations between the centre and the local (2000*b*) and the principles of good policy making and implementation (2000*c*).

The starting point for all these reports is the conviction that the functional organisation of government departments – the idea, coeval with the administrative state, that there can be some natural correspondence between the jurisdiction of problem-solving bureaucracies and the boundaries of core social problems – limits the possibility of addressing cross-cutting policy problems. Those limits are exacerbated by practices permitted but not entailed by the bureaucratic structures. These include, for example, a failure "to look at things from the perspective of the consumer", failure to work with local government, being "over-prescriptive in specifying the means as well as the ends", an increased focus on core business as a result of delegation, and perverse incentives.

In response, the reports suggest variants of what might be called a commando centre: a crack team of civil servants at the very centre of government who sue the powers of the bureaucracy to foster cross-cutting behaviours, and so transcend the structural limits without actually transforming the structures. The executive summary from "UK Cabinet Office Performance and Innovation Unit Report," February 2000, conveys the strategy:

- stronger leadership from Ministers and senior civil servants to create a culture which values cross-cutting policies and services, with systems of rewards and recognition that reinforce desired outcomes;

- improving policy formulation and implementation to take better account of cross-cutting problems and issues, by giving more emphasis to the interests and views of those outside central Government who use and deliver services;

- equipping civil servants with the skills and capacity needed to address cross-cutting problems and issues;

- using budgets flexibly to promote cross-cutting working, including using more cross-cutting budgets and pooling of resources;

- using audit and external scrutiny to reinforce cross-cutting working and encourage sensible risk-taking; and

- using the center (No. 10, the Cabinet Office and the Treasury) to lead the drive to more effective cross-cutting approaches wherever they are needed. The center has a critical role to play in creating a strategic framework in which cross-cutting working can thrive, supporting departments and promoting cross-cutting action whilst intervening directly only as a last resort.

The central message of the report is that simply removing barriers to cross-cutting working is not enough...A number of alternative approaches are described in the report...Creating the right environment in which these solutions can work is critical, and the signals which Ministers give civil servants about the priority they wish to be given to cross-cutting approaches is the key to it all.[6]

The reports give a lucid account of the balance that a successful commando centre will have to maintain between intensification and relaxation of control, without suggesting how in practice this balance is to be achieved. Thus the Cabinet Office's *Wiring It Up* paper insists that "conflicting priorities will be sorted out at a strategic policy level and not allowed to undermine efficient and effective service delivery" (Performance and Innovation Unit, 2000a, 5.1). But it also insists on "the need for the centre to recognise its limitations and...to look to service deliverers and end-users to signal where there are existing (or potential) failures to work cross-departmentally" (2000a, 11.4). The same report emphasises the value of "a clear over-arching framework of objectives and targets for each policy which can readily be translated into meaningful targets and objectives at lower levels of government" (2000a, 5.1). Yet it stresses as well that a sophisticated approach to local measures and targets is needed so that they "are not necessarily cascaded from those at national level but define what is needed at local level to deliver the national objective" (2000a, 7.22).

In a closely related paper for the Scottish Council Foundation, *Holistic Government: Options for a Devolved Scotland* (1998), Leicester and Mackay argue that creation of a new parliament and executive provides an opportunity to incorporate, from the start, the lessons of recent years. Drawing on the debates under discussion here, they too argue for selective use of many different types of civil-service structure – each suited to some tasks but suffering from distinctive limits as well – to promote

131|

effective, inclusive and democratic governance. But they emphasise participation and partnership at least as much as an eclectic reform of the civil service. In particular, they argue that the new Scottish Government must be designed to employ a range of processes or "operating codes" to make use of reformed structures singly and together. Besides the familiar forms of parliamentary debate, market contract and hierarchical administration, these include managing networks, diplomacy, partnership, problem-solving, deliberation and provisional consensus, direct democracy and participation, anticipatory government through scenario-planning, preventative government through both participation and new forms of measurement, and flexible government through combining insiders and outsiders.[7]

Many if not all the tensions just identified in these reform proposals will be familiar to their authors. They advance their proposals because they assume – often without stating they do – that it is both necessary and impossible to combine the advantages of largely informal, local knowledge passed in networks with the panoramic capacities of formal bureaucracy. The commando centre promises the necessary panorama. But creating a new bureaucratic elite with the flexibility to define cross-cutting projects invites a new centralisation: a Whitehall redux, cut off from local knowledge and therefore co-ordinating in the dark. Devolution to local networks might seem the countermeasure. But this is to put enormous faith in the self-co-ordinating abilities of society itself. It is to assume, as Perri 6 puts it, that "the best that can be hoped for is a constant and shifting process of negotiations, bargaining games and mutual adjustment across networks of organisations, without overarching objectives" (Perri 6, 1997, p. 70). (Notice that the National Performance Review – the re-invention of government agency created by Vice-President Al Gore, operating in a setting where the federal government never had the powers of even a chastened Whitehall – comes close to accepting this conclusion. Its current goal is to build "communities of practice" in which innovative local and state officials network with each other to create cross-cutting programmes.) Given these irreconcilable conflicts between the two types of organisation, and hence the need for trade-offs, some combination of commando centres and networked locales looks reasonably attractive under current conditions.[8]

At a sufficiently high level of abstraction this assumption is incontrovertible: only an omniscient being can have full knowledge of wholes and parts. But the assumption assumes away crucial, current innovations in the nature of organisation itself, which, blurring the distinction between bureaucratic formality and networked informality, allow for co-ordination in the changes of parts and wholes unattainable by conventional means. These breakthroughs, pioneered by but no longer limited to or even best exemplified by modern Japanese firms, are now commonplace in diverse industries, including automobiles, computers, semiconductors, athletic shoes and garments. The new model firm is introduced here to demonstrate the availability of an alternative to the principal-agent model that holds the promise of relaxing the constraints that models treat as inherent in relations between centre and locales.

4. The pragmatist firm and democratic experimentalism

The setting for the new model firm is the pervasive ambiguity of purpose and capacities just described. The principal-agent model takes for granted that principals know what they want, and the chief task of organisational design is to prevent opportunism by self-interested agents. The new model firm, and the form of public administration associated with it, assume on the contrary that the chief problem for organisations is determining what they and their collaborators, internal and external, should do, and how. Firms operating on principal-agent lines try, as we saw, to clarify goals to prevent agents from using ambiguities in the determination of ends to hijack the organisation. New model firms assume, like the scientists and citizens depicted in American pragmatism, that it is impossible, on the contrary, to eliminate such ambiguity. Instead, these pragmatist firms build organisations that allow for the clarification of ambiguous ends through the exploration of means, and vice versa: they deliberately perturb their beliefs by testing them in use, and unsettle what they learn from this by using it in new ways.

But note that in their emphasis on the search for means and ends, pragmatist firms do not presume collaborators to be selfless and without guile. The presumption is rather that the same mechanisms that allow for the collaborative exploration of means and ends also permit assessment of the reliability of collaborators. A comparison of the design practices and customer-supplier relations in the two types of firm illustrates the distinctive features of pragmatist organisation, and in particular the novel role of the organisational centre.[9]

In the standard firm, initial product designs aim to be integral and definitive. Products are conceived from the first as integral wholes: their major parts are customised to work only with other parts of the same make or model. This entails as well a striving for definitiveness from the outset in order to avoid inadvertent incompatibilities among the key components. Given the mutual specialisation of parts, the discovery late in the product-development cycle that, say, the car engine is unsuited to the proposed transmission means a costly, time-consuming reconfiguration not only of these, but also of the chassis, electric system and so on. Centralisation of design and timidity of design choices are by-products. The attraction of drawing on expertise outside the central design team is offset by fears that subordinates, even if well intentioned, might introduce innovations ultimately incompatible with other parts of the tightly connected design. With centralisation goes timidity. Fear of possible incompatibilities also leads to the (re-)use of already proven components, at the cost of innovation. In practice, of course, the standard firm is not as centralised or timid as this schematic suggests. Rather, it knows the cycles of decentralisation and recentralisation, networking and commando centralism familiar from the discussion above.

Design proposals in the pragmatist firm are modular and provisional. The product is conceived from the first as a system of sub-systems or modules, each

133

defined by and compatible with the others so long as it meets a set of performance criteria. The first outline of the eventual design is elaborated by benchmarking: a central team reviews the characteristics of the best competing products, evaluates the possibility that potential innovations will move from research lab to market during the current design cycle, and then proposes a design reflecting feasible improvements and market-ready innovations. The design team then identifies module-makers with the relevant expertise and asks them to evaluate and improve the module in their domain on the basis of their own benchmarking review of possibilities. As the parts are re-elaborated, the centre adjusts the overall design so that changes in one module remain compatible with the performance specifications of the other. Reciprocating changes in parts and whole continue (within time constraints imposed by the market) until a stable solution emerges.

This design process corresponds to an open or federated form of organisation, rather than a closed one; it invites, indeed depends on open consideration of alternatives rather than discouraging it. It would be pointless to call attention to new possibilities in the outside world through benchmarking only to dismiss them if their pursuit requires collaboration with outsiders. In effect, then, the organisation has to be configured so that it can be substantially re-configured in every product cycle. Indeed, such openness to "outside" points of view turns out to be an indispensable condition of the pragmatist organisation's success: by using each of many different design proposals as a foil for understanding the strengths and weaknesses of the competing ones, the pragmatist organisation can forgo much of the minute, initial analysis of design implications that standard firms require to ferret out hidden defects. This is why pragmatist organisations can manage the counter-intuitive trick of considering a greater number of design variants than standard firms while shortening the design cycle and reducing design errors in the bargain.

These differences are in turn reflected in differences in the kinds of components standard and pragmatist firms buy from other companies, and the conditions under which they buy them: their customer-supplier relations. Because product designs are integral and parts, specialised for each, are suited to only one make or model, the standard firm buys little of consequence from outside suppliers. It is the only customer for its crucial components, and the only producer able to make them. This is vertical integration. But even firms that are vertically integrated in this general way are not completely self-sufficient. They buy commodities – parts or materials whose relevant characteristics can be fully catalogued – in the open market; they buy products less fully specified than commodities, but not so enmeshed in the particulars of the design as a whole as those made internally from outside suppliers via long-term or relational contracts, i.e. agreements recognising that ambiguities in contractual specifications will lead to conflicts, and which therefore provide a mechanism such as arbitration for resolving them. (By fully specifying all the obligations of service-providers in contracts, the NPM aimed at undercutting the need for vertical integration in the provision of services, thereby stripping the legitimacy from monopoly providers, especially government. Contractualisation also made it harder for interest groups and civil servants to play on their expertise to enter into self-serving relational contracts with the government.)

In the pragmatist firm, in contrast, there is at the limit no difference between an inside and an outside supplier. Indeed, it is unclear whether the firm need have any in-house production capacity at all. Any entity that can engage in co-design, and then produce modules that meet the agreed performance standard, is a candidate supplier. Given the importance of keeping abreast of outside developments through benchmarking, and the risk that internal units can become mired in habit, external suppliers, themselves able to learn from a wide range of customers, may even be advantaged in competition with internal units that can learn only from one.

Similarly, because the parties cannot say in advance what they intend to do together, they cannot regulate their relations by means of either spot contracts, used to exchange commodities, or relational contracts, which suppose clarity about essentials while providing for the resolution of marginal disagreements. They have recourse instead to what are artlessly called new supplier agreements: slim documents by which they obligate themselves to provide the information necessary to advance the collaboration (by fixing, for instance, one timetable for proposing design solutions, and another for responding to the proposals of other collaborators). As this same information provides a detailed look at the performance and promise of the other parties, it serves a crucial governance function as well. Given the agreed flow of information, each collaborator can periodically assess the capacities and reliabilities of those on whom it depends. (More generally, because this method of collaboration gives early warning of possible breakdowns in co-operation, outsiders can enter the system by undertaking relatively demanding tasks, and then work their way up through the tiers of subcontractors as they demonstrate greater proficiency.)

On the one hand, therefore, the pragmatist firm is more decentralised than the standard firm, and its boundaries more contestable. The design centre of the pragmatist firm lacks the conclusive authority of its standard counterpart. On the other hand, specialised collaborators, above all those outside the formal boundaries of the firm, have powers of initiative in the pragmatist model that are denied them in the standard setting.

But on another, deeper level this contrast is misleading. It suggests that the power of decision making must be held either by the centre or by the specialised locales. So the gains of one are always the loss of the other. But what we observe in the innovations of the pragmatist organisation is something else again: the roles of centre and periphery are being redefined in ways that moot the question of the distribution of power between them, at least as measured by the yardsticks of the standard model. In the pragmatist organisation the centre proposes broad projects, facilitates reconciliation of alternative solutions, and monitors performance along the way. The locales propose solutions and adjust them, with the help of the centre, in the light of proposals by others. As projects change, so too does the circle of collaborators. This is an organisation that, from the traditional point of view, is neither centralised nor decentralised, and lacks clear boundaries without being diffuse or boundless. Strange as it seems by conventional measures, this organisation is, to judge by the epochal changes under way in the economy, more competitive than standard forms. The next section looks at how pragmatist organisations are emerging in public administration as potential answers to the wicked problems of co-ordination.

5. Democratic experimentalism and the new centre in public administration

As pragmatist institutions are at home with ambiguity and complexity, the world of public problem-solving is as much their habitat as the world of production and exchange. Indeed, they are particularly suited to addressing the wicked problems, whose solutions change in time, must be differentiated to suit varied contexts, and therefore require organisations that somehow combine apparently irreconcilable features of formal bureaucracies and informal networks. They do this in the public sector as in the private one by establishing a novel kind of formal relation between centre and locales that provide transparency and possibilities for systematic learning unavailable in informal networks, without creating the fixity that limits the capacity of bureaucracies to adapt. To show in some detail how this new centre works, and to indicate the very general conditions under which it can arise, this section will examine the case of school reform in Chicago.[10]

The focus is on school reform because it represents in sharp relief a series of developments, culminating in governance innovation, observed in the United States in areas as diverse as environmental regulation, the treatment of substance abusers, provisional child protection and other services to at-risk families, as well as reform of the police and many other aspects of the criminal justice system. After decades of skirmishing, inveterate antagonists (in the case of education: school administrators, teachers and parents) exhaust confidence in their respective strategies and relax doctrinal commitments (more resources for the public schools as against privatisation), not least because the partial successes of each side cast doubt on the validity of its larger programme (more money for schools does not by itself lead to improved performance by pupils; pilot programmes to privatise schools show how hard it is to write effective performance contracts to discipline providers). Facing urgent problems (crumbling schools and disastrous drop-out rates), the actors agree to explore new solutions without agreeing to put aside the differences in values that originally divided them (whether government is in principle good or bad). As they institutionalise their experimental efforts they stumble on arrangements that permit the piecemeal reelaboration of complex wholes through the reconsideration of their parts. Local actors (individual schools and the parents, teachers and students that constitute them) are

136

given substantial liberties to set goals for improvement and the means for accomplishing them. In return they must propose measures for assessing their progress and provide rich information on their own performance. The centre (the municipal or state school department) pools the information provided by local actors and ranks them according to (periodically revised) performance measures that give substance to standards of excellence and definitions of inadequacy. In the best cases the centre provides assistance to those who are not improving as quickly as their likes. At all events it eventually sanctions those whose continuing failure seems incorrigible. The system increases local innovation by allowing those on the spot to test, within broad limits, their assumptions of what works best. At the same time it makes the exercise of local discretion sufficiently transparent to assure public accountability, allowing each locale to learn from the experiences of the others, and the polity as a whole to draw lessons from the experience of all. Thus is created a framework for establishing what is currently feasible, how those who fall short can work to achieve it, and how those doing well can do better still. These arrangements allow the parties to get a grip, in a way to be specified in a moment, on problems whose complexity once seemed to put them beyond the reach of public action. They create new possibilities for citizens to steer public institutions that affect their vital interests by involving them in forms of problem-solving that unsettle encrusted beliefs. Because this architecture, like that of the pragmatist firm, takes its own starting points as arbitrary, and corrects its assumptions in the light of the results that they produce, it can be called experimentalist.

The author focuses on the Chicago reforms in particular for three reasons. The first is simply their scope and complexity. The Chicago school system is big enough, including the 560 elementary (K-8) and high (9-12) schools in the city limits, so that key aspects of the new relations between local schools and the superintending centre established in Chicago could plausibly be a model for large-scale change. Second, the progress of reform in Chicago shows that it is possible to advance by deliberately disruptive half-measures or bootstrapping: taking a step that both loosens the grip of the old system and prompts an exploration of alternatives, from which emerges a next step that does the same. The protagonists had good reasons for their actions every step of the way, yet came to understand the architecture of the new system they were building and how it avoided the apparently inevitable choice between bureaucratic centralisation and market-mimicking decentralisation only when construction was far advanced. Thus we do not have to learn exactly the right lessons from Chicago (or anywhere else) to address wicked problems as they did. Finally, the reforms are exemplary in their results so far. They demonstrate that large school systems can be made manageable in the sense that particular schools can say what they intend to do by way of reforms, and then actually do what they intend (or be held to account if they do not).

Chicago was one of the last of the large American cities to adopt the progressive programme of removing the public schools from what was presumed to be (and often was) the despoiling grasp of elected officials, and entrusting it to professionals accountable to their own best, scientific understanding of their responsibilities, and of hierarchical organisations as uniquely efficient and – because of their formalism – incorruptible. But starting in 1947 a central office set budgets and made purchasing and personnel decisions for all the schools. In time, selection of textbooks and the scheduling of the school day were centralised as well.

Even as the system was becoming more rule-bound and hence less responsive to changes in its environment, the rise of the Civil Rights movement and insistence on school desegregation placed new demands upon it. A study commissioned by the school board in 1963 found that the new administration ignored the needs for local diversity. Central regulations, moreover, blocked local adjustment: teachers could not even schedule discussions of possible changes in their home schools without headquarters' permission. The only sequel to the report was more reports confirming a worsening situation. By the mid-1980s citizens were so frustrated that advocacy of school decentralisation had become a social movement including business interests, local groupings focused on problems in particular schools, and broad groups such as Designs for Change, that they elaborated decentralisation programmes and built networks of supporters through discussion of the ideas.

The first, deeply disruptive break with the old system came in the period from 1987 through 1996, and produced a thorough, but still largely conventional, form of decentralisation. The immediate impetus to change was a teachers' strike – the ninth in the preceding nineteen school years – which came to symbolise the paralysing system's self-absorption. The conflict seemed to require engagement by wider circles, whose projects were in any case merging. The result was an alliance between Designs for Change and reformers in the business community in favour of state legislation providing for site-based governance.

Under the legislation, each school in the Chicago system was to be governed by an elected local school council (LSC) composed, for elementary schools, of six parents, two teachers, two community members, and the principal. High school LSCs were to add a twelfth, student member. The LSCs were given the power to hire and fire the principal, prepare the budget, and develop comprehensive three-year school improvement plans. As part of the compromise with business interests, proponents of decentralisation accepted system-wide monitoring of results by a central office created for the purpose. Early results were mixed: some school councils made wise use of their powers, others did not. There were cases of corruption. The reality of decentralisation brought to mind the virtues of centralised administration.

The next and decisive development of reform was passage in 1995 of further legislation clarifying the relation between local and central governance institutions and making manifest the novel division of labour emerging between them. The new law simultaneously increased the powers and capacities of local school councils to pursue their own course of action, and the powers of the central office to intervene in case the results of local decisions are unsatisfactory. For example, to increase local autonomy and capacity, monies previously passed from the central office to the schools for use for specific purposes – such as the construction of playgrounds – would now be available to them as block grants to be spent as changing local circumstances suggested. Authority over building engineers and janitors passed from the central office to the LSCs. Determination of class size and the schedule of the academic year were excluded as subjects of central bargaining between the Chicago public schools and the teachers union, and thus left to local negotiation. The law required additional training (funded by the central office) in the preparation of school budgets and improvement plans, as well as the selection of principals. To increase local accountability the law authorised the central authority to intensify scrutiny of poorly performing schools and place the poorest performers – those where fewer than 15% of the students tested met national standards – on probation or remediation lists. Listed schools would be inspected by an "intervention team" that advised the LSC and school staff on instructional, administrative and governance improvements.

In practice the LSCs are autonomous enough to undertake fundamental reorganisation of local schools, while the central intervention teams have the remedial capacities to establish accountability, but in a way that reduces the dangers of reversion to centralised control at either the school level or above. Thus, in their three-year school improvement plans the LSCs can propose specialised programmes in, say, dance or business; innovative methods for teaching disciplines such as mathematics; or new, project-based, collaborative pedagogies broadly applicable to nearly the whole curriculum. In the same plans the LSCs can also obtain financing for construction that facilitates curricular reforms, or makes the school more hospitable. An ambitious LSC can reorient the school and its methods to put learning at the service of a social project and vice versa: in one case a school was rededicated as an academy teaching an Afro-centric curriculum by drill methods (Direct Instruction) thought by the principal and the LSC (but only a small minority of education experts) to be especially beneficial for disadvantaged students.

For their part, officials in the new centre exercise their authority to complement, not challenge, the local autonomy. Even when a school is failing so badly that dissolution is imminent, the new centre issues no directives for reconstruction. Instead, the chief purpose of the intervention teams is to help the LSC prepare a "remediation" plan for removing the blockages to local discussion and decision making that prevented improvement by normal means. Only if these turnaround plans fail is the school finally "reconstituted", and teachers and the principal required to reapply for jobs. This means that the intervention consists far more in analysing with the local participants the causes of their past difficulties than proposing, let alone imposing, concrete measures for reorganisation. Accountability in the form of remediation plans does not, in other words, plant the seeds of recentralisation.

139

First indications are that the new institutional machinery works. A crude measure of the interest and participation of local parents in school reform is that elections to LSCs are orderly and attract competent candidates in sufficient numbers. Although it might be expected that only wealthy communities have the wherewithal to profit from the new institutions, poor communities have made as good use of local control as better-off ones. Studies that rank LSCs by the effectiveness of their use of school improvement plans find the best performers as likely to be located in poor catchment areas as middle class or rich ones. Test scores are rising but not, so far, in a pattern that can be connected to the effects of decentralisation.

The one incontestable achievement so far is that, as noted at the outset, local schools are manageable again. Reform plans are made and enacted. This is not, to be sure, a sufficient condition for effective reform: enacting a bad plan does not improve a school or a school system, except insofar as it warns others away from a dead-end. But manageability is a necessary condition of reform. Unless plans can be made and implemented, any success is a matter of chance – the result of stumbling upon something that works – and efforts to learn from it will be haphazard as well. In making the schools manageable, therefore, Chicago decentralisation creates a foundation on which further efforts to tackle the wicked problem of education can be built.

A more complete account would have to be at once more expansive and more cautious. More expansive, because it would have to show how states such as Texas, Kentucky and Florida are developing elaborate institutions for assessing performance of schools and pupils. Instead of setting minimum acceptable levels for the performance of teachers and pupils, as was commonplace in the 1980s, the new systems set standards for the improvement of schools, and reset these periodically in the light of actual experience. Instead of focusing exclusively on global outcome measures (math scores, graduation rates), the new systems provide more fine-grained measures of learning (ability to formulate a mathematical problem, ability to choose and manipulate the appropriate formalism). These operational or guiding standards are more like the measures of inventory turns or error rates that pragmatist firms use to improve their performance, than measures like stock price or growth rate that investors use to judge overall performance. They allow teachers and students to see where problems arise, and correct them before they ramify. Finally, instead of sanctioning poor performers, the new systems provide resources in the form of programmes in professional development for teachers, infrastructure for the exchange of experience, and funds for planning local school improvement. In short, these states and many others following their example are becoming new, experimentalist centres, thus complementing and re-enforcing the governance reforms illustrated in the Chicago experience.[11]

But the fuller account would have to be more cautious as well, underscoring the ways that old antagonisms – between, say public school advocates and privatisers

– can be fought out in new settings. By making standard tests very demanding and failure a bar to promotion and graduation, and by refusing aid to students or schools that do badly, opponents of public education aim to precipitate an immediate crisis of the schools, with profit to the privatisation movement from the resulting frustration. But while old conflicts can still be revived, doing so takes an ever less likely alignment of the political stars. That in itself is a crude measure of how much has already changed.

The trajectory of analysis has taken us from the breakdown of an old order housed in the familiar regulatory state, to fumbling adjustments of traditional solutions to changing circumstance, to halting elaboration of what is here called experimentalist alternatives. Then comes the realisation that this alternative will entrain further changes in the background institutions that frame it. From here the way forward branches.

At one pole are readers whose reflexes have been trained by modern social science. They will likely suspect that experimentalism works in cases such as school reform or environmentalism because of conditions particular to these domains, and is unlikely – at least in an obvious way – to obtain in society generally. Why, they might wonder, did experimentalism emerge with particular clarity in these areas, and not, say, in health care or labour relations? (There are signs of a change in this direction in both. But developments in these areas have not proceeded as far as in the examples chosen here, and it is certainly pertinent to ask why.) Such readers will accordingly be inclined to think that the best to way to learn more about experimentalism (assuming they are still interested in it at all) is by investigating why it emerges in some places rather than others.

The reflexes of other readers will be very nearly the opposite. Think of this as the artificer's or the activist's response. For such persons, cases of novel, experimentalist success will not prompt questions of why here, not there. Every new thing, after all, arises in some places before others. What they will find remarkable is that experimentalism could succeed at all, given the apparent intractability of the problems it addresses and the way its operation violates familiar assumptions about the impossibility of direct participation, the organisational superiority of hierarchy, and so on. They will wonder accordingly how its success changes our sense of our possibilities for acting together through politics. The first line of questioning truncates reconsideration of deep assumptions in the light of innovation, by shifting attention to what "causes" experimentalism before we know what "it" is. The second invites this reflection, but only by according experimentalism a kind of provisional reality it may not warrant.

Ultimately both lines of inquiry have to be pursued; indeed, insofar as they are both concerned with aspects of the generalisability of the new innovations, they converge. For now the focus is on the second, because it offers two immediate gains. First, reflection on the broadly political implications of experimentalism helps connect bottom-up discussion of problem-solving to current worries about the efficacy and legitimacy of modern democracies formulated, in different ways, at the heights of political and theoretical debate in the United States and the European Union. Unless these connections are established it is easy to dismiss the reforms considered – and many others – as irrelevant to the big picture. Second, establishing these links helps in turn connect the apparently disparate US and EU debates on these themes. As will be seen next, the combination of local innovation and public accountability characteristic of experimentalism speaks to the mutual monitoring of public institutions emphasised in the United States on the one side, and to the need for social learning increasingly key to EU debates on re-imagining solidarity and justice on the other.

6.   Accountability in experimentalist democracy: A preliminary response to the democratic deficit

It is an historical fact that in the United States, democratic innovations in democratic governance, however effective they promise to be, must be reconciled with our Madisonian tradition to be legitimate. Power in the Madisonian scheme is carefully parcelled out among rival branches and levels of government. Deliberation – preference-changing reflection in the service of the public interest – is the province of a senatorial élite buffered from the immediacies of everyday concerns. The rivalry among branches and levels of government safeguards liberty by providing checks and counterweights to the excessive ambitions of any part of the machinery of government. By blurring the division of labour among the branches and levels of government and tying the ultimate resolution of large questions of policies to daily collaborative problem-solving, experimentalism seems to repudiate this Madisonian legacy, perhaps putting our liberties at risk.

And yet the experimentalist accountability established by problem-defining legislation and the broad grant of problem-solving authority to local entities could nonetheless be considered a *neo-Madisonian* generalisation of the original design for three reasons (Dorf and Sabel, 1998; Sabel, Fung and Karkkainen, 2000, pp. 109-112). First, it too harnesses a form of competition among institutions to ensure that they all act in the public interest. Where the design of the 1787 Constitution relies on the rivalries among specified branches and levels of government, the emerging "constitution" of experimentalist institutions like the Chicago schools combines the mechanisms of strict performance monitoring, comparative benchmarking, and the pooled experience of diverse, often rivalrous jurisdictions into an engine of accountability that disciplines state action regardless of the precise subdivisions of government. Second, instead of seeing deliberation as possible only in the exceptionable circumstances of insulated chambers, neo-Madisonianism emphasises the capacity of practical problem-solving activity to reveal new possibilities in everyday circumstances. It thus opens the way for solutions that are as different from the vector sum of current interests as those achieved by senatorial deliberation, but sees these solutions as the result of the activity of the many, not the repose of the few. Finally, in an era in which the sub-national governments themselves have responsibilities and apparatuses larger than those of 19th century nation states, the emerging architecture of monitored local experimentation disassociates "central" and "local" from familiar jurisdictions of government, and allows their meaning to vary as problem-solving within the emergent design of co-ordination suggests. Like the older federalism, neo-Madisonianism lays the foundation for a resilient mutual accountability between centre and locality, dispassionate expert and engaged citizen. But it makes the division of labour among territorial units the provisional and corrigible result of the work they do, not the expression of historically entrenched responsibilities. Put another way, neo-Madisonianism simultaneously denaturalises our frame of government – because the boundaries of mutually accountable, problem-solving units are no longer taken as given – while connecting it more directly to the surprising contingencies of citizens' lives – because the problem-solving units are shaped and reshaped by practical deliberation directed to uncovering and making sense of these surprises.

Europeans, and European social democrats in particular, are likely to take all this worry about protecting the government from the people and the people from the government as a parochial affair: a legacy of the Tudor polity that the United States inherited from Great Britain, and another demonstration, as though one were needed, of the American inability to understand the concerns for social and universal justice that animated the welfare state and the Enlightenment. From this point of view experimentalism, regardless of any possible fidelity to US constitutional tradition, must address two pressing problems if it is to be more than an administrative or managerial curiosity.

The first has to do with solidarity. Those who press it most urgently stand in the tradition of reform tied to the social welfare state. In retrospect the success of the welfare state depended on the common ethos or ethical identity of its citizens: only if citizens recognise one another as fundamentally alike will they agree to redistribute resources in favour of those who fare poorly in market exchanges. As heterogeneous peoples are forced to amalgamate into composite polities under the pressure of globalisation, the common basis of redistributive solidarity is jeopardised. Because there is no "European" people, this worry goes, the harmonisation of law that makes an efficient common market will lead typically to regulatory races to the bottom, as each national group abandons costly protective rules so domestic producers can keep up with less-regulated competitors. How can experimentalism contribute to the reconstitution of solidarity under conditions of radical diversity? (Scharpf, 1999).

The second concern is with norms of justice, broadly conceived as obligations we owe our fellow human beings; those most ardent in urging it continue the Enlightenment tradition of universalising reform. They too fear that democracy may be reduced to an economic constitution under the pressure of competition. But they are suspicious of the ethical uniformity of the nation state, fearing that any people that identifies justice with the way it lives may oppress dissidents within its midst and turn bellicose against other nations that live differently. They look instead to the capacities we share as reasonable beings or as speakers and hearers bound – as conditions of mutual intelligibility – by norms of veracity and probity that make communication itself an occasion for self-reflection. Their hope is that these capacities, shaped and reshaped by the history we make, can give rise to ties of fellowship as powerful as those rooted in sentiments of solidarity, but less easily perverted by parochialism. But the recrudescence of group conflict of many kinds and the erosion of life worlds sheltered enough from strategic market exchange to admit of self-reflective communication give pause. Perhaps even universal conceptions of justice depend on widely diffused but historically shared values? Habermas, whose life's-work shows how theories of the moral constraints inherent in human capabilities can guide and be guided by effectively radical democratic politics, calls this substratum "constitutional patriotism." The worry is that the same forces undermining the ethics of national solidarity are sapping moral capabilities as well. Can experimentalism rekindle solidarity, while connecting it to respect for broad principles of justice? (Habermas, 1996, 1999).

To see how experimentalism responds to both these concerns – and in a way that helps resolve the tension between them – it is necessary to return to the relation between values, strategies, and programmes from which experimentalism arises, and which it in turn helps make politically and institutionally tractable. Experimentalist programmes, recall, emerge where actors, having lost confidence in long-standing, broad-gauge strategies (more market, more state), and without agreeing on deep values (the primacy of the individual as against the group, or vice versa), are nonetheless convinced of the need to respond to urgent problems.

This condition itself bespeaks a kind of interdependence born of radical indeterminacy or complexity. If the actors had workable projects, they would act alone or in concert to realise them. Because they do not, they must collaborate with others whose orientations and general goals will differ from their own to uncover new possibilities and discover dead-ends before incurring ruinous costs. In such a world, "strong" actors cannot rule out the possibility that they will come to depend on solutions discovered by "weak" ones. Even the strongest favour some division of investigative labour to going it alone. Homogeneity is here more nearly a threat than a buttress to this solidarity of uncertainty. Experimentalist search in turn strengthens these incipient ties. It institutionalises the commonality of initial uncertainty in the very process of creating a common language for expressing the results of joint exploration. With the articulation of this language comes deep familiarity with others that creates a kind of intimacy precisely because it facilitates surprising discoveries about oneself.

Such collaborative exploration, finally, occupies a middle ground between the exfoliation of common values in the historical ethos of a nation state and the evolution or discovery of norms of universal justice through the exercise of the capabilities of reasonable, communicative beings. Unlike the first, which is a form of self-explication indifferent to alien viewpoints, the experimentalism of directly deliberative democracy invites evaluation of one's own choices with the choices of others. Although comparison focuses on broad but concrete problems, and not explicitly on values, the result is to change the parties' sense of possibilities in a way that cannot but change their ideas of how it is good to live, and so, indirectly, their deep criteria of evaluation. Unlike the second, this discovery procedure and the self-reflection it occasions cannot claim to be an algorithm for hitting upon (nearly) universal truths. Its promise is to spare us the parochial, not to deliver the (nearly) transcendent.

To be more than a *jeu d'esprit*, this sparest sketch of directly deliberative democracy would have to be extended in two directions. First, beginning with responses to such currently pressing problems as the harmonisation of the EU laws, does the emergent regime give evidence of providing a web of rules and related services that together give its citizens protections against untrammelled market operations arguably equivalent to those enjoyed under the welfare state? Second, it would have to be shown that this link or entanglement leads not to the recognition of a solidarity of sentiment, but to an institutional acknowledgement and commitment to sustain a commonality of capabilities. Of these the ability to engage, as citizens, in common forms of problem-solving that underpin, and render mutually intelligible, the efforts dedicated to separate projects would be especially important. The resulting web of connections might (indeed very probably would) redistribute resources from one group to another. But redistribution would be the consequence of a solution adopted first and foremost to address broad common problems (above all, the problem of maintaining the ability to address together, as a democracy, unforeseen problems), not to correct social or economic imbalances. Standards requiring that citizens be provided with adequate levels of environmental protection, workplace health and safety, and education and vocational training, where "adequate" is continuously redefined in the light of experimental advances in the respective areas, would have this result.

A look at the vast literature on EU harmonisation suggests that there is quite arguably motion in this direction. In policy arenas such as health and safety, environmental regulation of products and production processes, competition policy, telecommunications standards, and others, there is no race to the bottom as feared (Joerges and Voss, 1999). Are the reasons to be sought in some lucky and limited accidents of the administrative structure of the EU and member states that allow public-minded actors to prevail over selfish ones? Or, without forgetting the caprices of the Brussels bureaucracy, the limits to parliamentary supervision and the other elements of the "democratic deficit" in the EU, can it be that directly deliberative structures, analogous to those emerging in the United States, are taking shape behind the screen of "comitology"? If one inchoate democratic renewal, why not two? Or many?

Notes

1. This paper draws on "USA: Economic Revival and the Prospect of Democratic Renewal", published in *Internationale Politik und Gesellschaft*, No. 1/2000; and "Democratic Experimentalism: What To Do about Wicked Problems after Whitehall (And What Scotland May Just Possibly Already Be Doing)", co-authored with Rory O'Donnell and presented to the OECD Conference on Devolution and Globalisation, Glasgow, Scotland, February 2000.

2. See story in *The New York Times*, 29 September 2000: "Danish Voters Say No to Euro" by Roger Cohen.

3. For representative projects see http://www.buildingterritories.org.

4. The cover of an authoritative book on recent transformations of British democracy reads, simply, *The End of Whitehall*. You must turn to the title page to uncover the cautionary addendum: *Death of a Paradigm?* (Collin Campbell and Graham K. Wilson. Blackwell, 1995).

5. An excellent survey is Jonathan Boston *et al.*, *Public Management: The New Zealand Model*, Oxford University Press (1996).

6. The full report can be found at http://www.cabinet-office.gov.uk/innovation/1999/wiring/Accountability/contents.htm.

7. See also Perri 6, *Holistic Government*, London (1997), on which much of this is based.

8. These impressions arose during discussions with officials at the National Partnership for Reinventing Government in Washington, DC, between October 1999 and January 2000.

9. The following draws on Charles Sabel, John Paul MacDuffie and Susan Helper, "Pragmatic Collaborations: Advancing Knowledge while Controlling Opportunism", in *Industrial and Corporate Change*, 9:3, 2000.

10. The account of reform in Chicago schools is based on Archon Fung, "Street Level Democracy: A Theory of Popular Pragmatic Deliberation and Its Practice In Chicago School Governance and Community Policing", 1988-97 (Ph.D. thesis, 1999).

11. For details on these cases see Charles Sabel and James Liebman, "Emerging Model of Public School Governance and Legal Reform: Beyond Redistribution and Privatization", working paper (2000).

Bibliography

BOSTON, Jonathan *et al.* (1996),
   Public Management: The New Zealand Model. Auckland: Oxford University Press.

CAMPBELL, Colin and Graham K. WILSON (1995),
   The End of Whitehall: Death of a Paradigm? Cambridge, Mass.: Basil Blackwell.

COATES, Ken S. and Paul G. McHUGH (1998),
   Living Relationships. Wellington: Victoria University Press.

DORF, Michael and Charles SABEL (1998),
   "A Constitution of Democratic Experimentalism", *Columbia Law Review.*

DURIE, Mason (1998),
   Te Mana, Te Kawanatanga. Auckland: Oxford University Press.

FRIEDRICH, Carl (1940),
   "Public Policy and the Nature of Administrative Responsibility", *Public Policy*, 1.

FUNG, Archon (1999),
   "Street Level Democracy: A Theory of Popular Pragmatic Deliberation and Its Practice In Chicago School Governance and Community Policing", 1988-97 (Ph.D. thesis).

HABERMAS, Juergen (1996),
   "Between Facts and Norms: Contributions to a Discourse Theory of Law and Democracy". Cambridge, Mass.: MIT Press.

HABERMAS, Juergen (1999),
   "The European Nation State and the Pressures of Globalization" in *The New Left Review*, 235 (May/June), pp. 46-59.

HUNTINGTON, Sam, Michael CROZIER and Joji WATANUKI (1975),
   "Crisis of Democracy: Report on the Governability of Democracies to the Trilateral Commission". New York: New York University Press.

JOERGES, Christian and Ellen VOSS, eds. (1999),
   EU Committees: Social Regulation, Law, and Politics. Oxford: Hart Publishing.

LEICESTER, Graham and Peter MACKAY (1998),
   "Holistic Government: Options for a Devolved Scotland". Scottish Council Foundation, at http://www.scottishpolicynet.org.uk/scotpol/scf/publications/paper_5/frameset.shtml.

PERFORMANCE AND INNOVATION UNIT (2000a),
   "Wiring It Up: Whitehall's Management of Cross-Cutting Issues", January, at http://www.cabinet-office.gov.uk/innovation/2000/wiring/index.htm.

PERFORMANCE AND INNOVATION UNIT (2000b),
"Reaching Out: The Role of Central Government at Regional and Local Government", February, at http://www.cabinet-office.gov.uk/innovation/2000/regions/index.htm.

PERFORMANCE AND INNOVATION UNIT (2000c),
"Professional Policy Making for the Twenty-First Century", at http://www.cabinet-office.gov.uk/moderngov/policy/index.htm.

6, Perri (1997),
Holistic Government. London: Demos.

RHODES, R.A.W. (1997),
Understanding Governance: Policy Networks, Governance, Reflexivity and Accountability. Philadelphia: Open University Press.

SABEL, Charles (1996),
Local Partnerships and Social Innovation: Ireland. Paris: OECD.

SABEL, Charles, Archon FUNG and Bradley KARKKAINEN (2000),
Beyond Backyard Environmentalism. The New Democracy Forum Series, Josh Cohen and Joel Rogers, eds. Boston: Beacon Press.

SABEL, Charles and James LIEBMAN (2000),
"Emerging Model of Public School Governance and Legal Reform: Beyond Redistribution and Privatization", working paper.

SABEL, Charles, John Paul MacDUFFIE and Susan HELPER (2000),
"Pragmatic Collaborations: Advancing Knowledge while Controlling Opportunism", Industrial and Corporate Change, 9:3.

SCHARPF, Fritz (1999),
Governing in Europe: Effective and Democratic? Oxford: Oxford University Press.

SCHMITTER, Philippe, ed. (1977),
"Corporatism and Policy-making in Contemporary Western Europe", Special Issue of Comparative Political Studies 10, No. 1, April.

SUNSTEIN, Cass (1990),
After the Rights Revolution. Cambridge, Mass.: Harvard University Press.

Chapter 6

Society as Social Diversity: The Challenge for Governance in the Global Age

by
Martin Albrow
Woodrow Wilson International Center for Scholars, United States
and University of Surrey Roehampton, United Kingdom

1. Introduction[1]

In 1900, governments in the West defined class and the threat of revolution as their social problem. In 2000, governments everywhere face the challenge of social diversity and ethnic conflict. They resolved the old problem with representative democracy and the welfare state; today, they look to governance to solve the new dilemmas.

The similarities of conditions at the two points in time provide the major premises for the analysis that follows. In each case, economic developments threaten an old ordering of society by releasing new and powerful social forces. The governing powers respond through a policy of social reconstruction. In each case, movements of capital create the problems for, and limit the capacities of, the governing powers.

The minor premises distinguish the two cases. In 1900 national governments asserted sovereign power internationally and sought to integrate society around the state. The outcome of the social transformation they effected, followed by global economic development, combine in 2000 to create a new politics of identity. The old national solution to class conflict had its costs: warfare on an international scale. The task of governance in our time is to find a solution to ethnic conflict at lesser cost.

We are, therefore, considering governing power as it exists today, in a global polity dominated by America and the rich countries. In their own interests, they have enlisted society, collectivities, networks and identities of all kinds, in a transformation of government into governance. This involves a much wider diffusion of

149

sovereignty, and hence responsibility for co-operation on the part of all agencies. In the Global Age, governance permits no free riders. At the same time, economy and society, in their course and effects, are global. The pursuit of governance cannot stop short of the shaping of global institutions and a more generous non-national citizenship. The welfare and security of each country now depends on all.

2. Society retrieved

In the 1990s, "society" returned to become a favoured term in political discourse. Whether qualified as "information society" or "knowledge society", or – in the guise of community – "civil society", "third sector" or "social capital", national leaders acknowledged afresh that society was one of their concerns.

It was a renewed interest, overshadowed only by the dramatic rise of globalisation as the key marker for the decade. The rise of the one and the return of the other, in the same period, was no mere coincidence. For, although globalisation was construed mainly in economic terms, there was a general loosening of the bonds holding together that bundle known as the "country", or the "nation state".

Not just the economy, but culture and the environment, appeared as transnational forces and issues. The idea that society was held in the confines of the nation state, and was even coterminous with it, came into question. The welfare and social security systems that cemented society to the state had already come under stress through the fiscal crises in Western countries in the 1970s. Acquiescence in and support for globalisation by national leaders in the 1990s added to a general sense that there were no longer any agencies in control of the world. At the same time, influential academic discourse promoted an image of society in disarray.

Indeed, just as business and national leaders again invoked society as partner for state and economy, intellectuals abandoned it in favour of diversity, difference, identity, agency and movement.[2] In what is often called the cultural turn, society dissolves into shifting flows of symbols, reappearing as "ethnoscapes", landscapes of group identity (Appadurai, 1996).

Even the state itself has not been exempt from the general sense of flux. Governments find it difficult to behave as controlling agencies. The rise of the term governance expresses revised expectations of the kind of control that the state can exercise over society in a transformed world. Steering (not rowing) is the preferred metaphor (Osborne and Gaebler, 1993), and there are many hands on the tiller. Economic management is enabling, rather than directing.

Instead of targeting society for administration, the state solicits it for social support. The first challenge, then, that social diversity issues to governance is to secure its own basis in the face of diversity. For if representative government once expressed the will of the people in the nation state, governance is now the state's representation of the social condition of diversity.

This new relation of state and society is doubly reflexive. Each reflects and is the condition of the other. They thus tend to magnify each other's instabilities. When they are both also open to multiple impacts and influences from economy, culture and environment, then the quest for stable axioms and points of reference becomes urgent.

We can see governance in a simple way as the management of society by the people. More profoundly than that, it is implicated in the constant reconstitution of society, as much an intellectual as a logistical engagement. The second challenge to governance from social diversity is, therefore, to rethink society. A knowledge society requires a self-knowing society.

In that spirit, the author argues in this chapter against the view that social diversity heralds the dissolution of society. Rather, we need to think of diversity in global terms if we are to understand the new forms of social relations that constitute contemporary society. It is the diversity of humankind, globally, which generates the problems for local governance, but also makes absolutely necessary a variety of different country solutions.

The long-term practical problems for governance are global and require appropriate institutional inventiveness. However, any new institutions will have to provide for diverse solutions. The noisy recriminations following the IMF's handling of Russia and the East Asian economic crises testify to the inadequacy of the view that globalisation provides one-size-fits-all solutions. If countries are increasingly becoming agencies for the globe, their structural positions become quite as differentiated as their unique histories.

Globalisation is the problem, not the solution. The old modern society in the West was divided primarily along class lines. The welfare state was the solution to the capital-labour cleavage. The sources of instability in the new global society are the shifts in the distribution of capital that threaten to open up the wounds of old ethnic, religious and cultural cleavages and to create new ones like the digital divide.

In the modern age, which is past, problems of class conflict were absorbed by mobilisation for national ends in the ultimate preparation for and pursuit of war. After 1945, the West got used to thinking that the problem of social order in capitalist conditions had been solved. Indeed, it promoted capitalism as the solution to that problem, and as "modernisation", sought to extend it to the rest of the world.

Today, in the global economy of the postcolonial, post-Cold War era, capital movements translate into the mobilisation of differences, especially of an ethnic and religious kind. Diversity presents as a problem not just overt ethnic conflict; it is reflected in unequal opportunities, in deprivation and poverty, addiction, crime and oppression.

At the end of the 19th century, class was the social problem: at the beginning of the 21st, it is diversity. Not that it is in the nature of class and diversity to be social problems. In each case they become problems because of instabilities precipitated by the behaviour of capital. The 21st century state can no longer adopt the old national solution of preparing for war. It is to governance and not to the mobilisation of the nation that we have to look for solutions.

The transformation of government into governance in the last twenty years has been challenging for anyone working in public service. It has not been just a matter of learning new methods and unlearning the old. It has meant rethinking what work is needed, who should do it, and whom it serves. If it is the good society which is the intended outcome of the work, then the message that society no longer exists can hardly inspire ever renewed effort.

In sum, social diversity issues two challenges to governance in the coming period. The first is to secure its own continuing renewal under changing global conditions. The second, which is essential to meet the first, is to rethink the ideas of state and society.

3. Transformation and globalisation

At the beginning of the 20th century European states had a lot in common. They looked to expand trade through colonies, or at least to expand trade and build empires. They competed for influence with each other and prepared for war, signalling readiness to assert their interests. Their industrial development had revolutionised communications and transformed their societies. The new capitalists swept long-established feudal relations aside. Everywhere, an industrial proletariat threatened disorder. This was the social problem for the ruling classes of the time.

It was different in the United States, Russia, China and Japan. In particular, the colonial impetus was less, but each was equally exposed to the disruptions of industrialisation and urbanisation, and the demand for democracy. But for them, as for European powers, these were challenges to be met within a national frame of reference. The call went out for total individual commitment to the nation as a whole. Patriotism was the supreme duty.

One hundred years later there are 188 sovereign countries in the world. If we take the rich ones, like the 29 Member countries of the OECD, they have shed, or never had, colonies. They no longer make peace by preparing for war. They are bonded into complex multilateral arrangements all the way up to the United Nations. Their citizens look to the state to provide support at every stage of life, especially with education, health and social security. The rights of citizenship are well nigh universal – though the enjoyment of these varies with wealth, the distribution of which becomes ever more unequal even as it grows year on year. Individual freedom of movement, self-expression and free association have reached unprecedented levels, while the obligation to perform military service has almost disappeared.

In the rest of the world democracy is often unstable. Industrialisation and urbanisation produce the same social unrest as they did in Europe a century before. However, rich and poor countries alike are exposed to a revolution in communications and a deepening of their dependence on each other. Instead of national projects there are regional and global threats. Sovereign states have less sense of control over their affairs than their European predecessors a hundred years before, even while the technology of control has advanced out of all recognition.

The most popular label for this overall transformation is globalisation. In the 1990s it displaced postmodernity as the intellectual catch-all term. We have to be careful here. There is no overall process of globalisation, in the sense of a single movement taking us in one direction. If we want to signal a rupture with the past and, at the same time, the openness of the future, it is perhaps best to refer to the "Global Age" (Albrow, 1996). There are multiple globalisations, often contradictory, and there are many points where policies make a difference. The term globalisation refers to at least three quite distinct concepts; for the purposes of analysis we need to distinguish:

- *Interdependence* – in defence, trading relations, cultural policies, investment in technology and communication networks, and in macroeconomic policy, countries cannot act alone without taking unreasonable risks. It is an aspect of the general connectedness of our time, "the network society" (Castells, 1996) or our "age of connexity" (Mulgan, 1998) The phenomenon is just as likely to produce regional or sectoral groupings as global organisation.

- *Globality* – the capitalist financial system, world population and health trends, air transport, water resources, forests and climate change present global issues. But "global" here has two distinct senses: belonging to the planet (e.g. climate change) and an aspect of a totality (e.g. capital markets). Responses to these issues are always "local", hence "glocalisation" (Robertson, 1992). They have to be situated somewhere, even if that means a website.

- *Delinkage (or decoupling)* – we no longer expect the big life-spheres of culture, economy, environment, nation and society to coalesce around the state, or to coincide in their boundaries with each other. They float free and collide in unpredictable ways. Thus people and products travel far from their origin, and correspondingly, in any one place, we can find wild

153

cultural juxtapositions, e.g. McDonald's in Beijing, sushi bars in New York. These are the "disjunctures" of our time (Appadurai, 1996).

The complex cultural interweavings of the new knowledge economy and society produce new configurations, recombinations of elements from the delinked spheres. Environmentalism, Islamic fundamentalist states, e-commerce, the European Union, rock concerts, derivatives trading, Silicon Valley and Scientology are new phenomena dependent on globalised conditions. None of them existed a hundred years ago. In an earlier period these novelties might have been represented as "modern progress". The implausibility of this claim for so much of what is new today is sufficient to prompt us to think of our time as postmodern.

Globalisations of many kinds have played an important part in the transformation that took us into the Global Age. They include human rights and technology, education and religion, laws and markets. These varied globalisations work neither in unison, nor toward a preordained goal. In each case contradictory tendencies claim our attention and allegiance. Similarly with society, for the "social diversity" transformation only conveys part of the story. From the point of view of governance, however, it is the key issue.

The author argues that it is the contemporary challenge to the nation state that accounts for the bundling of these three distinct concepts into one. When we take account of the various, even contradictory, meanings of interdependence, globality and delinkage, we begin to make sense of a situation where the state has become more powerful, sovereignty is ever more restricted, and the nation and governance go their separate ways. This is the absorption of the nation state into the global polity of territorial states. The globe then also takes on a symbolic importance as an alternative focus for loyalty. In globalisms of all kinds, the globe supplants the national flag as the totem.

Transformation, then, is not a matter of extrapolating separate trends. It happens when previous directions are reversed, come into conflict with each other, or are subject to transvaluations in experience and language. Transformation is peaceful revolution, which is why we apply the idea to the events of the early 90s in Eastern Europe and the Soviet Union. The earlier "Great Transformation", of which Karl Polanyi (1944) spoke mid-century, entailed the nation state's assumption of control over society. In our time new agencies in society vie with each other for control of a transformed state. They seek to assert a role in governance that stops at nothing short of global reach.

4. Society as social diversity

Just as economists are having difficulties in locating the new economy in a new paradigm, so sociologists have problems in recodifying their conceptual frameworks for a new age. In both fields, the problems arise in part from the need to move from the national to the global as the frame of reference. One people's diaspora is another country's diversity. Either way we are talking global social relations.

Diversity is not new.[3] Amartya Sen (1992) sees the inherent diversity of human beings in society as the premise for our interest in equality. It is also the normal condition of society – differentiation of people by gender, age, origin, language, religion, occupation, economic position and so on. They are the face sheet data of surveys and the records that the national census collects. They are also attributes of individuals as registered by the wider society, and are often referred to as identities.

Diversity and difference in society mean more than just differences between individuals. The reference is to shared life-chances or fates with some, and separateness from others. In this respect differences assigned at birth of nationality, gender, religion or race have enduring consequences for both individuals and social differentiation. In American usage social diversity often is synonymous with ethnic group membership (Hero, 1998), but its generalisation to all kinds of social differentiation is widely accepted (Anderson, 1996).

The social recognition of difference confers some similarity in life-chances on those who share an identity. For all kinds of purposes, governments, corporations and individuals make collective reference to people who share identities. Minority is a frequently used collective term for them. But this is a leftover from a time when society appeared as a national structure divided on class lines, with minorities outside the mainstream. Women, motorists, gun-owners, internet users, black people, the British, and scientists are hardly minorities in that sense, and all can be "identities".

Moreover, identities today are potentially viable sites of collective sentiment that can be mobilised to political ends, exactly as class could be once. If the social question for governing elites in 1900 was the containment of working class solidarity, the key issue for governance today is the reproduction of social order under conditions of multiple conflicting identities. This calls for both different social technologies and different kinds of sociological analysis.

Once it is accepted that identities are potential sites for solidarity, the national society no longer provides the exclusive frame for political mobilisation. Community may also attach not merely to residence in a local area but also to occupations, believers, sexual orientations and lifestyles. None of these are inherently confined by territorial boundaries to national societies. For identities, the nation state is the local service provider; society is global.

There are other configurations of social relations characteristic of the Global Age. The nation state society is a set of cultural, economic, political and technological relations between people, loosely but effectively expressed as a "country". The very loose nature of this bundle draws attention to other bundles of the same factors of differing strengths and histories – households, schools, factories, cities, regions. Under global conditions they acquire a new autonomy. Thus, regions like Silicon Valley acquire a global identity as economic "hot spots", cities like New York become global in their economic functions (Sassen 1991). Adapting Bruno Latour's (1993) suggestion, we can call these collectivities. Their internal relations are local, their external are global. For the state, they represent the real world.

We understand from our experience of nation states that people are not confined in their social relations by the boundaries of collectivities. Indeed people bond collectivities together through their ties across boundaries, enmeshing the globe with their networks. The idea of the social network achieved prominence first in anthropological studies of kin relations, then in studies of influence and markets. Now the internet is the technological apotheosis of the power of networks.

Manuel Castells (1996) sees networks as the defining feature of contemporary society. They, together with collectivities and identities, are intrinsic to human society anywhere, but now have to be in the foreground of any analysis that tries to capture the special character of global society today. All three depend in different ways on a still more elementary unit of analysis, the social relation.

Instead of viewing identities as the contemporary clash of individual and society, we can see them as potential social relations, power in the context of governance. Whites, women, blacks, men, gays, Hispanics, Arabs, seniors, teenagers, migrants and bureaucrats are identities in contemporary discourse that may mobilise for self-determined ends. They may be the bases for collective agency and as such work through, or in tension with, established social institutions.

In recent years, law, economics, political science and international relations are disciplines that have accorded institutions renewed close consideration. In sociology, Anthony Giddens (1984) sees them as central for explaining the reproduction of society. Institutions are widespread, sanctioned social practices. In the context of the governance of social diversity, institutions appear in the guise of the state, including law, marriage, property, and as its protectorates. The market cannot exist without the state. The state is the institution that regulates institutions, yet they possess no inherent centre, not even government itself. They are the shape and organisation of practices. The subjects of those practices are agencies, like governments, corporations, voluntary associations and citizens.

The term "institution" has also been used confusingly to refer to great sectors of national life, such as the economy, education, culture, religion, or politics. These were all once considered necessary for a nation state, equated with a functioning society. In a post-Cold War period, we can recognise that these are, above all, spheres of life for individuals, where they join with others in exercising their creative capacities. The nation is neither central to nor the core condition for these.

Agencies, collective and individual, despite their recognition and incorporation through the legal institutions of the nation state, may achieve most when they cross its boundaries. Human capacities, like human rights, are not intrinsically national, either in origin or scope. One of the major challenges for governance in the coming period is the development of institutions that match those capacities. This means reshaping the state.

5. Updating the state concept

Despite global transformation, the prevailing concept of the state remains one forged in the furnace of nation state rivalry at the beginning of the last century. Max Weber (1921) found the modern state to be organised around the monopoly of the legitimate use of force in a defined territory. This was the sociological rendering of the claim to sovereignty by the nation state. It is time to update it to contemporary global conditions.

Even in his own time, Weber's formulation strained at the reality. It did not allow, for instance, for the many ways in which force remained and still remains open as a legitimate resort in families, workplaces and public spaces. Today force has retreated in public life in most OECD countries, but if we then look to the organisation of collective force, the military, we find that it has marched forward to the international alliance, from which national armies are hard to extricate. Collective security means precisely that the guarantee of world order is transnational.

What nation states have in common are their juridical existence, and the sovereign rights they accord each other through mutual recognition. It is this mutuality, however, which gives rise to a global discourse of governance and the development of institutions in an interconnected global polity. For some, this points to the realisation of the dream of world government.

We should, however, be ultra-cautious here, because this global framework of international institutions, including the United Nations, is as much a contingent outcome of historical circumstances as any other. It is not the perfection of rationality, and in contests between it and nation states, the only court of appeal is world opinion. It does, nonetheless, point to increasing practical limits on sovereignty accompanying economic and technological interdependence. This is the much-trumpeted "decline of the nation state", which is really only a decline of the national content of the state.

The state as such is an abstraction, the concrete shape of which we will forge afresh as circumstances require. The state, in the general and abstract, is the successful enforcement of public goods. This definition allows for multiple agencies of enforcement, diverse goods and different kinds of coercion. Nation states – or better, territorial states – are still the most important concrete instances of the state, and their governments are its most important representatives. However, in the contemporary world, there are other agencies to partner governments in securing public goods. Citizens, voluntary organisations and corporations are transforming the state's interface with society, reshaping the old public-private divide.

Those agencies also work to limit positivist, power-based justifications of nation state sovereignty. They often invoke international law and conventions, especially in human rights and commerce, against national governments. Justice and power may then be locked in conflict. Both sides can claim victories, but in the contemporary world they are pyrrhic. Thus, governments claim they retain their sovereignty when they incorporate international conventions into their state law, but they then concede the effectiveness of extraterritorial jurisdiction. International agencies produce new binding accords and legal judgements, but then they have to rely on national agencies to enforce them.

These tensions between local force and universal principles are drivers of institutional change. When territorial states are durably – often, in effect, indissolubly – bonded in a wider system, the nation as a factor in public policy has to give way to a wider rationality. Governments can then buck neither markets nor laws. The fact that they signed up to the broader agreements in the first place only highlights their loss of sovereignty. Global federalism is an incipient, if very incomplete, fact.

There are only slight prospects for a global government, but that should not cloud our understanding of the growth of a global state or polity. Governments are agents for states, but there is no inherent necessity for a single central agent for each state. The territorial state has many agents: local governments, public corporations, police forces, schools and museums. The global state has similar affiliates, including a central agency, the United Nations. But, as Wolfgang Reinecke (1998) says, this is "governing without government". Federal systems are complex layers of subsidiarity and autonomy, and arise in many forms. The growing interdependence of territorial states is itself producing a complex global federation, in which regional alliances are subsidiary instances. In this global transformation of the state, government becomes governance.

6. From government to governance

Under conditions of social diversity, rethinking society and updating state organisation constitute the central strategic task of governance. This is what earlier was called the continuing renewal that social diversity requires of governance. For responsible agents in this process, the two broad areas of concern are how appropriate collective agencies are best organised and what contribution citizenship makes.

These are considered here in discussing new organising of the public-private divide and performative citizenship. The section following will consider the challenge of social diversity where governance has yet to find an adequate response.

Bridging the public-private divide

It is safe to say that in the modern period there has been no task too sublime or too trivial to be brought, at some time, into the public sphere and backed by the state. Religion in England; reproduction in Nazi Germany; space exploration in the United States; language in France – these have nothing in common except enforcement by the state.

Conversely, any task that the state has assumed historically has at some time been in private hands – except that, by definition, "private" enforcement of goods makes a claim to share in statehood. With that proviso, no tasks are essentially public or private, and different traditions and circumstances, rather than alternative rationalities, explain why the share of state expenditure in the gross domestic product of national economies varies between the 35% of the United States and the 60% of Sweden.

Questions of the balance and extent of state activities have to be seen in context, against particular historical experiences. Privatisation also, therefore, proceeds relative to prevailing conditions. What has been different in the 1980s and 90s has been the extent to which criteria of economic efficiency have prevailed over considerations of social justice in tipping the balance towards divesting tasks. Economic competition between nation states has for instance led to a retreat from direct involvement in production where that has proven less efficient. The international economy provides criteria for the efficiency of state expenditure. It also sets limits on raising revenue. Electoral success in a democratic state is the bottom line for decisions on taxes and benefits, but with open borders, states cannot get out of line with their competitors for fear of erosion of revenues and increasing burdens on those who pay taxes.

It was the relation between taxes, state expenditure and the comparative wealth of nations that was the central concern of the founder of modern economics, Adam Smith. His *Wealth of Nations* (1776) set the terms of subsequent debate on the division between the public and private. For him, the duties of sovereign states were limited to the provision of defence, internal justice, and the maintenance of public works and institutions, especially those for commerce and education.

However, by the late modern era, when T.H. Marshall (1964) contributed the classic statement of social citizenship, the nation state was expected also to secure the productive base of society and the lifelong economic security of its citizens. The welfare state repaired the class cleavage that had preoccupied the ruling élites of nation states by extending public ownership to the means of production and making public provision for private well-being.

These extensions of the activities of the state involved a parallel organisational development. The other side to the social citizenship that Marshall advocated was the rise of bureaucratic organisation in both the corporation and the state. It was the massive scale of the new national projects, bringing the same organisational principles into play in business and government, that obscured Smith's public-private divide. The collective organisation of society appeared increasingly to fulfil Max Weber's dire predictions of a comprehensive bureaucratic cage encasing human experience.

The increased scale of organisation accompanying the extension of the activities of the state raised issues of control that challenged representative democracy. The paradox of modern development was that the public sphere was now the area out of control. The incongruity was even greater because the operations of the business corporations were increasingly subject to public scrutiny. It was a matter of public concern that their collective organisation should be transparent. What was now public was the whole area of collective organisation, however owned, and the private reverted to the individual and personal. The fall of public man (Sennett, 1977) thus coincided with the rise of the corporate state.

From this point of view the involvement of the business sector in contemporary governance is only the latest phase of a long-standing engagement, noticed more than incidentally by Marx, and not the product of late 20th century neo-liberalism. The business sector has always been hybrid, public and private, and since the invention of the public incorporated company, intimate with the state. The idea of corporate governance has centred on issues like directors' responsibilities to shareholders and to other stakeholders, voting, and rules for accounts and auditing – and these are public concerns. It is their organisational intimacy that has given business the opening to push the state towards the new governance.

The exponents of reinventing government now ask not for more or less government, but for "better governance" (Osborne and Gaebler, 1993, p. 24). Its missionaries are (significantly) professionals, consultants and journalists, rather than professors or philosophers. This in itself challenges assumptions of an earlier period when government was synonymous with bureaucracy, hierarchical organisation, central direction, regulations, paper records and career advancement by seniority. But in these respects the large corporation was not dissimilar. There are fewer reasons all the time to regard state organisation as different from the corporation. Corporations and nation states scan the environment, identify threats, frame policy, set direction and strengthen their capabilities.

Both state and nonstate organisations have shared in a general transformation in which hierarchy has become flatter, authority less authoritarian, and participation more flexible. To this extent, we can call contemporary organising postmodern (Bergquist, 1993; Albrow, 1997). The development of governance rides on the back of the reinvention of the corporation, not as the bureaucratic monolith envisaged in the 1950s, but as self-monitoring, repositioning capital investment possibilities around technology and human resources. Organisational structure ceases to be a given and becomes merely a contingent element in the pursuit of profit.

There is no single factor underlying this broad transformation of work, organisation and society. The obvious changes are strategic, political and economic. An important result of changes in warfare is that it relies less on mass conscription. The chief interface of society and the military is through science and not discipline. As we saw above, political aims now demand less central mobilisation for national projects. Finally, the informatisation of production and the rise of new service occupations place a premium on flows of knowledge rather than commands.

Overall, then, the shift from government to governance involves decentring, flexibility, professionalisation, and forms of authority that rely on reputation and demonstrated competence rather than coercive control. Leadership is achieved through exemplary performance and encouragement of others. At the same time information flows laterally, not only within government and within corporations and associations, but across their boundaries. The lattice is the frame for organising in society as a whole. There is an affinity between diversity in society and the new delivery of governance. Diversity prompts the recognition of alternatives and the quest for alternatives is the imperative of efficiency-led market solutions.

The course of computerisation runs parallel to changes in organising. Initially seen as the obvious way to build databanks and enhance central control, the computer now enhances access to information by citizens, and permits interactive communication of messages and data within and across different agencies. At the same time, the matching for so many purposes of personal identification numbers (PINs) from passports, identity cards, credit cards, bank accounts and driving licences, and their potential consolidation in the smart card, permits unprecedented intrusions on privacy. The knowledge economy knows its consumers as well as its factors of production, outputs, and returns on capital. But, it is precisely the diversity of consumer identities that makes the knowledge so valuable and as important to governance as it is to the corporation.

This shared flexibility of state and corporation has been matched by changes in career structures. Those with professional and business expertise can move in and out of government, corporations and associations. The status of a public official carries less esteem in its own right and is less likely to be a career for life. The new technology has itself transgressed old occupational boundaries, created new job descriptions and required flexibility on the part of both employers and employees. The new flexibility extends to the agencies as well as the methods of delivery. The shift in the basis of state control from coercion to knowledge makes boundaries permeable and empowers agents. Coercion divides, knowledge penetrates. Moreover, the state's encouragement of citizens to take responsibility precisely co-opts them into performing state functions.

The idea of responsibility is at the heart of governance. It is the counterpart of the new authority, depending on leadership legitimated through example, not dictat (Sennett 1980, Albrow, 1997). This authority cannot be narrowly circumscribed, and it relies on public acceptance in the sense of what is in the open. Secret authority is an oxymoron. This broader sense of "public" always challenges narrow definitions of the state. It brings the delivery of public goods into the public domain.

The reinvention of government, impelled by ideas of public choice and resistance to higher taxation, has led the state, like business, to adopt performance measures, management by objectives and strategic planning. Value for money becomes as much an operational requirement for government as profit for the business enterprise.

But the core difference remains between a corporation, with its duty to earn profits for its owners, and a state agency, with its duty to spend public money wisely and efficiently. Their collaboration is advertised as an example of new flexibility. But flexibility in organisation can mean exactly flouting open and recognised institutional procedures. The capabilities which make it easy to switch jobs between corporate and state sectors can result in opaque arrangements that challenge both democratic accountability and corporate governance: "lockbox" government (Roberts, 2000).

The increasing exchange of jobs between state and business sectors, led by the technical similarity of the work, can easily lead to the conversion of knowledge at work into the professional secret, offering possibilities of personal gain way beyond regular salary. This is more than managerialism or technocracy. "Knowledge plutocracy" comes closer to the reality.

The new affinities between employment in government and business put an even greater premium on institutions to regulate both, to serve the people as a whole and not privileged strata in society.

Performative citizenship

In combating the appropriation of governance by its professional practitioners, citizenship becomes the critical agent and raises the question of ownership. Hindy Schachter (1997) recalls a time in the United States (1907-14) when "efficient citizenship" was the watchword for administrative reform. She has argued effectively that the reinventing of government needs a new metaphor for citizenship, owner rather than customer. That takes us into the issue of the relation of institutions to governance.

Only the general public can own institutions; that is, they cannot be owned by anyone in particular. Agencies can never own them. So, no one can own the institution of property, if anything is to be called property. It does not belong to a faction, or to the lawyers – not even to individual citizens. Tangible and intangible goods can be property, not institutions. The citizen owner, therefore, is only an agent for the public interest and ever alert to the misuse of public property. At the same time, instititutions are upheld only through the practices of people who observe them. The state itself, however much it depends on enforcement, relies for its existence on people performing their duty towards it, either as its direct agents, or as voters, taxpayers or simply law-abiding citizens.

The campaigning citizen asserts citizen rights in a positive sense for the collective interest. The consuming citizen gets a bad press. Yet, the heritage of the nation state is the expectation held by its educated citizenry that the state is to provide the institutional infrastructure of daily life, and citizens are no longer required to participate in great national projects. Citizens, as consumers, use the social infrastructure the state provides as the space in which they can choose culture, religion, entertainment, sport, travel, lifestyle. They rely on the state management of labour markets, education and housing. Their demands fill the discourse of the state and justify its operations.

They have, moreover, not been idle in filling the space vacated by national projects to pursue new public missions for playgrounds, to save the rain forests, against apartheid, for or against gun control. They act as responsible agents, engaging in discursive democracy (Dryzeck, 1990). As such, they look beyond the country's boundaries to global causes, to human rights, peace, children and the environment. There has never been such a widespread sense of public responsibility in the service of what Ronald Inglehart (1990) has called our post-materialist values. When national leaders plead for even more responsibility, they tend to forget that citizens deem the public sphere to be transnational.

Invoking responsibility in the abstract enlists citizens to do their duty towards the causes to which they feel obligation. It does not necessarily encourage patriotism. At the same time, it vests the state in the individual. One of the most important themes in Western political thought has been to deconstruct the state as leviathan and to conceive of its existence in individual practices like voting and paying taxes. If these practices fall into abeyance then the state falls with them. The responsible citizen then performs the state. Rights of free association when exercised are also responsible performances of the state, enforcements of public goods, even if only as public demonstrations. In this sense too, on the streets of Seattle as well as in the deliberations of the WTO, the global state is at work.

Where citizens join in associations for mutual benefit or form campaigning organisations for public goods, we find common reference to Daniel Bell's (1973) "third sector", or (since the 1980s) "civil society". Neither formulation is adequate to the full potential of citizen organisation. The new citizenship continually generates alternative visions of society because it expresses social diversity. This is not a "third sector", but the foundation of any and every sector. It is "civil society" not in the attenuated version of the 1990s, but as it was in the 1770s – namely, the peaceful assertion of civilised political values.

In the past, both government and business have been able to reject citizen engagement on the grounds of its lack of professionalism and organisational capacity.[4] In the new knowledge society, citizens put their professional knowledge to use in the public service, on the street or the net. They can mobilise an identity as easily as a corporation markets a brand. On the street, they perform their identities for a global media audience. The "performativity" of identity politics (Nealon, 1998) and performance indicators for public corporations then inhabit the same world. They stem from the same transformations of the state and society where public responsibility flows through governments, corporations and citizens alike.

7. Countries, the globe and public policy

In a basic sense, governance is the positive acceptance of diversity by the state – pluralistic forms of organising, multiple lifestyle choices, flexible work patterns, free markets. It is therefore tempting to represent it simply as a straightforward and necessary adaptation to a changing world. In fact, it is not as easy as that. There may be an affinity between the flexible economy and social diversity, but the new technology and the politics of identity have different points of origin and do not necessarily work in unison.

From the outside, diversity is flux; on the inside, it is struggle. Social diversity results from mobilised differences, voices of identities once mute, or new voices altogether. Diversity is not assimilation into a pre-existing social order, but a state of society where order is constantly renegotiated. In the conditions of identity politics, governance involves balancing the claims of one group against another, in terms of their respective contributions to the economy as well as their social rights. The rights of women will be weighed differently whether they are considered as consumers, producers or voters, and then they have to be put on the scales with those of men, seniors, employers, immigrants, and so on. The budgetary process becomes the fine-tuning of diversity.

Governance is successful ongoing renegotiation – but what if it does not succeed? Unsuccessful governance arises from the failure to negotiate identities, in large part by clinging to old models and failing to adapt to new global conditions. Very often, failed governance is diagnosed as the terminal decline of the nation state in the face of globalisation. Rather, the nation state has been transformed into an agency in the global institutional frame. It is now simply the "country".

In the past two decades there has been yet another reworking of the public-private divide, also enmeshed in a new world-frame, namely the globe. The great life-spheres have been decoupled from the nation state. Networks extend beyond boundaries, institutions have become transnational, agencies other than government deliver public goods. In this context, direction of countries is under constant internal and external review. Far-sighted leadership has understood that successful governance arises from repositioning countries in relation to the globe. The country, not "the nation state", becomes an agency in the global institutional frame.

Cleavage and social exclusion

It will help our considerations to recall here an older account of the integration of nation state society. It held that social order depended on an established social division of labour and hierarchy of occupational status. Society could be plural, heterogeneous in terms of religion, ethnicity or language, but it was still integrated by consensus on core values. The American dream, with the assimilation of immigrants in the melting pot, was the archetypical case.

On this account, the European nation state, though threatened by class division, contained conflict through its institutionalisation. German *Mitbestimmung*, co-determination between the social partners, was the prime example. In their different federal ways, the United States and the Bonn republic were quintessential examples of the nation state, creations of modernity. If there was a threat to their existence, it was of outside origin. Within, order reigned.

However, there were discrepancies for this account, like the civil rights movement in the United States, or the Turkish *Gastarbeiter* in the Federal Republic of Germany. By the 1970s, those kinds of issues were prompting a widespread reappraisal in social theory, and diversity began to be registered. The old account was not, however, finished. Two concepts arose to reinvigorate it, cleavage and social exclusion.

Cleavage refers to the consolidation of shared profiles of social characteristics, thus dividing one group of people from another. Cleavage can turn into a threat to social order. Thus, the divide between owners of capital and property-less workers extended into every life-sphere, and through every collectivity. The welfare state, the New Deal, the Great Society were all responses to that threat. All involved the management of society to greater national ends, the enlistment of citizens in return for broadly conceived rights of security, welfare, education and health.

Cleavage overrides some differences by creating a bigger one. Thus, class often suppressed differences of ethnicity, religion and language, but they reemerged as the modern nation state resolved the problem of its internal class divide (Parkin, 1979). Cleavages involving the Québecois in Canada, the Northern Ireland conflict, the language divide in Belgium were examples.

The cleavages just mentioned either arise out of social processes long predating the nation state, that the latter seeks to suppress or contain, or originate in the economic division of labour. There is a variant, however, which is generated by the process of social integration itself. As Emile Durkheim (1893) pointed out, community-building around common norms has a necessary counterpart in deviance, which might or might not be criminalised. In industrial society, unemployment itself drops people outside class, into what has been called an underclass. The local clustering of factors like unemployment, drug abuse, domestic and street violence, bad housing, educational failure and conflicts with neighbours creates "no-go" areas in cities.

For national governments, the consolidation of these factors presents both an economic problem as a drain on resources and loss of productive potential, and a political problem as demands increase to restore law and order. These phenomena certainly testify to a failure to deliver state aims, such as universal literacy or full employment. However, the roots of that failure are to be found in integrationist aims, which generate social exclusion, as in any technical defect.

Ethnic cleavage and social exclusion constitute a challenge to contemporary governance when there is a failure to acknowledge the inherent limits of nation state citizenship. These are the formal limits, which in their nature create the non-citizen, and the substantive limits, where, in confronting global economic forces, the nation state fails to deliver the expectations it has raised among its citizens.

National citizenship is, after law itself, still the key institution in contemporary governance. It is also unable to deliver solutions to problems arising from its exclusionary nature. While its obligations are usually couched in universal terms, citizenship is still normally limited to the nationals of a single country. The nation state made entitlements to benefits of all kinds the keynote feature of citizenship: access to health, education, and security in old age, as well as rights to political participation.

Marshall (1964, p. 116) insisted this was social citizenship, not simply political, but confined it to a "population united in a single civilization" and thus neglected the problems of internal ethnic division or relations with foreign residents. To the present, concern for social exclusion as lack of social integration assumes this notion of citizenship (Berghman, 1995, p. 19). Social rights are blind to the cleavages generated by citizenship itself. The most important cleavage in world society is the one constituted by the modern nation state, that ubiquitous transnational institution, diverse in itself and dividing ethnicities, religions and languages one from another.

Stemming the mobility of people and ideas across boundaries is hardly a possibility in our networked interdependent cyberworld. Within countries, the provision and securing of the social infrastructure is a preoccupation for governance. Under global conditions, it has to respond to demands from citizens to have full access to the rest of the world, and to the needs of foreigners, be they immigrants, workers, tourists, or visitors. Today integration for a country can only be achieved in a global frame.

As David Lockwood (1992) has pointed out, the classic contributors to the sociological approach to social integration, Marx and Durkheim – both in their very different ways – saw capitalist development as disruptive of social order, not because it brought division but because it unsettled the ordering of old divisions. Societies have long accommodated fundamental divisions without collapse – India is the most cited example in this respect. The point is that capitalist development undermines older configurations of inequality, especially status orders and established privileges of all kinds.

Neither of their solutions to the new disorder, Marx's collective ownership or Durkheim's new bonds of solidarity, envisaged global society with economic growth as a central value and the ongoing reconstitution of society as the permanent problem of governance. These aspects of our globalised world are a fundamental departure from the assumptions of the nation state social order. A long-established distinction in sociological theory can help here to illuminate the nature of the departure.

"Social integration" refers to bonds between people, "system integration" to the linkage between institutions. It was a feature of the integrationist theory of the nation state that it deemed its core institutions to be limited to its nationals, thereby creating its social integration. Today the bonds between people are sited in identities, collectivities and networks, societies all, non-national and transnational, of greater and lesser size. Institutions are the practices that allow people to move in and between these societies.

While the International Institute for Labour Studies (1996) reports that institutions, including both citizenship and markets, can be exclusionary, it treats them as belonging to the nation state and fails to draw the inference that both need to be open. Indeed, it reports a tension between "globalization and democracy, in that increasing economic interdependence may undermine national efforts to institute citizenship rights" (p. 24). Increasing citizen rights precisely opens up a greater divide between citizens and noncitizens. It is the issue of human rights that is key.

Both cleavage and social exclusion are concepts that identify problems in nation state society as failures of governance, or, expressed another way, as an excess of diversity which threatens integration. In the terms of an older political jargon, they prompt reactionary measures when the response is to seek a return to the *status quo ante*. For a progressive account we need to acknowledge that governance is not intrinsically national: it is non-national and transnational too. Diversity has its roots beyond and outside the nation state, and solutions to what are defined as cleavage and social exclusion will have to be sought both across country boundaries and at local level.

The challenge to countries

One of the most frequently encountered assertions about the impact of globalisation is that it restricts the range of policy options open to nation states and that they are all bound to converge on the same model. We used to hear the same thing in the 1960s about industrialism and the convergence of socialism and capitalism. In fact, every country had its own model. The United States relied more on safety nets and welfare capitalism, the Federal Republic of Germany on constitutionally guaranteed corporate welfare, the United Kingdom on a central state insurance system. The Soviet Union, with its state-controlled welfare, collapsed.

Certainly there were common features. In the Western democracies, the best distribution of an individual's well-being over a lifetime became a matter of a cost/benefit calculation for both the individual and the state. Pensioners, the unemployed, the disabled, families with children became the identities of a new social diversity, entitlement classes.

Determining the exact mix to give the best outcome for economic stability, growth and social justice is now central routine political issue in social democratic states. In market economies, social rights are resourced through taxation, and one person's welfare is another's expense. The management of the economy and the distribution of social benefits are, therefore, intimately interrelated in the political process.

Now at the beginning of the Global Age, national governments in their promises of prosperity and welfare to citizens neither can restrict their freedom to move abroad, nor can sensibly exclude foreigner workers and tourists. They have to accept foreign ownership of national brands. They face immigrant claims to welfare benefits. Even as the call goes out to become involved as responsible citizens, nationals invest their capital overseas. While proclaiming national independence, governments submit to external jurisdictions on trade and human rights. In the global economy the institutional prerequisites for social order under conditions of social diversity become a transnational concern.

This epoch is as self-contradictory as any other. An educated citizenry in a national system is empowered to follow non-national lifestyles of their choice. States have achieved recognition of their nationhood at the expense of losing command over their culture. Governments have acquired a deeper understanding of their economies even as – indeed, economists would say because – the economy has become more independent of the state. The forms of state intervention in society become ever more sophisticated, while the forces which direct society increasingly are beyond state control.

These are the paradoxes of the knowledge economy that is also the risk society (Beck, 1992). Increases in knowledge are not scoops from a diminishing pot of ignorance. Our knowledge *of* the economy *in* a knowledge economy is restricted to the calculation of the effects of small interventions. We don't know when the business cycle is going to peak, which countries will succeed, where the next hot spot will occur.

Even more important is the collective understanding that increased attempts at control do not deliver the desired results. It is this salutary recognition that gives us governance through the partnership of citizen participation and professional intervention. Responsibility requires judgement in situations of uncertainty, and governance devolves that responsibility onto a diversity of agencies and agents. We may not know when the next recession will come, but officials, lobbying groups and lone mothers can all have special knowledge of the impact of a tax concession for child care. They all, in their respective ways, have their responsibilities.

What is continually underestimated under these conditions is the range of choices open to governments in the provision of social infrastructure. Even with fiscal stability, balanced budgets and low inflation, a formidable array of policy instruments is available to government: coercion, mass media, legislation, conventions, currencies, licences, standards, interest rates, public employment, taxation, and expenditure on health, education, environment and social security. Even as governments cease to direct society, the instruments for fine-tuning become more refined.

As far as policy sectors are concerned, the new organising facilitates cross-departmental approaches to diverse identities. In the United Kingdom, for instance, "joined-up government" "mainstreams" policy for lone mothers as well as setting up special units close to the centre, like the Social Exclusion Unit.[5] Since taxation is at the interface between society, economy and government, the economics ministry – the Treasury – collaborating closely with such new units and departments, becomes the fine-tuning workshop for the management of contemporary social diversity.

The rhetoric of a general reduction of taxation and level of state expenditure is usually a red herring for the new governance. What is important for the governance of diversity is that governments, over the economic cycle, use balanced budgets in any redistribution of both benefits and burdens. Any measure then has at least a double effect: what is given to one side is taken from another.

When it comes to ethnic diversity and the position of women, management of the economy through interventions in the labour market is equally social policy. It becomes a pragmatic matter whether it is better to encourage good practice with employment legislation, mount affirmative action programmes, or let market forces work.

Sometimes these are not dilemmas – different forces move in the same direction. Under conditions of full employment, the profit motive can expand job opportunities to disadvantaged groups. In segmented labour markets, the enlightened firm gains an advantage over prejudiced competitors who refuse employment to qualified persons. Governments also have a fiscal motive for reducing ethnic disadvantages in the labour market. Here they have various policy options, like training programmes targeting ethnic groups and setting targets for minority employment in a framework of equality of opportunity legislation.

Within countries, the range of policy alternatives, the uneven geographical incidence of diversities and the variety of agencies involved combine to produce widely differing patterns and outcomes of governance. The differences between the fifty American states are sufficient to suggest that ethnic diversity is a key factor in their politics and policies (Hero, 1998) but also that there is no single model of governance on which they converge. There is a widespread view that pragmatism has supplanted ideology with a kind of centrist uniformity. Nothing could be further from the truth. The escape from the one-dimensional left/right alternative takes political choice into a multidimensional space in which identity politics is just one of inputs. We can expect ever-growing differences between units of any kind, local, regional or national.

If this is the case within a federal national state system with a common political heritage, we can scarcely be surprised to find the same among the countries of the globe. Differences between countries become specific bases for national competitive advantage in the global economy (Porter, 1990). The sheer heterogeneity of nation states defies easy generalisation. If Singapore and the United States, China and Luxembourg are equally sovereign states, it is hardly surprising if national aims diverge and if degrees of internal diversity vary enormously. Even in countries with similar population size, internal diversity can range between the overwhelmingly Japanese speaking people of Japan to Nigeria with approximately 300 languages.

The challenge for the national leaders today is to position their countries to take advantage of social diversity. Ethnic identities provide social relations across boundaries that can bond countries both economically and politically. This means building the inclusive political community that provides for diversity while at the same time differentiating the identity of the country from that of any other. The discourse of responsibility requires most from those who proclaim it from positions of highest responsibility. National leaders now bear responsibility for the image of their country abroad and recognise the global importance of national images. They therefore are bound to defend non-nationals and risk nationalistic backlash from their own electorates. Competition between territorial states today is in the frame of a global cultural economy where images matter more than weaponry. The institutions that matter in this peaceful competition are the ones that build bridges between countries and permit diversity to flourish in all.

Social capital and capital

Frequently, building bridges is made more difficult because the plans resurrect design concepts from an older period. It is difficult to reconcile transnational institutions with old ideas of social integration. But co-operation across boundaries no more standardises identity than company law produces one-size, one-shape firms, or patent law eliminates difference between products. Interests will be infringed to be sure, in particular those that seek to preserve local power and privilege, but countries can differentiate themselves more effectively in an agreed transnational environment. Globalisation and diversification operate in conjunction for business, culture and countries.

One illustration of the persistence of old integrationist thinking, even when the concept is new, is the idea of social capital. It highlights trust in others, positive reciprocity and co-operation. Along with ideas of the "third sector", "community" and "civil society", it has done much to bring society back into consideration as a strategic factor for public policy. It has been promoted in political science (Putnam, 1995), economics (Dasgupta and Serageldin, 2000), and in sociology by rational choice theorists (Coleman, 1990). Notwithstanding this surge of interest, what it leaves out is quite as important as what it includes.

Partha Dasgupta (2000) has pointed out the difficulties in finding accounting prices that could measure social capital. Put another way, trust, though an asset in trade, is not tradable. There is an even profounder disjunction between economic and social capital. Economic capital in the form of fixed assets, buildings, machinery, raw materials or money can be converted by labour into outputs. A money value can attach to each and profits can be calculated. Valuation of the outputs in moral or political terms does not belong to the economic calculation. In Kenneth Arrow's words, "The essence of social networks is that they are built up for reasons other than their economic value to the participants" (2000, p. 4).

Social capital is inherently based on moral considerations and mutual recognition of worth. It involves choosing to associate with some and neglecting, even shunning others. Honour among thieves exists. However, it also exists among police. In a society of police and thieves, does their mutual distrust negate the aggregate of their separate social capitals?

171

In fact, considerations of social capital take us away from the world of economic growth and into questions of ownership, distribution, control, negative reciprocity and conflict. What one misses in the discussions of social capital is precisely the social relations *of* capital, and it is these that frequently are the hidden and sometimes determining factor in governance.

If we take the public-private partnership, for instance, more is involved than linking the profit and public service motives. Beyond that, two different principles of governance are involved: plutocracy and democracy. In the private sector, those who own most have most say. The equal weighting of shareholders and the general public in partnership gives more weight to the few. The shareholders count twice over, as a special interest and as members of the public.

Corporate governance in the Anglo-American mould especially is based on the principle that wealth means power (Dunlavy, 1998). In the world of responsible citizens, corporations and governments in partnership it is wealth, not the ballot, that energises the project. Indeed, without access to wealth it is impossible to gain the highest office in the United States.

Social capital is important for wealth creation certainly. An obvious case is the social capital of the family. The ties of kinship go beyond contract and provide the security, both emotional and in resources and income, that can underpin career support and business start-up. The importance of family ties for economic development was the factor that surprised the West with Asian economic success, and is now being re-evaluated for Western countries. Moreover, this exports. For example, Asian families dominate the small business sector in the United Kingdom, thus showing how social networks challenge integrationist ideas of national community.

The case of Asian business challenges old assumptions in many ways. Traditional family ties are not anti-capitalistic. Indeed, for that very reason they are not confined by national boundaries. The family network becomes a transnational medium for the circulation of capital arising mainly in small corner retail shops. This is only a microcosm of the global movement of capital, culminating in the one and a half trillion dollars a day that changes hands in the foreign exchange markets.

Global financial flows have only remote connections with the money of the Asian family business, but those connections constitute economic capital and its circulation depends on specific social relations. These are what determine whether wealth produces income, income becomes consumption and consumption produces well-being. These are the basis for evaluating the significance of concentrations of wealth where the assets of 225 billionaires equal the annual incomes of half the world's population (OECD, 1997). Those assets can generate income in diverse ways and feed (figuratively and literally) networks of vastly different character. These networks are the basis of the entitlements that translate into welfare and security.

At the same time, networks undermine national attempts to regulate entitlements. Avoiding taxation on capital is the one of the main reasons for family trusts and deposits in the offshore accounts. Paradoxes abound. Tax breaks in America encourage ostentatious displays of philanthropy. Rapacity of rulers in poor countries supports kin or ethnic affiliations. The capacity of governance to respond to its challenges has ample support from social technology and citizen involvement. Undermining it continually are both sudden and stealthy movements of capital. When social capital seeks to protect itself from the risks of mobile economic capital, then economic capital mobilises its strength in the political process. The biggest challenge governance faces is from capital, and the only adequate response is the building of new institutions.

Democratising global institutions

The modern nation state sought to create the impression that institutions were its own creation, products of its own unique constitution. The contemporary world exposes that for the fiction it has always been. Institutions bridge societies as much as constitute them: peace and war are the outcome of relations between peoples, not the property of one or the other; national currencies are worth only what the world market determines. National governance is sustained and limited by its global recognition.

In a knowledge economy, governance equally depends on knowledge, and ignorance of the ownership and transfer of capital is a major source of uncertainty. The transparency of the American political system permits public scrutiny of the influence of capital on building public support, on the legislative process, and on elections. The issue of corruption is correspondingly more exposed, but revelations are less explosive than in the more secretive European regimes.

Since the crises of the East Asian and Russian economies particularly, transparency has become a central concern for governance worldwide, from the workings of the International Monetary Fund downward (Center of Concern, 1998). Thus it is the relative lack of transparency as much as the lack of labour market flexibility that brings the German social partners concept into question today. Globally, the consequences for society of the constitutional arrangements for foreign investment proposed in the draft Multilateral Agreement on Investment have given rise to an internet debate of citizens of the world engaging in discursive democracy (Schneiderman, 1999).

International agencies with global responsibilities like the World Bank or the IMF have relatively little autonomous control over the levers of a global public policy except through and with the approval of the United States. But, one of the consequences of Seattle is to show that movements invoking First Amendment values are able to focus world opinion. The historic positioning of the United States as a new society established on principles of universal rights provides for dynamic interaction around these. In terms of its own commitment to those values, the new doctrine of global intervention in sovereignty on behalf of the human rights of minorities cannot be unilateral.

In some respects the domestic policies of countries are more globalised than policies for the globe. In fact one of the most striking developments in work on social diversity is the lead given to governments by international agencies. The main lines of national policies on equal opportunity derive from conventions countries sign under the auspices of the United Nations and to which they report. Thus British policy towards women reports on the individual articles of the Convention on the Elimination of All Forms of Discrimination against Women and covers the whole range of policy levers down to the policing of domestic violence.

Ethnic division has been treated as the key cleavage in the social diversity of the nation state, but the biggest challenge to governance, overshadowing and destabilising it, is the cleavage between rich and poor countries (Stavenhagen, 1990). The diversities of gender and age are also reflected in and through the overall division between rich and poor countries. In the rich countries the connections between gender equality in the workplace, low rates of reproduction, an increase in dependency ratios, the anomie of young males, demand for immigrant labour and racist attacks are well enough understood. A whole range of problems for governance, including sexual exploitation, AIDS, drug crime, weapon control and environmental protection, are essentially global in scope and reflect that cleavage.

The worldwide implementation of global policies for social diversity is now a possible future. At the same time, there is a dilemma besetting all policies for diversity. It is built into the actual Charter of the United Nations. Whether dealing with social exclusion or apartheid, internal or external to country boundaries, the rights of peoples clash with the rights of individuals. This is a conflict only resolvable on a pragmatic, case-by-case basis. The spirit of toleration and the readiness to defend people's rights by force remain in permanent tension. The task for government in the 21st century is to find the institutional frame for humankind to manage the process without disasters. Within that frame, countries will still remain the main agencies, provided they reshape their own democratic institutions.

One commentator, Nicholas Negroponte (1995) has suggested that cyberspace will make national space irrelevant to governance, and that nothing short of the world will be its frame in the future. But the global frame cannot exclude territorial organisation of some kind.

Democratic institutions within nation states have shown many signs of declining vitality. Institutions only work if people use them. Parliaments dominated by one party, assemblies without power and elections with minimal participation are danger signs. However, these factors may be less important than the growing sense that the big issues are global. There is now a huge democratic deficit in global institutions, which events in Seattle in November last year dramatically illustrated.

The main requirement is to register and listen to the multiple allegiances of the contemporary world. Here, governments need transparency as much as international institutions. They can also work to extend democracy not only to other countries but also to non-governmental agencies, by providing for representative assemblies for ethnicities, by recognising the rights of peoples without states, and by according democratic representation and reciprocal rights to foreigners. The day-to-day governance of diversity requires states to overcome the exclusionary nature of national citizenship, the major obstacle to the revitalisation of democracy (Jordan, 1997).

In the end, residence and local territory will always be a core concern for any system of governance, global, national, or regional. The current decline of democracy also includes the loss of power by people over the area in which they live. But it can be sustained through global co-operation.[6] The new technology can just as easily revitalise locality as it can provide for global governance. Governments have been slow to recognise the potential the new technology affords for closer involvement of both absent citizens and resident noncitizens for the reinvention of democracy.

Here again, however, there are dilemmas. The recent decision to allow electronic voting in the Arizona primary elections rejected the view that it would disadvantage ethnic minorities. The digital divide is certainly a new source of inequality. But electronic elections and regular referenda need in principle be no more difficult to organise online than lotteries, which command widespread support. The governments of the world may have to move quickly if they want to forestall the entrepreneurial intervention that establishes global polling as an alternative source of legitimacy.

8. Conclusion: Rethinking the future

Broadly, for the purpose of this chapter, disaster scenarios have been avoided and governance considered under long-term conditions of worldwide economic growth. This is not Panglossian. It does not preclude recessions or disaster. It makes every sense to measure the Antarctic ice cap, to monitor asteroid orbits, to prevent the terrorist acquisition of biological or nuclear weapons, to destroy the Y2K bug, and to guard against collapse of the global financial system. These are genuine global threats.

But the very global co-operation that they prompt is what highlights the diversity of world society. Globalisation provides no single direction for society. It greatly diversifies the range of considerations for governance. Thinking about
175

governance in the future therefore has to be as much about new thinking as it is about the future. The diversity of human activities precludes us from postulating a single line to the future. The same diversity compels us to join together in facing it.

The availability of differing models of social diversity, both in the historical record and as living practices handed down over the generations, reminds us of the unforeseeable variety of social arrangements that governance worldwide must seek to manage, both within space and as possible futures. Therefore, we should not even assume a cycle, or oscillation around a trend line.

There may well be an argument for saying that the future is going to be more like the past than the present is. But which past and which present? Considering the containment of social diversity, there are quite different models in existence in the United States, Canada, and Europe. That in itself should suggest to us that there is no reason to see, say, India and Brazil as having to tread the same path. The new Chinese "socialist market capitalism" is built as much on age-old Confucian relations as on communism.

Nor need there be continuity. Feudalism, in the sense of economic activity within bonds of dependency, is a recurring phenomenon within capitalist economies. Diversity indeed depends on drawing upon values that transcend time or place. The difficulty is that the contextual experience of any set of values in particular cultures interferes with communication across boundaries. We are stuck in our particular cultural experiences and historical traditions.

The West itself is insular even in its claims to universality. As a result we often cannot share our problems, or we remain tied to formulations that applied in the past but cannot handle the novelty of the present. We therefore continually have to update our language for any general diagnosis of our time and rewrite our history to reflect new understandings. Currently the most important task is to rewrite modernity as the past, not the future.

There are at large two dire contradictory images of the future of society. One sees it as tied to the front of the Juggernaut of globalisation, gathering speed and doomed to crash at some unspecified time in the future. The other sees it as the home of Pandemonium, going nowhere and powerless in the face of forces it cannot control. Both images are of course tied to mythic narratives with their roots in the transformation of modernity and the decline in belief in Progress.

True, there has to be some story to underpin the account of the world we inhabit. Yet it does not have to be either doom-laden or clap-happy. State agencies have as many choices open to them as corporations. No CEO imagines that the future is so predetermined that there are fixed and certain answers to decisions on whether to go global or local, to merge or divest, to downsize or invest. The corporation's very existence will depend on these critical choices. National governments in particular have equally serious options before them.

The OECD Forum for the Future has explored the new "knowledge economy" as the "driver" of change. Broadly the author has no quarrel with the view that the knowledge economy, a complex of factors, is driving contemporary changes. But it destabilises much more than it determines the diversity of society, and it leaves open a vast variety of alternative social and political coping arrangements, not to speak of individual lifestyles.

The choices in governance today extend far beyond nation versus market. In every sector there are equivalently acute dilemmas: the rights of peoples as opposed to those of the individual; freedom for or from monopoly power; freedom of speech or freedom from offensiveness; right to free association or defence of the state. These are issues where we know that the decision can never arise out of purely rational considerations. It is the tacit understanding of the limits of rationality and the importance of society that makes appointments to the Supreme Court of the United States so sensitive. If it were not for the profound importance of diversity in society, the appointment of the first Hispanic judge would go unnoticed.

That illustrates again the general point of this chapter. The old concept of society integrated around the nation state is inadequate for understanding the requirements of the new governance. Social diversity challenges us to understand society as global in order to arrive at a diagnosis of local problems.

Notes

1. The author is grateful to Barrie Stevens and Riel Miller of the OECD Secretariat, to Willemijn Dicke of the University of Nijmegen and to Marian Zulean of the University of Pittsburgh for their comments on earlier versions of this chapter.

2. For examples see Mann (1986, p. 2), Touraine (1998). Somers and Gibson (1994, p. 70) reject "society" for being "falsely totalizing", and prefer "relational setting". The author's view is close to Bauman (1992) who rejects the equation of society with the modern nation state. We can usefully retain the term society for complexes of social relations anywhere, any time.

3. In contemporary political rhetoric diversity refers to social differences between people. It covers two kinds of difference, which rigorous analysis of social structure keeps distinct: heterogeneity, which simply refers to membership of different groups; and inequality, which ranks people by some criterion. In social structural analysis, "diversity" is a statistical concept referring to dispersion of a population on a ranked order of positions (see Blau, 1977).

4. Schachter points out that the Rockefellers killed "efficient citizenship", preferring to deal with professionals rather than with the public (1997, pp. 49-54).

5. "Mainstreaming" itself emerges from the discourse of diversity – see Jahan, 1995.

6. A typical instance of contemporary global networking for local ends is provided by the Jaipur (India) Declaration of the World Mayors' Conference on the New Role of Mayors in a Changing Global Scenario, January 1998. The first resolution is an interesting expression of local governance in global conditions:

    In a changing scenario of globalisation, liberalisation, democratisation and decentralisation, we will strive to make our cities productive, efficient and equitable, with care and concern for all sections of society, especially for the poor, the socially disadvantaged, handicapped, women and children. We will promote goals of "adequate shelter for all", "health for all" and "literacy for all", and make our cities clean, healthy and safe habitats for citizens. (Quoted in Chit Dukhira, 1998.)

    The paradox is reserved for the last word. This statement of aims for the governance of diversity limits itself to citizens. Perhaps it means citizens of the world. Otherwise foreign residents and visitors appear to be excluded.

Bibliography

ALBROW, Martin (1996),
   The Global Age: State and Society Beyond Modernity. Cambridge: Polity.

ALBROW, Martin (1997),
   Do Organizations Have Feelings? London: Routledge

ANDERSON, Mary B., ed. (1996),
   Development and Social Diversity. London: Oxfam.

APPADURAI, Arjun (1996),
   Modernity at Large: Cultural Dimensions of Globalization. Minneapolis: University of Minnesota Press.

ARROW, Kenneth (2000),
   "Observations on Social Capital" in Partha Dasgupta and Ismail Serageldin (eds), *Social Capital: A Multifaceted Perspective*. Washington, DC: The World Bank, pp. 3-5.

BAUMAN, Zygmunt (1992),
   Intimations of Postmodernity. London: Routledge.

BECK, Ulrich (1992),
   Risk Society: Towards a New Modernity. London: Sage.

BELL, Daniel (1973),
   The Coming of Post-Industrial Society: A Venture in Social Forecasting. New York: Basic Books.

BERGHMAN, Jos (1995),
   "Social Exclusion in Europe: Policy Context and Analytical Framework" in Graham Room (ed.), *Beyond the Threshold: The Measurement and Analysis of Social Exclusion*. Bristol: Policy Press, pp. 9-28.

BERGQUIST, William (1993),
   The Postmodern Organization. San Francisco: Jossey Bass.

BLAU, Peter M. (1977),
   Inequality and Heterogeneity: A Primitive Theory of Social Structure. New York: The Free Press.

CALHOUN, Craig, ed. (1994a),
   Social Theory and the Politics of Identity. Cambridge, Mass.: Blackwell.

CALHOUN, Craig (1994b),
   "Social Theory and the Politics of Identity" in Craig Calhoun (ed.), *Social Theory and the Politics of Identity*. Cambridge, Mass.: Blackwell, pp. 9-36.

CASTELLS, Manuel (1996),
   The Rise of the Network Society. Oxford: Blackwell.

CENTER OF CONCERN (1998),
   "IMF Study Group Report: Transparency and Evaluation". Washington, DC: Center of Concern.

COLEMAN, James S. (1990),
   Foundations of Social Theory. Cambridge: Harvard University Press.

DASGUPTA, Partha (2000),
   "Economic Progress and the Idea of Social Capital" in Partha Dasgupta and Ismail Serageldin (eds), *Social Capital: A Multifaceted Perspective*. Washington, DC: The World Bank, pp. 325-424.

DASGUPTA, Partha and Ismail SERAGELDIN, eds. (2000),
   Social Capital: A Multifaceted Perspective. Washington, DC: The World Bank.

DRYZECK, John S. (1990),
   Discursive Democracy: Politics, Policy and Political Science. Cambridge: Cambridge University Press.

DUKHIRA, Chit (1998),
   Local Governance in the Global Village: A Comparative Study of Contemporary Local Government. Mauritius: Cathay Printing.

DUNLAVY, C.A. (1998),
   "Corporate Governance in Late 19th-Century Europe and the U.S.: The Case of Shareholder Voting Rights" in Klaus J. Hopt, Hideki Handa, Mark J. Roe, Eddy Wymeersch and Stefan Prigge (eds), *Comparative Corporate Governance: The State of the Art and Emerging Research*. Oxford: Clarendon, pp. 5-40.

DURKHEIM, Emile (1933) [1893],
   The Division of Labor in Society. Glencoe, Ill.: Free Press.

GIDDENS, Anthony (1984),
   The Constitution of Society. Cambridge: Polity.

HERO, Rodney E. (1998),
   Faces of Inequality: Social Diversity in American Politics. New York: Oxford University Press.

INGLEHART, Ronald (1990),
   Culture Shift in Advanced Industrial Society. Princeton, NJ: Princeton University Press.

INTERNATIONAL INSTITUTE FOR LABOUR STUDIES (1996),
   Social Exclusion and Anti-Poverty Strategies. Geneva: IILS.

JAHAN, Rounaq (1995),
   The Elusive Agenda: Mainstreaming Women in Development. London: Zed Books.

JORDAN, Bill (1997),
   "Citizenship, Association and Immigration: Theoretical Issues" in Maurice Roche and Rik van Berkel (eds), *European Citizenship and Social Exclusion*. Aldershot: Ashgate, pp. 261-272.

LATOUR, Bruno (1993),
  We Have Never Been Modern. Hemel Hempstead: Harvester Wheatsheaf.

LOCKWOOD, David (1992),
  Solidarity and Schism: "*The Problem of Disorder*" *in Durkheimian and Marxist Sociology*. Oxford: Clarendon Press.

MANN, Michael (1986),
  The Sources of Social Power. Volume 1, A *History of Power from the Beginning to* A.D. 1760. Cambridge: Cambridge University Press.

MARSHALL, T.H. (1964),
  Class, Citizenship and Social Development. New York: Doubleday.

MULGAN, Geoff (1998),
  Connexity: Responsibility, Freedom, Business and Power in the New Century. London: Vintage.

NEALON, Jeffrey T. (1998),
  Alterity Politics: Ethics and Performative Subjectivity. Durham: Duke University Press.

NEGROPONTE, Nicholas (1995),
  Being Digital. New York: Knopf.

OECD (1997),
  The World in 2020: Towards a New Global Age. Paris: OECD.

OSBORNE, David and Ted GAEBLER (1993),
  Reinventing Government. New York: Plume.

PARKIN, Frank (1979),
  Marxism and Class Theory: A Bourgeois Critique. London: Tavistock.

POLANYI, Karl (1944),
  The Great Transformation: The Political and Economic Origins of Our Time. New York: Rinehart.

PORTER, Michael E.(1990),
  The Competitive Advantage of Nations. London: Macmillan.

PUTNAM, Robert (1995),
  "Bowling Alone: America's Declining Social Capital", *Journal of Democracy* 6, pp. 65-78.

REINECKE, Wolfgang H. (1998),
  Global Public Policy: Governing without Government? Washington, DC: Brookings.

ROBERTS, Alasdair (2000),
  "What Follows Reinvention? Lockbox Government", *Government Executive*, Vol. 32, No. 5.

ROBERTSON, Roland (1992),
  Globalization. London: Sage.

SASSEN, Saskia (1991),
  The Global City: New York, London, Tokyo. Princeton, NJ: Princeton University Press.

SCHACHTER, Hindy Lauer (1997),
  Reinventing Government or Reinventing Ourselves: The Role of Citizen Owners in Making a Better Government. Albany: State University of New York Press.

SCHNEIDERMAN, David (1999),
"The Constitutional Strictures of the Multilateral Agreement on Investment", *The Good Society*, 9, No. 2, pp. 90-96.

SEN, Amartya (1992),
Inequality Re-examined. Oxford: Oxford University Press.

SENNETT, Richard (1977),
The Fall of Public Man. New York: Knopf.

SENNETT, Richard (1980),
Authority. New York: Knopf.

SMITH, Adam (1776) [1976],
An Inquiry into the Nature and Causes of the Wealth of Nations. R.H. Campbell *et al.*, eds. Oxford: Oxford University Press.

SOMERS, Margaret and Gloria D. GIBSON (1994),
"Narrative and Social Identity" in Craig Calhoun (ed.), *Social Theory and the Politics of Identity*. Oxford: Blackwell, pp. 37-99.

STAVENHAGEN, Rodolfo (1990),
The Ethnic Question: Conflicts: Development and Human Rights. Tokyo: UN University Press.

TOURAINE, Alain (1998),
"Sociology Without Society", *Current Sociology*, 46, No. 2, pp. 119-143.

WEBER, Max (1921) [1978],
Economy and Society, 2 volumes edited by G. Roth and C. Wittich. Berkeley: University of California Press.

Chapter 7

The New Governance, Subsidiarity, and the Strategic State

by
Gilles Paquet
Centre on Governance
University of Ottawa
Canada

"Anchor new solutions in stand-alone principles"
– A.J. MacEachen

Introduction[*]

Many observers have announced the demise of the Westphalian nation state as the dominant system of territorial governance. Supposedly, the erosion of this dominant jurisdiction is ascribable to a nexus of forces: from the pressure emanating from the ever expanding expectations of the citizenry to the weaker capacity to govern of the nation states in the face of greater mobility of the factors of production. The territorial nation state has become, if one accepts this scenario, less congruent with the contemporary realities, and less capable of providing an effective governance system.

It is the author's view that much remains in the existing process of governance that is mediated by the national state context, and by nation state regimes (McCallum, 1995; Nitsch, 2000). While governance capabilities are not necessarily as tightly packaged in national territorial niches as they were in earlier times, the territorial nation still plays a role of echo box through which much must be arbitrated (Paquet, 2000a). However, there has been a rather fundamental transformation of the innards of territorial governance systems in the last decades. New forms of distributed governance

[*] This paper draws significantly on the work done over the past few years at the Centre on Governance. The help of the Fellows of the Centre is gratefully acknowledged although they should be spared any guilt by association for the use I have made of their counsel.

183

arrangements, based on a more diffused pattern of power and on a new valence for various meso-systems, have emerged (Storper, 1996; Elkins, 1995).

These new territorial connections have woven a new pattern of geo-governance that is still without a formal name. Some still insist on "national packaging" as a matter of convenience, but the new realities bear little resemblance to the old Westphalian construct. This new pattern has vested infra-national communities with new powers, has built on new principles of co-operation/competition within and across national boundaries, and has been rooted in new capabilities that are much less state-centred (Paquet, 1999a).

The new dynamic involves more complex mixes of intertwined relations, networks and regimes, and governance capabilities that are more diverse and seemingly more disconnected than was the case in the old nation state-centred governance world. But these new complexities do not change the fact that territory remains a fundamental underpinning of governance systems.

This chapter proceeds in three phases. First it sketches a very simple geo-governance framework based on social learning as the most useful lens through which the current challenges can be examined. Second, it is argued that the only workable governance scheme in this context is bottom-up governance based on a new strategic state capable of effecting major architectural repairs to the existing nation state. The third phase is to examine the ecology of collaborative governance at the source of a more effective governability and a refurbished territorial governance.

1. A primer on geo-governance

"Geo-governance" (i.e. territorially-based governance) refers to ways of achieving effective co-ordination in a world where knowledge and power are distributed. The technology of governance refers to the many ways in which 1) individuals and institutions (public, private and civic) manage their collective affairs, 2) the diverse interests accommodate and resolve their differences, and 3) these many actors and organisations are involved in a continuing process of formal and informal competition, co-operation and learning (Carlsson and Ramphal, 1995).

Throughout the 20th century, geopolitics has attempted to make sense of the complex and at times seemingly chaotic political/economic realities, to define a map of how power is allocated. This map has echoed the dominant power/knowledge infrastructures of the day. It was shaped by imperialism in the early part of the 20th century, by the East-West divide and the Cold War in the period following the Second World War, and by globalisation and the erosion of the powers of the Westphalian nation state in the more recent past. Geopolitics has proposed different faultlines of competition/ co-operation, various linkages between the local/regional and the world as a whole, and different discourses to rationalise them for these different eras.

But, as the compilers of a recent reader in geopolitics boldly state, "geo-politics is not a science", it is "a field of contestation" (Ò Tuathail *et al.*, 1998). It presents very partial images of the geo-governance process, and this has never been more true than after the fall of the Berlin wall. The extensive recent literature on geo-governance continues to define faultlines and interfaces in unduly simplistic ways: Luttwak's pronouncements that economic priorities and modalities are dominant; Luke's insistence that security and political issues continue to dominate the scene; Huntington's suggestion that clashes of civilisation are the defining interfaces (Luttwak, 1990; Luke, 1991; Huntington, 1993).

While each of these arguments has merits, each of these families of forces may at best be said to have completely dominated the scene only episodically. Strict geo-economic, geo-security and geo-civilisational arguments remain, therefore, unpersuasive in accounting for the evolving pattern of geo-governance; they are unduly crippled by overly macroscopic and Manichean (either/or) interpretations that provide none of the nuances necessary to take into account the extraordinary diffraction of the governance structures, or the new vertical (continental/regional/local) division of labour that has ensued on the governance front.

Governance as pattern of power-sharing

A *problématique* that deliberately explores the diverse sites over which the authority has become diffused and draws on a multiplicity of factors (in the economic, political and social spheres) to explain the vertical, horizontal, and transversal diffusion of powers formerly vested in the nation state should prove more promising as a way to explore the geo-governance dynamics of the present world order (Paquet, 1997*a*).

François Perroux (1960) and Kenneth Boulding (1970) have proposed a simple conceptual scheme to map out this terrain. Both identified three generic ensembles of organisations characterised by different mechanisms of integration: *quid pro quo exchange* (market economy), *coercion* (polity), and *solidarity* (community and society). These mechanisms had been explored by economic anthropologist Karl Polanyi (1957) as dominant features in concrete socio-economies of the past. Perroux and Boulding fleshed out the idea and applied it to the modern context.

This approach provides a rough cartography of the organisational terrain into three domains where the rules, arrangements or mechanisms of co-ordination are dominated (more or less) by three different principles: the economic/market domain (B), where supply and demand forces and price mechanism are the norms; the state domain (C), where coercion and redistribution are the rules; and the civil society domain (A), where co-operation, reciprocity and solidarity are the integrating principles. This corresponds roughly to the standard partitioning of human organisations into economy, polity and society. Each of these mechanisms of integration, in its purest form, is located at one of the apexes; all the inner territory represents organisations and institutions embodying different mixes of these integrative mechanisms. A lightly modified version of the resulting triangle is presented in Figure 1.

Figure 1. **The Boulding Triangle**

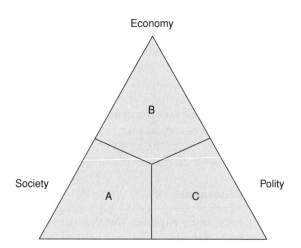

Source: Boulding, 1970.

The three sectors need not have equal weight. A century ago, the state portion was quite limited; the terrain was dominated by the other two sets of organisations. From the late 19th century to the 1970s, government grew in importance to the point where, at the end of the period, probably half of the *measured* activities fell into the general ambit of state and state-related activities. The boundaries have been displaced accordingly over time. More recently, there has been a vigorous counter-movement of privatisation and deregulation that has caused a reduction of the state sector, and a reverse shift of the boundaries (Paquet, 1996-97).

In parallel with these swings giving more valence to one or another of the family of integration mechanisms, there has been a tendency for the new socio-economy to trigger the development of an ever larger number of *mixed* institutions, blending these different mechanisms (market-based public regulation, public-private-civic partnering, etc.). This has translated into a much denser filling in of the Boulding triangle. Mixed institutions have emerged that are capable of providing the basis for co-operation, harmonisation, concertation, and even co-decision mechanisms involving elements from the three sectors (Laurent and Paquet, 1998, Chapter 8). This has entailed a fuzzification of the boundaries between A, B and C, and a new division of labour within and among the three sectors.

Contrary to the thrust that emerged from most of the recent analyses of geo-governance (Luttwak, Luke, Huntington), none of the sectors has had a dominant role in defining the faultlines, or in imposing hegemonic constraints on the others. In reality, the relationships among sectors have been *heterarchical*: it is not a world with a pecking order. Heterarchy introduces *"strange loops"* of authority "under conditions of time and place" very much like the "game of paper, rock, and scissors where paper covers rock, rock crushes scissors, and scissors cut paper" (Ogilvy, 1986-87). Any sector may at times have a dominium over the others: the three sectors co-evolve.

Indeed, the ecological concept of *co-evolution* provides an apt way to synthesise the links among these three universes. Co-evolution in biology refers to an evolutionary process based on reciprocal responses of closely interacting species, as in the co-evolution of the beaks of hummingbirds and the shape of the flowers they feed on. The concept can be generalised to encompass feedback processes among interacting systems (social, economic, political) going through a reciprocal process of change. The process of co-evolution becomes a form of *organisational learning*: joint learning and inter-adjustment of economy, society and state.

The macroscopic analytical schemes in good currency have failed importantly in probing the infra-nation-state realities where much of the co-evolution has occurred. While nation states have been readily aggregated into broad ensembles when it has proved convenient for analytical purposes, there has been a reluctance to acknowledge the growing importance of the new network of city-regions that has redefined the map of the power world. The new texture of infra-national realities is clearly making the whole notion of territoriality much more complex, but this dimension is at the core of the new governance.

Moreover, such schemes have carefully expurgated the subversive content that the notion of governance has acquired as it has become associated with arrangements based on the recognition that knowledge and power are inevitably distributed, that no one is omniscient or omnipotent, that local and nonstate actors are bound to become more important, and that collaboration is the new categorical imperative.

Distributed governance and governability

In times of turbulent change, organisations (micro and macro, economic, political and civic) govern themselves by becoming capable of learning both what their goals are, and the means to reach them *as they proceed*. This is done by tapping the knowledge and information that active citizens possess, and getting them to invent ways out of the predicaments they are in. This leads to a more distributed governance that deprives leaders of their monopoly on the governing of organisations: for the organisation to learn quickly, everyone must take part in the *conversation*, and bring forward each bit of knowledge, wisdom and capabilities they possess that has a bearing on the issue.

Distributed governance does not simply mean a process of dispersion of power toward localised decision making within each sector: it entails a dispersion of power over a wide variety of actors and groups within the Boulding triangle. This diffraction of power has evolved because it triggers more effective learning in a context of rapid change, through decentralised and flexible teams woven by moral contracts and reciprocal obligations negotiated in the context of evolving partnerships (Nohria and Eccles, 1992).

In the transition period from the present nation state-dominated era to the newly emerging era of distributed governance and transversal co-ordination, there has been a tendency 1) for much devolution and decentralisation of decision making (i.e. for the meso-level units in polity, society and economy to become prominent), 2) for the rules of the game of the emergent order to be couched in informal terms, and 3) for the emergent properties of the new order to remain relatively unpredictable as one might expect in a neural-net-type world (Ziman, 1991; Norgaard, 1994; Paquet, 1993, 1995).

The new form of transversal co-ordination now in the making unavoidably generates a loss of central control and a weakening of the national state *imperium*. A different sort of *imperium*, adapted to the network age, is emerging, reminiscent of the Roman empire under Hadrian, where the institutional order was a loose web of agreements to ensure compatibility among open networks (Guéhenno, 1993). We are entering an era where the governance process is becoming a game without a master – and, for many observers, this diffraction of power has raised the spectre of non-governability.

Governability is a measure of the organisation's capability for effective co-ordination within the context of the environment within which it is nested: it corresponds to the organisation's capacity to transform, its capacity to modify its structure, its process, and even its substantive guidance mechanism and orientation (Kooiman, 1993, pp. 259-260). At any time, the gaps between governing needs and capabilities transform the governance pattern. This tends over time to trigger the emergence of a fitful degree of decentralisation and differentiation, to bring forth a variety of partnerships and joint ventures to respond to the challenges posed by knowledge dispersion, motivation and implementation problems, and by the need to correct some of the important side-effects of the existing governance structure.

The central thrusts of this evolving process are *resilience* (the capacity for the economy-polity-society nexus to spring back undamaged from pressure or shock through some slight rearrangements that do not modify the nature of the overall system), and *learning* (the capacity to transform in order to improve present performance through a redefinition of the organisation's objectives, and a modification of behaviour and structures) (Paquet, 1999*b*). Resilience and learning would appear to point in contradictory directions (maintaining coherence versus structural transformation), and they do. They must be balanced, for they are both necessary to underpin sustainability.

The governance system has evolved considerably over the past few decades as a result of the important shocks emanating from both the internal milieu and the external context, and of the need to learn faster (Paquet, 1999*c*); a number of rounds of adaptation have been necessary to provide the requisite flexibility and suppleness of action. The ultimate result of these changes is a composite governance system, built on unreliable control mechanisms in pursuit of ill-defined goals, in a universe that is chronically in a state of flux: this composite governance process has emerged as the result of cumulative efforts to harness complexity that have blended in a new way the different integrative mechanisms within organisations (Axelrod and Cohen, 1999; Paquet, 2000*b*).

Social learning and co-ordination failures

In a learning economy, wealth creation is rooted in the mobilisation of knowledge: learning is harnessing the collective intelligence of the team as a source of continuous improvement. This in turn commands new modes of production of knowledge and new modes of collegiality, alliances, and sharing of knowledge; a degree of co-operation to take advantage of positive externalities; economies of scale and scope; and strong cumulative experience-learning processes. But these processes do not necessarily work perfectly (Argyris and Schon, 1978; Gibbons *et al.*, 1994; Lundvall and Johnson, 1994).

While much know-what and know-why has been effectively codified, and can be produced and distributed as quasi-commodity, know-how and know-who have remained tacit and socially embedded (Foray and Lundvall, 1996). Consequently, the production and distribution of this latter form of knowledge have been more problematic: they depend a great deal on social cohesion and trust, on much trespassing and cross-fertilisation between disciplinary fields, and on the development of networks capable of serving as two-way communication links between tacit and codified, private and shared knowledge, between passive efficiency-achieving learning and creative/destructive Schumpeterian learning (Boisot, 1995). In this complex world, there are ample possibilities for co-ordination failures that can slow down the process of learning.

Co-ordination failures may be ascribable to a variety of problems (legal, organ-isational, etc.), and as they materialise they are bound to generate dysfunctions and some performance deterioration. This in turn puts pressure on the learning or-ganisation to modify its conventions and relational transactions, i.e. its *functioning*. When such adjustments in the functioning of the governance system prove insuffi-cient to restore good performance, more serious modifications to the *structure* of the governance of the learning economy become necessary.

But neither set of modifications are usually sufficient. In addition to these plumbing-type repairs, new forms of social ligatures must be put in place to forge a new dominant logic capable of replacing the logic of centralisation-cum-redistribu-tion of the old nation state. This new "soul" or *"imaginaire"* or "north star" of the new governance system is unlikely to emerge solely as a result of some tinkering with structure/functioning, for it must construct nothing less than a new set of reference points to replace the fundamentally territorial co-ordinates of the nation state.

In lieu of the administrative territorial order imposed by the logic of top-down control (with its requirements that clearly delineated borders be respected, good fences be erected, interregional flows be regulated, and jurisdictions be enforced), one must invent a way to deal with the new fluid order, still anchored somewhat in territorial proximities but to a much lesser degree than ever before. This "revenge of nomadism over the principle of territoriality and settlement" (Bauman, 2000, p. 13) is the result of 1) the *"révolution commutative"* that is allowing each individual to disconnect at will and reconnect differently (Guillaume, 1999); 2) the revolution in connexity that has transformed the way we maintain and develop a community – from raising barriers and boundaries to feeding relationships and networks (Mul-gan, 1997; Lévy, 2000); and 3) the new diffuse "bridging capital" that has come to re-place the old bonding tightly connected with the geography of proximity (Putnam, 2000).

The new "lightness and fluidity of the increasingly mobile, slippery, shifty, eva-sive and fugitive power" (Bauman, 2000, p. 14) is not completely a-territorial: it is characterised, however, by new forms of belonging that escape the control and reg-ulation of the nation state to a much higher degree than before, by virtual agoras, liquid networks, variegated and overlapping terrains where citizens may "land" temporarily. The fabric of these new "worlds" is defined by the new dominant logic of subsidiarity in all dimensions: it welds together assets, skills and capabilities in-to complex temporary communities that are as much territories of the mind as any-thing that can be represented by a grid map.

In the shorter run, co-ordination failures may be eliminated through *process ar-chitecture*, i.e. eliminating obstacles to the collaboration of the different stakeholders within the learning cycle and developing the relationships, conventions or relation-al transactions required to define mutually coherent expectations and common guideposts. These conventions differ from sector to sector: they provide the requisite coherence for a common context of interpretation, and for some "cognitive routinization of relations between firms, their environments, and employees" (Storper, 1996, p. 259).

Such coherence must, however, remain somewhat loose: the ligatures should not be too strong or too routinised. A certain degree of heterogeneity, and therefore of social distance, might foster higher potentiality of innovation because the different parties bring to the "conversation" a more complementary body of knowledge (Granovetter, 1973). More fruitful synergies ensue, although too much social distance and too much "noise" can prevent an effective harnessing of collective intelligence and sabotage the learning process. Modifying relational transactions transforms the very nature of the power map. But as collective intelligence comes to depend less on geographical proximity than on other proximities in cyberspace (Lévy,1994), the pattern of effective relational transactions is changed. This does not exorcise territoriality but it transforms its role. "Smart communities" are a good illustration of the new comparative advantages derived from the compounding of these different types of proximity.

In the longer run, co-ordination failures may be eliminated more radically through *organisational architecture*, i.e. the transformation of the structural capital defining the capabilities of the learning economy. This redefines the networks and regimes to ensure the requisite coherence necessary for an effective learning economy.

Coherence and pluralism are crucial in the organisational architecture of a learning concern. This is what makes federal structures so attractive from a learning point of view: they provide co-ordination in a world where the "centre...is more a network than a place" (Handy, 1995a). This is also the reason why federal-type structures have emerged in the different sectors in most continents. Potentially, federalism represents a sort of "fit" or effective alignment between the different components of structural capital in the sense of Saint-Onge (1996) – i.e. the systems (processes), structures (accountabilities and responsibilities), strategies, and culture (shared mindset, values and norms). And since there is always a significant probability of misalignment between these components, there is often a need to intervene directly to modify the organisational architecture in order to ensure effective learning.

But social learning is unlikely to proceed apace (despite process and organisational repairs) unless the new dominant logic of the strategic state generates a new public philosophy and *outillage mental* capable of serving as a gyroscope in the learning process.

While these three ways of correcting co-ordination failures (process and organisational architecture and a new public philosophy) are of necessity intertwined in

---

the operations of the new strategic state, there is some merit in dealing with them separately, for they represent different degrees of intrusiveness by the state in the learning economy. They are examined separately and in a general way in the next section, but the one following will attempt to deal with them together.

2.   The strategic state: process, organisation and public philosophy

The existing co-ordination failures in the learning economy cannot be eliminated by the conventional panoply of policy instruments in good currency in the nation states, based on fence-keeping, centralisation and redistribution. The new strategic state, focused on enabling effective social learning, must develop the required new instruments by effecting a significant reframing of the vocation of the state – away from tinkering with static resource allocation and redistribution, and toward a significant involvement in fostering dynamic Schumpeterian efficiency and enhancing the collective learning power of the economy.

As suggested in the last section, this can be effected in different ways.

Catalysing the social learning cycle

Collective intelligence is defined by Pierre Lévy as "une intelligence partout distribuée, sans cesse valorisée, coordonnée en temps réel, qui aboutit à une mobilisation effective des compétences" (1994, p. 29). Such an intelligence is continuously producing new knowledge and sharing it with all the partners, for its main purpose is social learning and the effective mobilisation and co-ordination of the continually growing competencies of all the partners.

To catalyse social learning, one must have some view about the ways in which collective intelligence works, and be in a position to intervene to remove any obstacles likely to hinder such learning. In an effort to identify the major obstacles (and therefore to guide the process architecture interventions), Max Boisot has suggested a simple mapping of the social learning cycle in a three-dimensional space – the information space – which identifies an organisational system in terms of the degree of abstraction, codification and diffusion of the information flows within it. This three-dimensional space defines three continua: the farther away it is from the origin on the vertical axis, the more the information is codified (i.e. the more its form is clarified, stylised and simplified); the farther away from the origin laterally eastward, the more widely the information is diffused and shared; and the farther away from the origin laterally wesward, the more abstract the information is (i.e. the more general the categories in use) (Boisot, 1995).

The social learning cycle is presented in two phases, with three steps in each phase: Phase I emphasises the cognitive dimensions of the cycle, Phase II the diffusion of the new information.

In Phase I, learning begins with a scanning of the environment and of the concrete information widely diffused and known in order to detect anomalies and paradoxes. Following this first step, one is led in step 2 to stylise the problem (p) posed by the anomalies and paradoxes in a language of problem solution; the third step of Phase I purports to generalise the solution to the more specific issue to broader families of problems, through a process of abstraction (at). In Phase II, the new knowledge is diffused (d) to a larger community of persons or groups in step 4. Then, there is a process of absorption (ar) of this new knowledge by the population and its assimilation so that it becomes part of the tacit stock of knowledge in step 5. In step 6, the new knowledge is not only absorbed but has an impact (i) on the concrete practices and artefacts of the group or community.

Figure 2 below identifies the different blockages through the social learning cycle. In Phase I, cognitive dissonance in (s) may prevent the anomalies from being noted; epistemic inhibitions of all sorts in (p) may stop the process of translation into a language of problem solution; blockages preventing the generalisation of the new knowledge because of the problem definition being encapsulated within the *hic et nunc* (at) may keep the new knowledge from acquiring the most effective degree of generality. In Phase II, the new knowledge may not get the appropriate diffusion because of property rights (d), or because of certain values or very strong dynamic conservatism which may generate a refusal to listen by those most likely to profit from the new knowledge (ar), or because of difficulties in finding ways to incorporate the new knowledge (i).

Figure 2. **Learning cycle and potential blockages**

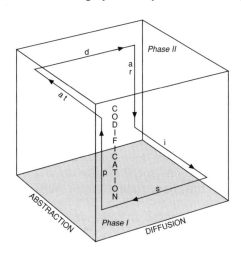

Source: Max Boisot, 1995, pp. 237, 190.

Interventions to remove or attenuate the negative effects of such blockages always entail some degree of interference with the mechanisms of collective intelligence. In some cases, like the modification of property rights, the changes in the rules appear relatively innocuous but government interferes with the affairs of the mind: correcting social learning blockages modifies relational transactions and therefore the psycho-social fabric of the organisation.

These interventions at the cognitive level often have unintended consequences – and may even aggravate the dysfunctions. At the core of these difficulties is the illegitimacy still attached to government being involved in the "politics of cognition" or, in general, in the realm of the mind (Tussman, 1977). This has led to very costly delays in process through which the state has accepted to shoulder these new fundamental responsibilities in a knowledge-based and learning socio-economy, and has invested in discovering effective ways of intervening.

Redesigning the organisational architecture

Eliminating the blockages in the social learning cycle cannot suffice, however; we must not lose sight of the importance of the required longer-run changes to the organisational architecture of the governance of the learning economy. New structures are needed to generate the requisite collaboration among stakeholders, and to correct the high degree of disconcertion that has marred the operations of a large number of nation states (Paquet, 1997b).

The state, in the past, has played housekeeping roles and offsetting functions. These functions required minimal input from the citizenry. The state must now, in complex advanced capitalist socio-economies, play new central roles that go far beyond these mechanical interventions. It must become involved as a *broker*, as an *animateur* and *partner* in participatory planning, if the requisite amount of *organisational learning*, co-evolution and co-operation with economy and society is to materialise.

In order to be able to learn, the state must develop a new interactive regime with the citizenry to promote the emergence of a *participation society* (where freedom and efficacy come from the fact that the individual has a recognised voice in the forum on matters of substance and procedures in the public realm, and, more importantly, an *obligation to participate* in the definition of such matters). The citizen should not be confined to living in a rights-society where the dignity of individuals resides exclusively in the fact that they have claims (Taylor, 1985).

The design principles for a social architecture that is in keeping with this mandate are clear.

First is the principle of *subsidiarity*, according to which "power should devolve on the lowest, most local level at which decisions can reasonably be made, with the function of the larger unit being to support and assist the local body in carrying out its tasks" (Bellah *et al.*, 1991, pp. 135-6; Millon-Delsol, 1992). This applies in the three realms (private, public and civic); the level of empowerment and decentralisation may call for the individual or the family or a minute constituency in the market, society or polity to take charge.

The rationale for this principle is that the institutions closer to the citizen are those likely to be the closest approximation to organic institutions, i.e. to institutions that are likely to emerge "undesigned", to emerge from the sheer pressure of well-articulated needs, and likely to require minimal yearly redesigning. While subsidiarity reduces the vertical hierarchical power, it increases in a meaningful way the potential for participation.

This is not the death of central government, but the demise of big government as the morphological assurance of resilience. If the ground is in motion, the bulkier and more centralised governments are more likely to flounder. The lean new central strategic state must deal with norms, standards, general directions, and values. The process of ministering to the public and of delivering a service well-adapted to its needs must be devolved to the local level.

The second design principle is that of *effective, citizen-based evaluation feedback* to ensure that the services produced, financed or regulated by the public realm meet with the required standards of efficiency, economy and effectiveness, and are consonant with the spirit of the agreed standards or norms. Some may argue that this is essentially what democracy is all about. However, the democratic political process is hardly a fast and unfailingly effective machinery. The intent here is to strengthen considerably the cybernetic learning loop feature at the core of the refurbished state. It is essential if organisational learning is to proceed as quickly as possible (Crozier, 1987).

This sort of evaluation (rooted in collective reporting and a recognition of the necessity of collaborative governance) ensures that the process of participation is significantly strengthened. It provides partially some content to the *silent relation* or *implicit contract* that prevails between the state and the citizenry. This sort of feedback cannot be presumed to materialise organically. Its objective would be to ensure that the state activities, standards and rules have legitimacy in the beneficiaries' eyes, and that they are compatible with everyday morality rather than incentives to lie or misrepresent their situations. It would allow the ordinary citizen to be heard better, for "politics is not only the art of representing the needs of strangers; it is also the perilous business of speaking on behalf of needs which strangers have had no chance to articulate on their own" (Ignatieff, 1985).

These sensible principles may entail a somewhat *decoupled organisational form* of social architecture: since the centre focuses on norms and the periphery on delivery, there is the serious possibility of lack of co-ordination unless 1) a clear sense

195

of public purpose materialises; 2) new partnerships and new skills (strategic management, consultancy and advice, evaluation, etc.), along with new moral contracts binding the partners, are developed to weave this whole enterprise together; and 3) the agencies are granted the necessary powers to organise activities in a way consonant with the principle of subsidiarity and become *negotiating arenas* in which there is i) significant space for interaction between the agency and the citizens, ii) scope for defining and redefining activities, and for reorienting them "under conditions of time and place", and iii) ample provision for dynamic monitoring from above and for continuing feedback from below.

Centrally important in this context is what Charles Lindblom has labelled "preceptoral politics": leaders become educators, *animateurs*, persons called upon to *reframe* our views of the public realm, to design the organisation of mutual education, and to "set off the learning process" necessary to elicit, if possible, a latent consensus (Marquand, 1988). Such learning is unlikely to occur easily in a postmodern society through a forum organised exclusively through national institutions. The requisite institutions will have to be *middle-range* or *meso* institutions, networks designed to promote communication and co-operation on a scale of issues that mobilises existing communities, and meso-forums (regional and sectional) likely to remobilise the commitment of the citizenry in organisations in ways that suit them.

The strategic state must bet on a flexible exercise of control, and on extremely effective organisational learning through such meso-forums. Their triple role – as mediating structures, as setting patterns for the provision of services, and as educating individuals in their mutual and civil commitments – needs to be revitalised accordingly (Etzioni, 1983).

Many officials have expressed great concern about the improper devolution of authority from elected officials to bureaucrats and citizens (Schaffer, 1988; Auditor General of Canada, 1991). Such complaints are ill-founded. This exercise of power is not improper, or illegitimate, or inefficient. In fact, cumulative decision making by bureaucrats and citizens, *working within and with a public philosophy appropriately defined*, enables the postmodern state to learn faster through decisions based on the particulars of the case, while maintaining basic standards. Clinging rigidly to the old "parliamentary control framework" of the Westminster model years is not necessarily enlightened: what is essential is the development of a *modified* framework, better adapted to the needs of a strategic state.

The new *kind* of institution requires the government to be satisfied with providing a problem setting, with framing the context of the situation and the boundaries of public attention, while allowing the bureaucrats and citizens to use a lot of their tacit knowledge and connoisseurship to deal with specific situations, and to arrive at decisions on the basis of a "reflective conversation with the situation" (Schon, 1983; Argyris *et al.*, 1985). This in turn calls not only for a very decentralised structure but also for new forms of horizontal accountability for the system of governance to be effective.

Rethinking foundational values

It is not sufficient to remove obstacles to social learning or to improve organisational architecture. One must also provide the dominant logic (requisite infrastructure + public philosophy) to ensure that the new centrality of social learning is a permanent feature of the new governance, for these guiding values and design principles – and the language to articulate them – are not cast in stone. Any ideal can be dropped as learning proceeds: our desires and ideals "are not like our limbs: they are not a fixed part of us" (Schick, 1984).

The challenge is that of producing a language adequate for our times, a language of belonging and common citizenship, a language of problem definition that provides the citizen with a translation of his or her needs, usually expressed in unspecialised language, into categories that are both relevant and inspiring. This would be a language of human good that would serve as an arena "in which citizens can learn from each other and discover an 'enlightened self-interest' in common" (Dionne, 1991).

The new dominant logic of the strategic state is a response to the failures of the Keynesian state. The main critiques of the Keynesian state that emerged in the period following the Second World War have been well documented. They may be subsumed under a number of headings (Duncan, 1985):

1. *Overgovernment and government overload.* The state is presented as "a kind of arthritic octopus, an inept leviathan" unable, despite massive growth, to do much to meet the demands of the citizenry; as a result, it has triggered weakened citizen compliance, growing civic indifference and much disillusionment (King, 1975).

2. *A legitimation deficit.* The depoliticised public has by now ceased to believe that the state has any moral authority or technical ability to deal with the issues at hand; this would explain the disaffection and the withdrawal of support by the citizenry (Habermas, 1973).

3. *A fiscal crisis.* Revealing the incapacity of the state to reconcile its dual obligation to attenuate social difficulties, and to foster the process of capital accumulation without generating fiscal deficits that are in the long run unbearable (O'Connor, 1973).

4. *Social limits to growth.* The three crucial dimensions of our social organisation (liberal capitalism, mass democracy, and a very unequal distribution of both material and symbolic resources) cannot coexist easily: democratic

197

egalitarianism (in society) generates compulsive centralism (in the polity) to redistribute more and more resources with little success in reducing inequality, but growing shackles on the productive capacity of the economic system (Hirsch, 1976).

This overall crisis of the Keynesian state has been analysed historically as a two-stage process: 1) it evolved first as a crisis in the *economic realm*: co-ordination failures became more and more important in advanced market-type economies, thereby creating a demand for intervention and regulation by the state – the economic crisis was therefore shifted to the state; 2) the *state crisis* developed as the legitimation deficit grew: the state was failing to mobilise the requisite commitment of citizens to do the job, and out of despair it made an attempt to effect an "epistemological coup", to obtain a "blank cheque" from the citizenry. The argument was that since the management problems were so technically complex, the citizenry should pay its taxes and demand no accountability from the professional experts. This coup has failed, and "cognitive despotism" has not succeeded in suppressing the autonomous power of the community to grant or withhold legitimacy (Habermas, 1973; Wiley, 1977; Paquet, 1977). The polls have recorded this story line.

Why has such a situation developed?

The central reason would appear to be that the public institutional framework built by the Keynesians in the postwar period was presented to the citizenry as designed for *instrumental purposes*: to combat a depression, to raise standards of living, to provide public goods not otherwise produced, to assist the needy, etc. As a result, citizens have come to define the state in terms of *claims* they could make on it: "claimant politics began to overshadow civic politics". By comparison, "the activities of the private sphere were seen as ends pursued for their own sake". It is hardly surprising that the instrumental goods of the public sphere were regarded as subordinate to the intrinsic goods of private life (Bellah *et al.*, 1991).

Even though the governments were major funders, underwriters and regulators, and therefore the fundamental bedrock on which the economy and society prospered from the 40s to the 70s, a number of countries have continued to occlude the importance of the state. This ideology of Lockean individualism has continued to prevail despite the fact that government activities had grown so much by 1980 that very little remained absolutely private in a meaningful sense.

In a more and more globalised context, the private sector made ever greater demands on public institutions, at a time when the capacity to supply services from the public sphere could not expand further. This was due to the fact that participation, trust, and creative interaction (on which politics and the public sphere are built) had all but disappeared, as had the sense of community that underpinned civil society and the collective/private ways of meeting the needs of strangers.

In this world of rugged individualism, where most citizens are strangely unaware that the government has been the prime mover in the postwar period of prosperity, *private enterprise at public expense has become the rule*. The lack of commitment of emotional, intellectual, and financial resources to refurbish the public infrastructure could only lead to demand overload, and the frustration generated by the policy failures of the 1970s set the stage for citizens to suggest that the best way to strengthen democracy and the economy was to weaken government.

At the core of our difficulties is a *moral vacuum*. The notion of public purpose is alien to us. We need first and foremost a *philosophy of public intervention*, a *philosophy of the public realm* (Marquand, 1988): the recognition that despite statements from social scientists, and the fact that it is not fashionable to say so, *the state is a moral agent* and not a morally neutral administrative instrument. Both on the left and on the right, there is a longing for civil society to organically provide the well-defined codes of moral obligation that underpin the realisation of the good society. However, the "built-in restraint derived from morals, religion, custom, and education" that were considered by Adam Smith as a prerequisite before one could safely trust men to "their own self-interest without undue harm to the community" are no longer there (Hirsch, 1976).

The disappearance of this socio-cultural foundation has been noted and deplored, and much has been written about the need to rebuild it. However, it has also become clear that it is futile to hope for some replacement for these values to come about by "immaculate conception" in civil society. So many have called on the state and on political leaders to accept their responsibility as second-best moral agents (Mead, 1986; Wolfe, 1989). Political leaders are called upon to provide a *vision*, to propose a *sense of direction*, a commitment to ideals, together with the *public philosophy* to realise them. Such a public philosophy is both *constraining* (in the sense that it echoes some fundamental choices and therefore excludes many possibilities) and *enabling* (in the sense that it provides a foundation on which to build a coherent pattern of institutions and decisions in the public realm).

The choice of a public philosophy must be rooted in the basic values of civil society, and on the criterion of *enlightened understanding*. This calls not for the least constraining public philosophy, but for one recognising that the optimal amount of coercion is not zero. Such a position would be the choice of citizens if they had "the fullest attainable understanding of the experience resulting from that choice and its most relevant alternatives" (Dahl, 1989). The challenge is to bring about that sort of "fullest understanding" in the population. It means that government can no longer operate in a top-down mode, but has a duty to institute a continuing dialogue with the citizenry.

This will require a language of common citizenship, deeply rooted in civil society: the citizens have goals, commitment and values that the state must take into account. But the citizens must also insist that they want an active role in the   199 formation of these values, goals and commitments, and in the making of policies supposedly generated to respond to their presumed needs (Sen, 1987). Only through a rich forum and institutions that enhance citizens' competence as producers of governance is an *enlightened understanding* likely to prevail – both as a result of, and as the basis for, a reasonable armistice between the state and the citizenry.

The fluid and seemingly scattered – baroque – system of governance (Paquet, 2001) likely to ensue must, however, be anchored in a clear sense of direction. So there must be a *plan*. Most state leaders in advanced socio-economies outside of North America have such a plan, a direction for strategic intervention, and a public philosophy that will articulate and rationalise it. "They do not publish their plan because it would never gain consent. Yet it is not what one ought to call a conspiracy...The plan is not entirely conscious or systematic, and it cannot be as long as it is not written, published, debated, revised and so on. But it is not what you could call a secret" (Lowi, 1975).

The importance of this *unwritten plan* is that it serves as a gyroscope in the definition of actions taken by the personnel of agencies and ministries. It serves as the basis for a *double-looped learning* process, as organisational learning must be (i.e. not only finding better means of learning to do what we do better, but also, and more importantly, finding the right goals, learning whether the objectives we pursue are the right ones).

Such learning cannot be accomplished by elected officials alone. Elected officials, bureaucrats and citizens must work symbiotically, and elected officials must learn to devolve a greater amount of discretion to bureaucrats and citizens, not only in the delivery process, but in the governance process itself. Moreover, it must be recognised by all those who take on public service that the world is changing around them, that they need to refurbish continually their *outillage mental* in order to be equipped and able to develop new ways of getting things done, without running into political walls.

3. The ecology of collaborative governance

Whether one wishes to emphasise process architecture, organisational redesign, or the distillation of a new dominant logic, it is unlikely that anything will be accomplished without the development of new collaborative governance capabilities. But to foster the development of these new capabilities, one has to understand the ecosystem within which they blossom, and to optimise the ways in which organisations can capture the imagination of all the relevant players in order to make the highest and best use of collective intelligence.

As Dalum *et al.* suggest (1992), this entails intervening to improve the means to learn (and this goes much beyond the formal education and training systems), the incentive to learn (supporting projects of co-operation and networks), the capability to learn (promoting organisations supporting interactive learning, i.e. more decentralised organisations), the access to relevant knowledge (through bridging the relationships between agents and sources of knowledge, both through infrastructure and mediating structures), but also fostering the requisite amount of remembering and forgetting (act to preserve competencies and capabilities, but also compensate the victims of change and make it easier for them to move ahead). This in turn requires a well-aligned nexus of relations, networks and regimes.

States can be important catalysts in the construction of the new "loose intermediation" social capital: improving relationships here, fostering networks there, developing more or less encompassing formal or informal regimes at other places, and ensuring that the new dominant logic of the strategic state unfolds. This is the central role of what some have called the *catalytic state* (Lind, 1992).

Collaborative capabilities: relations, networks, regimes

Managers in the private, public and civic sectors have to exploit not only the favourable environmental circumstances but also the full complement of imagination and resourcefulness in the heart and mind of each team player; they have had to become team leaders in task force-type projects, quasi-entrepreneurs capable of cautious sub-optimising in the face of a turbulent environment. This sort of challenge has pressed public, private and civic organisations to design lighter, more horizontal and modular structures, to create networks and informal clan-like rapports, and to develop new rules of the game. In general, this has generated pressure for non-centralisation, for an expropriation of the power to steer that was held by the top managers.

These new modularised organisations cannot impose their views on their clients, citizens or members. They must consult, they must move toward greater use of the distributed intelligence and ingenuity of the members. The strategic organisation is becoming a broker, a prime mover, and in this network, a consultative and participatory mode obtains among the firm, the state and the communities (Paquet, 1994, 1995, 1996-7, 1997a).

That entails a major qualitative change. It introduces the network paradigm within the governance process (Cooke and Morgan, 1993; Castells, 1996, 1997, 1998). This paradigm not only dominates the transactions of the civic sector, but also permeates the operations of both the state and market sectors. For the network is not, as is usually assumed, a mixed form of organisation existing halfway along a continuum ranging from market to hierarchy. Rather, it is a generic name for a third type of arrangement, built on very different integrating mechanisms; networks are consensus/inducement-oriented organisations and institutions.

In the best of all worlds, learning relationships, networks and regimes would be in place as a response to the need for nimbleness in the face of increasing diversity, greater complexity and the new imperative of constant learning. Moreover, in such a world, organisational culture would have become an important bond that makes these networks and regimes operative and effective at collective learning.

Organisational culture refers to unwritten principles meant to generate a relatively high level of co-ordination at low cost by bestowing identity and membership through stories of flexible generality about events of practice that act as repositories of accumulated wisdom. The evolution of these stories constitutes collective learning, an evolving way to interpret conflicting and often confusing data, but also a social construction of a community of interpretation.

Unfortunately, one does not live in the best of all worlds. The requisite relationships, networks and regimes do not necessarily fall into place organically. Moreover, at any time, the organisational culture may not serve as the best catalyst to make the highest and best use of relationships, networks and regimes.

Arie de Geus uses an analogy from evolutionary biology to explain the foundations and different phases of collective learning and collaboration, and to identify the loci for action in correcting learning failures: the ability of individuals to move around and to be exposed to different challenges (new relations); the capacity of individuals to invent new ways to cope creatively in the face of new circumstances (new networks); and the process of communication of the new ways from the individual to the entire community (new regimes) (de Geus, 1997).

First, a certain heterogeneity is an important source of learning, since a community composed of identical individuals with similar history or experiences is less likely to extract as much new insight from a given environment. However, there must be a sufficient degree of trust to sustain learning. This in turn requires a cultural basis of differences that members recognise and share (Drummond 1981-82). This "cultural" basis of heterogeneity and trust, and the mastery of weak ties (i.e. the capacity to build strong relations on weak ties) are obviously dimensions that can be nurtured and represent a critical capability (Laurent and Paquet, 1998).

Second, learning is not about transmission of abstract knowledge from one person's head to another person's head – it is about the "embodied ability to behave as community members". It is fostered by contacts with the outside, by facilitating access to and membership in the community-of-practice. Trust is at the core of the fabric of such networks and communities-of-practice that transform "labourers into members", an employment contract into a membership contract (Handy, 1995*b*).

Third, belonging is one of the most powerful agents of mobilisation. Therefore what is required is an important "moral" component to the new membership contract, to make it less contractual and more interactive. This *new refurbished moral contract* is "a network of civic engagement...which can serve as a cultural template for future collaboration...and broaden the participants' sense of self...enhancing the participants' 'taste' for collective benefits"(Putnam, 1995, 2000).

These loose arrangements or regimes require a certain degree of interaction and proximity. Those are important features of the learning process. Regime institutions facilitate the adjustment of the group to external shocks through policy coordination, enabling the group to define more effective ways either to prevent a shock or at least to attenuate the impact through compensatory mechanisms, and collaboration capable of providing adequate forums for consultation and co-decision (Preston and Windsor, 1992).

Relations, networks and regimes constitute layers of collaborative capabilities of the governance process. They evolve as the socio-economy is transubstantiated but neither fast enough nor in an integrated way: the process is evolving slowly, bit by bit. As a result, the emerging governance process is much like a patchwork quilt becoming ever more complex as the environment evolves from being more placid to being more turbulent (Emery and Trist, 1965).

Assets, skills and styles behind these collaborative capabilities

In our new turbulent environment, strategic management is no longer sufficient. What is required is the development of capacities for collaborative action in managing large-scale reorganisations and structural changes at the macro level. The ground is in motion; acting independently not only may not ensure effectiveness, it may even make things worse and amplify disintegrative tendencies. What is required is collective action by "dissimilar organisations whose fates are, basically, positively correlated". This requires trust-enhancing mechanisms such as stronger relationships, networks and regimes.

The challenge is to succeed in finding ways to pragmatically resolve the sort of reconciliation that is possible between different but somewhat compatible perspectives or frameworks. This is the sort of compromise promised by *design rationality* – "the kind of limited reason that is feasible and appropriate in policy-making" (Schon and Rein, 1994). This is a pragmatic approach based on the assumption that there is no frame-neutral position in policy analysis.

Consequently, the only way to resolve these framework differences is to seek a "situated resolution" through efforts to reframe the debates in such a way as to make the differences manageable and agreement combining antagonism and co-operation reachable.

But this requires some probing into the assets, skills and styles of co-ordination that underpin governance capabilities.

203

First, in order for these collaborative capabilities (relationships, networks, regimes) to be created and maintained, there are several requirements: a mix of different sorts of 1) rights and authorities enshrined in rules, 2) resources, i.e. the array of assets made available to individuals and institutions such as money, time, information and facilities, 3) competencies and knowledge, i.e. education, training, experience and expertise, and 4) organisational capital, i.e. the capacity to mobilise attention and to make effective use of the first three types of resources (March and Olsen, 1995).

These various resources are obviously related in a dynamic fashion: governance through organisational capital reflects the tensions between the rights and rules in place, the resources available and the competencies and knowledge defining other possible configurations, but it also affects the evolution of the system through an erosion of existing rules, and the distillation of new patterns of authority, asset-holding and expertise.

Second, Spinosa, Flores and Dreyfus (1997) have shown that the engines of entrepreneurship (private sector), democratic action (public sphere), and cultivation of solidarity (civil society) are quite similar. They are based on a particular skill that Spinosa *et al.* call "history-making", which can be decomposed into three sub-skills: 1) acts of articulation – attempts at *"définition de situation"* or new ways to make sense of the situation, 2) acts of cross-appropriation – to bring new practices into a context that would not naturally generate them, and 3) acts of reconfiguration – to reframe the whole perception of the way of life. Such individual actions are necessary but not sufficient to generate new capabilities or to trigger the required renovation in the different worlds. As Putnam (2000) puts it, the renewal of the stock of social capital (relationships, networks, regimes) is a task that requires the mobilisation of communities. This in turn means that we must be able to ensure that these actions resonate with communities of interpretation and practice – what Spinosa *et al.* call "worlds".

This is at the core of the notion of institutional governance proposed by March and Olsen. For them, the craft of governance is organised around four tasks: developing identities, developing capabilities, developing accounts and procedures for interpretation that improve the transmission and retention of lessons from history, and developing a capacity to learn and transform by experiments and by reframing and redefining the governance style (1995, pp. 45-46). In a turbulent environment, the styles of the different worlds – but also the very nature of the equipment, tasks and identities – are modified. This transforms the organisational capital but also the rest of the asset base of the system; it stimulates a different degree of re-articulation and reconfiguration, and enriches the possibilities of cross-appropriation.

Disclosing new worlds

One cannot hope to transform these "worlds" (in the private, public and civic spheres) unless one can first disclose them (in the sense of the world of business or the world of medicine). "World" here means a "totality of interrelated pieces of *equipment*, each used to carry out a specific task such as hammering a nail. These *tasks* are undertaken to achieve certain *purposes*, such as building a house. This activity enables those performing it to have *identities*, such as being a carpenter". Finally, one may refer to the way in which this world is organised and co-ordinated as its *style* (Spinosa *et al.*, 1997, pp. 17-19). Articulation, cross-appropriation and reconfiguration are kinds of style change (making explicit what was implicit or lost, gaining wider horizons, reframing).

The distinctiveness of any territorial governance system is this ensemble of components: the way the system adopts certain patterns of assets and skills, distills capabilities, and constitutes a particular variety of partly overlapping and interconnected "worlds" corresponding to different games being played (political, bureaucratic, interest groups, media, electorate, etc.). All these worlds cast some sort of "territorial shadow" and disclose a particular space. The market economy space may not fit well with the political formation space or the contours of the civil society: indeed, the disconnectedness among these three spaces has been amply noted in the recent past.

The intermingling of all these worlds (with their infrastructures/equipments, their particular tasks or purposes, the variety of identities they bestow on individuals and groups, and the various styles they allow to evolve) adds up to a number of different spatial co-ordinates lending themselves to some extent to some sort of design. They all reflect frame differences (i.e. different notions of actors, criteria of effectiveness, etc.) and frame conflicts (when these perspectives clash). Indeed, the existence of the different frames corresponding to the different "worlds" or "styles of worlds" cause participants to notice different facts and make different arguments. The outcome of this cumulation of "worlds" is indeed what generates the territorial fabric that ensues. But these contours are truly unpredictable.

This is especially clear when one realises that those "worlds" are not only disclosed by reference to some underlying realities or facts, but may be contrived by perceptions and imagination. There are as many "imagined" economies, polities and communities as one may wish, with corresponding purposes, identities, styles and territorial imprints. In that sense, any entrepreneur, theorist or fanatic is a discloser of a new space that may or may not leave any scar on the territorial realities. But these in turn always have an impact (important or minute) on the world of assets, skills and capabilties.

This dynamic is synthesised in Figure 3. It depicts the political socio-economy as an "instituted process" characterised by a particular amalgam of assets, adroitly used and enriched by political, economic and civic entrepreneurs, through skillful articulation, cross-appropriation and reframing activities, and woven into a fabric of relations, networks and regimes defining the distinctive habitus of a political economy as a complex adaptive system.

Figure 3. **Radiography of the governance process**

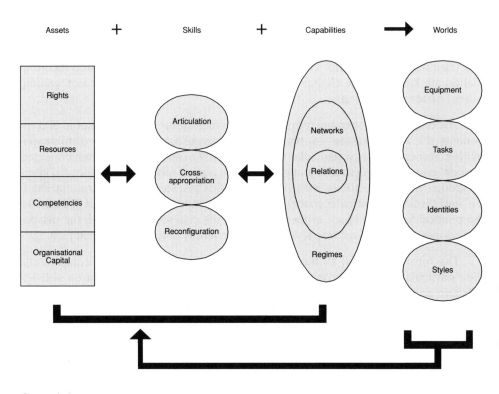

Such a complex world is disclosed by multiple examinations of its equipment, tasks and identities organised and co-ordinated in a variety of ways with particular styles. Modification in the structure of assets, skills and capabilities are echoed in a transformation of the "particular integrated world" that emerges as the synthesis of all these disclosed "worlds", a transformation that impacts back on the pattern of assets, skills and capabilities.

These various forces contribute to the shaping of the territorial connections that ensue, but it is impossible to state *ex ante* which one will turn out to be the defining one.

Conclusion

The strategic state undoubtedly has a role to play in jump-starting, catalysing and steering the process of social learning, while allowing the other two domains (the private and civic sectors) to occupy their own terrain as fully as possible. It should obviously be remembered that the new bottom-up and distributed governance elevates the citizen to the inescapable role of producer of governance, and imposes on the citizenry *in toto* a key role in the transformation of the overall capacity to make and implement decisions. But there is still some margin of manoeuvrability left for creative initiatives. Indeed, one may envisage two broad avenues that might deserve consideration, one that is modest and one more ambitious.

In the modest agenda, the strategic state does not aim at the *optimum optimorum* in this context, but only strives for ways of avoiding excesses, for a loose codifying of a sense of *limits*, for some reframing likely to lead to some workable agreement. This modesty stems from the fact that very few political questions can be handled by simple rules. Therefore, even a wise public philosophy and an efficient process of organisational learning are regarded as at best capable of establishing by negotiation nothing more than an agreement on what is *not* moral, what is *not* acceptable. Since we understand intuitively what is unjust more easily than what is just, the challenge is to find the path of minimum regret, for that corresponds to the only hope a leader may reasonably entertain in a postmodern state (Shklar, 1989).

In the more ambitious agenda, the challenge is a bit more daunting: the objective is not to seek the utopian just society of yesteryear, but to develop an active citizenship. This agenda is built on the following premises: 1) the *Tocqueville lament* about the peril of democracy is warranted: "not only does democracy induce to make every man forget his ancestors, it hides his descendants and separates his contemporaries from him; it throws him back forever upon himself alone, and threatens in the end to confine him utterly within the solitude of his own heart"; and 2) the *John Stuart Mill statement* about social obligations is also warranted: "every one who receives the protection of society owes a return for the benefit" (Buckley, 1990).

From these premises, three sets of actions follow:

- The search for a way to frame a public philosophy aiming at nothing less than a change in the national ethos.

- The citizen needs to become an "official", i.e. "a person with duties and obligations", not only to forgo private interests in the name of public duty, but also to "get the ruled to do what they don't want to do" because what the public wants, or thinks it wants, or thinks is good for it, may not be what the public good requires; this entails a duty to interfere.

- The citizen needs to be persuaded that he/she may act unjustly, not only by breaking a law, but also by remaining passive in the face of a public wrong; this means that the citizen has to be *educated* into an active citizenship that entails a duty toward solidarity (Tussman, 1977, 1989).

207

The public philosophy in good currency suggests that the modest agenda is the only viable one. Dwight Waldo, one of the foremost observers of the public administration scene over the last forty years, has reminded us recently that "we simply do not know how to solve some of the problems government has been asked to solve" (Waldo, 1985). For Waldo, the central feature in the discussion of the boundaries between the private and public spheres is the "growth of the 'gray area'... the fading distinction between public and private, caused and accompanied by increasing complexity of organisational arrangements where what is – or was – government meets and interacts with what is – or was – private, usually but by no means exclusively 'business'". And Waldo added somewhat sharply that any person who claims to have clear ideas about this "gray area" is "suspect as ideologue, scenario writer, or a con artist".

Yet the times may call for initiatives envisaging a real attempt at a somewhat immodest agenda: enlightened pragmatism, an emphasis on practice guided by a modest public philosophy, an ongoing and somewhat directed conversation with the situation, "under conditions of time and place" are the bedrock of the new modern and modest strategic state. But this enlightened pragmatism need not be amnesic and myopic; it must forge new concepts and new symbols, new options, and as "options are thus changed or expanded, it is to be expected that choice behavior will change too, and changed choice behavior can in turn be expected, given appropriate time lags, to be conceptualized or 'habitualized' into a changed set of values" (Mesthene, 1970).

This hemi/semi/quasi immodest agenda is not echoed in the triumphant "politics of principle" developed by supposedly "great" political leaders and likely to convulse society, but in the solution of "particular cases" in an innovative way. Already there is agreement on the profile of the new type of leader that the times call for; the key features are 1) a capacity to listen, to learn and to entice others to learn, to change and adapt to change, and to inform the public clearly and serenely about the general orientation of the guiding public philosophy, 2) the courage to change one's mind when circumstances and problems demand it, but centrally 3) an "ethical attitude" acting as a gyroscope and permitting no concession to opportunism (King and Schneider, 1991).

It is not clear whether what is needed to kick-start this transformation is a fully worked out *"projet de société"*, an *avventura comune*, or nothing more than what Aristotle identified as "concord" ["homonoia" – "a relationship between people who...are not strangers, between whom goodwill is possible, but not friendship...a relationship based on respect for...differences" (Oldfield, 1990)]. What is clear is that the leader of the strategic state needs to find a way to energise the nervous system of the economy, society and polity, for, as Joseph Tussman would put it, a modern democracy is committed to "governance not by the best *among* all of us but by the best *within* each of us" (1989, p. 11).

Bibliography

ARGYRIS, C. *et al.* (1985),
  Action Science. San Francisco: Jossey-Bass.

ARGYRIS, C. and D.A. SCHON (1978),
  Organizational Learning: A Theory of Action Perspective. Reading, Mass.: Addison-Wesley.

AXELROD, R. and M.D. COHEN (1999),
  Harnessing Complexity. New York: The Free Press.

AUDITOR GENERAL OF CANADA (1991),
  "Report to the House of Commons for Fiscal Year Ended 31 March 1991", Ottawa.

BAUMAN, Z. (2000),
  Liquid Modernity. Cambridge: Polity Press.

BELLAH, R.N. *et al.* (1991),
  The Good Society. New York: Alfred A. Knopf.

BOISOT, M. (1995),
  Information Space – A Framework for Learning in Organizations, Institutions and Culture. London: Routledge.

BOULDING, K.E. (1970),
  A Primer on Social Dynamics. New York: The Free Press.

BUCKLEY, W.F. (1990),
  Gratitude. New York: Random House.

CARLSSON, I. and S. RAMPHAL, eds. (1995),
  Our Global Neighbourhood – The Report of the Commission on Global Governance. Oxford: Oxford University Press.

CASTELLS, M. (1996),
  The Rise of the Network Society. Oxford: Blackwell.

CASTELLS, M. (1997),
  The Power of Identity. Oxford: Blackwell.

CASTELLS, M. (1998),
  End of Millennium. Oxford: Blackwell.

COOKE, P. and K. MORGAN (1993),
  "The Network Paradigm: New Departures in Corporate and Regional Development", *Environment and Planning* D: *Society and Space*, 11, 543-564.

CROZIER, M. (1987),
Etat modeste, Etat moderne. Paris: Fayard.

DAHL, R.A. (1989),
Democracy and its Critics. New Haven: Yale University Press.

DALUM, B. et al. (1992),
"Public Policy in the Learning Society" in B. Lundvall (ed.), National Systems of Innovation. London: Pinter, pp. 296-317.

de GEUS, A. (1997),
"The Living Company", Harvard Business Review, 75, 2, pp. 51-59.

DIONNE, E.J. (1991),
Why Americans Hate Politics. New York: Simon & Schuster.

DRUMMOND, L. (1981-82),
"Analyse sémiotique de l'ethnicité au Québec", Question de culture, No. 2, pp. 139-153.

DUNCAN, G. (1985),
"A Crisis of Social Democracy?", Parliamentary Affairs, 38, 3, pp. 267-281.

ELKINS, D.J. (1995),
Beyond Sovereignty. Toronto: The University of Toronto Press.

EMERY, F.E. and E.L. TRIST (1965),
"The Causal Texture of Organizational Environments", Human Relations, 18, pp. 21-32.

ETZIONI, A. (1983),
An Immodest Agenda. New York: McGraw Hill.

FORAY, D. and B.A. LUNDVALL (1996),
"The Knowledge-Based Economy: From the Economics of Knowledge to the Learning Economy" in Employment and Growth in the Knowledge-Based Economy. Paris: OECD, pp. 11-32.

GIBBONS, M. et al. (1994),
The New Production of Knowledge. London: Sage Publications.

GRANOVETTER, M. (1973),
"The Strength of Weak Ties", American Journal of Sociology, 78(6), pp. 1360-1380.

GUÉHENNO, J.M. (1993),
La fin de la démocratie. Paris: Flammarion.

GUILLAUME, M. (1999),
L'empire des réseaux. Paris: Descartes & Cie.

HABERMAS, J. (1973),
Legitimation Crisis. Boston: Beacon.

HANDY, C. (1995a),
Beyond Certainty. London: Hutchinson.

HANDY, C. (1995b),
"Trust and the Virtual Organization", Harvard Business Review, 73, 3, pp. 40-50.

HIRSCH, F. (1976),
Social Limits to Growth. Cambridge: Harvard University Press.

HUNTINGTON, S.P. (1993),
"The Clash of Civilizations?", Foreign Affairs, 72 (3), pp. 22-28.

IGNATIEFF, M. (1985),
The Needs of Strangers. New York: Viking.

KING, A. (1975),
"Overload: Problems of Governing in the Seventies", Political Studies, June-September, pp. 284-296.

KING, A. and B. SCHNEIDER (1991),
Questions de survie. Paris: Calmann-Lévy.

KOOIMAN, J., ed. (1993),
Modern Governance. London: Sage Publications.

LAURENT, P. and G. PAQUET (1998),
Epistémologie et économie de la relation: coordination et gouvernance distribuée. Lyon/Paris: Vrin.

LÉVY, P. (1994),
L'intelligence collective. Paris: La Découverte.

LÉVY, P. (2000),
World Philosophie. Paris: Editions Odile Jacob.

LIND, M. (1992),
"The Catalytic State", The National Interest, 27 (Spring), pp. 3-12.

LOWI, T.J. (1975),
"Toward a Politics of Economics: The State of Permanent Receivership" in L.N. Lindberg et al., Stress and Contradiction in Modern Capitalism. Lexington, Mass: D.C. Heath & Co., pp. 115-124.

LUKE, T.W. (1991),
"The Discipline of Security Studies and the Codes of Containment", Alternatives, 16 (3), pp. 315-344.

LUNDVALL, B.A. and B. JOHNSON (1994),
"The Learning Economy", Journal of Industry Studies, 1(2), pp. 23-42.

LUTTWAK, E.N. (1990),
"From Geo-politics to Geo-Economics: Logic of Conflict, Grammar of Commerce", The National Interest, 20 (Summer), pp. 17-24.

MARCH, J.G. and J.P. OLSEN (1995),
Democratic Governance. New York: The Free Press.

MARQUAND, D. (1988),
The Unprincipled Society. London: Fontana Press.

McCALLUM, J. (1995),
"National Borders Matter: Canada-US Regional Trade Patterns", American Economic Review, 85(3), pp. 615-623.

MEAD, L. (1986),
Beyond Entitlement: The Social Obligations of Citizenship. New York: The Free Press.

MESTHENE, E.G. (1970),
Technological Change. New York: Mentor Books.

MILLON-DELSOL, C. (1992),
L'état subsidiaire. Paris: Presses Universitaires de France.

MULGAN, G. (1997),
Connexity. Boston: Harvard Business School.

NITSCH, V. (2000),
"National Borders and International Trade: Evidence from the European Union", Canadian
Journal of Economics, 33(4), pp. 1091-1105.

NOHRIA, N. and R.G. ECCLES, eds. (1992),
Networks and Organizations. Boston: Harvard Business School Press.

NORGAARD, R.B. (1994),
Development Betrayed: The End of Progress and A Coevolutionary Revisioning of the Future. London:
Routledge.

O'CONNOR, J. (1973),
The Fiscal Crisis of the State. New York: St Martin's Press.

OGILVY, J.A. (1986-87),
"Scenarios for the Future of Governance", The Bureaucrat, pp. 13-16.

OLDFIELD, A. (1990),
Citizenship and Community. London: Routledge.

Ò TUATHAIL, G., S. DALBY, P. ROUTLEDGE (1998),
The Geopolitics Reader. London: Routledge.

PAQUET, G. (1977),
"Federalism as Social Technology" in J. Evans (ed.), Options. Toronto: The University of Toronto Press, pp. 281-302.

PAQUET, G. (1993),
"Sciences transversales et savoirs d'expérience: the art of trespassing", Revue générale de
droit, 24(2), pp. 269-281.

PAQUET, G. (1994),
"Reinventing Governance", Opinion Canada, 2(2), pp. 1-5.

PAQUET, G. (1995),
"Institutional Evolution in An Information Age" in T.J. Courchene (ed.), Technology, Informa-
tion and Public Policy – The Bell Canada Papers on Economic and Public Policy 3. Kingston: John
Deutsch Institute for the Study of Economic Policy, pp. 197-229.

PAQUET, G. (1996-97),
"The Strategic State", Ciencia Ergo Sum, 3 (3), 1996, pp. 257-261 (Part 1); 4 (1), 1997, pp. 28-
34 (Part 2); 4(2), 1997, pp. 148-154 (Part 3).

PAQUET, G. (1997a),
"States, Communities and Markets: The Distributed Governance Scenario" in T.J. Courchene (ed.), The Nation State in a Global Information Era: Policy Challenges – The Bell Canada Papers on Economic and Public Policy, 5. Kingston: John Deustch Institute for the Study of Economic Policy, pp. 25-46.

PAQUET, G. (1997b),
"Canada as a Disconcerted Learning Economy: A Governance Challenge", Transactions of the Royal Society of Canada, Series VI, Volume VIII, pp. 69-98.

PAQUET, G. (1999a),
Governance Through Social Learning. Ottawa: University of Ottawa Press.

PAQUET, G. (1999b),
"La résilience dans l'économie", L'Agora 7(1), pp. 14-17.

PAQUET, G. (1999c),
"Tectonic Changes in Canadian Governance" in L.S. Pal (ed.), How Ottawa Spends 1999-2000. Toronto: Oxford University Press, pp. 75-111.

PAQUET, G. (2000a),
"Canada 2015: The Challenge of Governance", Ivey Business Journal, 64(3), pp. 57-61.

PAQUET, G. (2000b),
"On Hemispheric Governance", Transactions of the Royal Society of Canada, Series VI, Vol. X, (in press).

PAQUET, G. (2001),
"Toward a Baroque Governance in the 21st Century" in C. Gaffield et al. (eds.), The Canadian Distinctiveness in the 21st Century. Ottawa: The University of Ottawa Press (in press).

PERROUX, F. (1960),
Economie et société. Paris: Presses Universitaires de France.

POLANYI, K. (1957),
"The Economy as Instituted Process" in K. Polanyi et al. (eds.), Trade and Markets in the Early Empires. New York: The Free Press, pp. 243-270.

PRESTON, L.E. and D. WINDSOR (1992),
The Rules of the Game in the Global Economy: Policy Regimes for International Business. Norwell, Mass. and Dordrecht: Kluwer Academic.

PUTNAM, R.D. (1995),
"Bowling Alone: America's Declining Social Capital", Journal of Democracy, 6, 1, pp. 65-78.

PUTNAM, R.D. (2000),
Bowling Alone: The Collapse and Revival of American Community. New York: Simon & Schuster.

SAINT-ONGE, H. (1996),
"Tacit Knowledge: The Key to the Strategic Alignment of Intellectual Capital", Strategy and Leadership, March-April, pp. 10-14.

SCHAFFER, D.L. (1988),
"Theodore J. Lowi and the Administrative State", Administration and Society, 19, 4, pp. 371-398.

SCHICK, F. (1984),
Having Reasons. Princeton: Princeton University Press.

SCHON, D.A. (1983),
The Reflective Practitioner. New York: Basic Books.

SCHON, D.A. and M. REIN (1994),
Frame Reflection: Toward the Resolution of Intractable Policy Controversies. New York: Basic Books.

SEN, A. (1987),
On Ethics and Economics. Oxford: Basil Blackwell.

SHKLAR, J. (1989),
"Giving Injustice Its Due", Yale Law Journal, 98, pp. 1135-1151.

SPINOSA, C., F. FLORES and H.L. DREYFUS (1997),
Disclosing New Worlds. Cambridge: The MIT Press.

STORPER, M. (1996),
"Institutions of the Knowledge-Based Economy" in Employment and Growth in the Knowledge-Based Economy. Paris: OECD, pp. 255-283.

TAYLOR, C. (1985),
"Alternative Futures" in A. Cairns and C. Williams (eds.), Constitutionalism, Citizenship and Society in Canada. Toronto: University of Toronto Press, pp. 183-229.

TUSSMAN, J. (1977),
Government and the Mind. New York: Oxford University Press.

TUSSMAN, J. (1989),
The Burden of Office. Vancouver: Talonbooks.

WALDO, D. (1985),
"An Agenda for Future Reflections: A Conversation with Dwight Waldo", Public Administration Review, July-August, pp. 459-467.

WILEY, N. (1977),
Review of Habermas' Legitimation Crisis in Contemporary Sociology, 6, 4, pp. 416-424.

WOLFE, A. (1989),
Whose Keeper? Berkeley: The University of California Press.

ZIMAN, J. (1991),
"A Neural Net Model of Innovation", Science and Public Policy, 18(1), pp. 65-75.

List of Participants

Chairman

Donald JOHNSTON
Secretary-General
OECD

Martin ALBROW
Senior Fellow
Woodrow Wilson International Center
and Research Professor in the Social
Sciences
University of Surrey Roehampton
United States/United Kingdom

Richard BLANDY
Professor of Economics
University of South Australia
Australia

Walter BRINKMANN
Executive Vice President
Coca-Cola
Belgium

Frederik von DEWALL
General Manager & Chief Economist
ING Bank
The Netherlands

Gunter DUNKEL
Member of the Board of Management
Norddeutsche Landesbank (Nord/LB)
Germany

David GARRISON
Senior Advisor to the Deputy Secretary
Representative to the Community
Empowerment Board of the
US President
Department of Health and Human Services
United States

Bob HAWKE
Former Prime Minister
The Bob Hawke Prime Ministerial
Centre
University of South Australia
Australia

Carlos HURTADO
Coordinator de Asesores Para Asuntos
de Politica Economica y Social
Presidencia de la Republica
Mexico

Sumiko IWAO
Professor of Social Psychology
Keio University
Japan

215

Tae-Dong KIM
Chairman
Presidential Commission for Policy
Planning
Korea

Jerzy KROPIWNICKI
Minister
Government Center for Strategic Studies
Poland

Antoni KUKLINSKI
Professor
European Institute for Regional and
Local Development
(EUROREG)
Poland

Roberta LAJOUS
General Coordinator
Matías Romero Institute
Ministry of Foreign Affairs
Mexico

Robert Z. LAWRENCE
Member
Council of Economic Advisers (CEA)
Executive Office of the President
United States

Jorge de LEMOS GODINHO
Ambassador
Permanent Representative of Portugal
to the OECD

Ruud LUBBERS
Former Prime Minister
President, WWF International
Centre for Economic Research
University of Tilburg
The Netherlands

Wolfgang MICHALSKI
Director
Advisory Unit to the Secretary-General
OECD

Geoff MULGAN
Special Advisor to the Prime Minister
Prime Minister's Policy Unit
United Kingdom

PERRI 6
Senior Research Fellow
Department of Government
University of Strathclyde
United Kingdom

William PFAFF
Journalist
The International Herald Tribune
France

Mario RODRIGUEZ MONTERO
Director del Grupo
Pulsar International
Mexico

Charles F. SABEL
Professor of Law and Social Science
Columbia Law School
United States

André SAFIR
Président
BIPE & Stratorg International
France

Peter Y. SATO
Advisor
Tokyo Electric Power Company
Former Ambassador to China
Japan

Sally SHELTON-COLBY
Deputy Secretary-General
OECD

Daniel TARSCHYS
Professor of Political Science
Stockholm University
Former Secretary General
Council of Europe
Sweden

Jean-Claude THEBAULT
Directeur
Cellule de Prospective
Commission Européenne

Kimon VALASKAKIS
Professeur honoraire
Université de Montréal
Canada

Kevin WELDON
Chairman
Weldon Group of Companies
Australia

Jahn WENNERHOLM
Director, Marketing and Strategic
Business Development
Ericsson
Sweden

Soogil YOUNG
Ambassador
Permanent Representative of Korea
to the OECD

**OECD Secretariat
Advisory Unit to the Secretary-General**

Barrie STEVENS
Deputy to the Director

Riel MILLER
Principal Administrator

Pierre-Alain SCHIEB
Principal Administrator

OECD PUBLICATIONS, 2, rue André-Pascal, 75775 PARIS CEDEX 16
PRINTED IN FRANCE
(03 2001 01 1P 1) ISBN 92-64-18541-0 – No. 51455 2001